Brexit and citizens' rights

Manchester University Press

Brexit and citizens' rights

History, policy and experience

Edited by

Djordje Sredanovic and Bridget Byrne

MANCHESTER UNIVERSITY PRESS

Published by Manchester University Press
Oxford Road, Manchester, M13 9PL

www.manchesteruniversitypress.co.uk

British Library Cataloguing-in-Publication Data
A catalogue record for this book is available from the British Library

ISBN 978 1 5261 6962 4 hardback

First published 2024

Typeset by Newgen Publishing UK

Contents

List of figures	vi
List of contributors	vii
Acknowledgements	x

Introduction: Brexit and citizenship in context – Djordje Sredanovic and Bridget Byrne	1

Part I History and policy

1	Empire and Brexit: rights, rollback and categorical exclusion – Devyani Prabhat	27
2	Brexit and legal status of Turkish nationals in the UK: a case study on the standstill clauses of the Association – Çiğdem Nas and Sanem Baykal	48
3	Understanding and explaining the practice of denaturalisation in the United Kingdom – Colin Yeo	68

Part II Experience

4	Citizenship and belonging in the times of Brexit: the case of Polish migrants in Manchester – Alina Rzepnikowska	91
5	'I will never be British': EU citizens and the illusion of belonging – Marianela Barrios Aquino	111
6	Brexit fears: anticipating and dealing with the loss of citizenship rights – Djordje Sredanovic	129
7	Brexit and Brits in Spain: lifestyle migration and political agency – Jeremy MacClancy	148
8	'We are the European family': unsettling the role of family in belonging, race, nation and the European project – Hannah Jones	166
	Conclusion: the long Brexit – Djordje Sredanovic and Bridget Byrne	191

Index	202

Figures

Contributors

Marianela Barrios Aquino, after obtaining her BA Hons in Sociology at the University of Salamanca in Spain, started her postgraduate education at the Institute of Social Sciences, University of Lisbon. During that time, she was also a Visiting Scholar at the Institute for the Study of International Migration, Georgetown University. She finished her PhD at the Sussex Centre for Migration Research, University of Sussex and is currently a post-doctoral research associate at the Centre for European and International Studies Research, University of Portsmouth. Her research interests include issues regarding the experiences of migration and citizenship, as well as decolonial and feminist methodologies.

Sanem Baykal is a Professor of EU Law at the TOBB-ETÜ Law Faculty. She graduated from Ankara University Law Faculty in 1990 and started her academic career as a research assistant in 1992 at the same university. She obtained her LLM (1994) from the University of London as a Jean Monnet Scholar and her PhD (2001) from Ankara University in EU law. During 2004–5 Sanem Baykal did post-doctoral research at NYU Law School as a Hauser Research Scholar and Emile Noël Fellow. She served as the director of the EU Law Directorate at the Turkish Ministry for EU Affairs between 2009 and 2012 and became a full professor at Ankara University Law Faculty in 2014. Sanem Baykal worked at the Department of Graduate Studies of the European Union, Ankara University between 2010 and 2018, where she was Head of Department, and the Deputy Director and Director of the EU Research Centre (ATAUM), Ankara University, between 2012 and 2018. Since September 2019 Sanem Baykal has been a faculty member of the TOBB-ETÜ Law Faculty, Ankara. Dr Baykal's research interests include European integration, EU law and Turkey–EU relations.

Bridget Byrne is a Professor of Sociology at the University of Manchester and Director of the ESRC-funded Centre of the Dynamics of Ethnicity

(CoDE). She works in the areas of citizenship, race, class and gender. In 2014 she published *Making Citizens: Public Rituals and Personal Journeys to Citizenship* (Palgrave). She has also published in journals such as *Citizenship Studies*, *Journal of Ethnic and Migration Studies*, *Sociology*, *Ethnic and Racial Studies*, and *Sociological Review*. Her latest book *All in the Mix: Race, Class and School Choice* was published by Manchester University Press in 2019, and she was the lead editor of the open access book *Ethnicity, Race and Inequality in the UK State of the Nation*, published by Policy Press in 2020.

Hannah Jones is a Professor of Sociology at the University of Warwick. She writes, researches and teaches on racism, belonging and migration control, power and emotion, and critical public sociology. She is the author of *Violent Ignorance: Confronting Racism and Migration Control* (Zed/Bloomsbury, 2021), co-author of *Go Home? The Politics of Immigration Controversies* (Manchester University Press, 2017), co-editor of *Stories of Cosmopolitan Belonging: Emotion and Location* (Routledge, 2014), and author of *Negotiating Cohesion, Inequality and Change: Uncomfortable Positions in Local Government* (Policy Press, 2013), which won the BSA Phillip Abrams Prize 2014 for best first book in UK sociology.

Jeremy MacClancy is Professor of Social Anthropology, Oxford Brookes University. He has done major fieldwork in the South Pacific archipelago of Vanuatu and the Basque region of northern Spain. Since the 2000s he has been conducting fieldwork in Alicante province, southeast Spain, studying the British residents there. He has written six books and edited another 15. Topics covered include cultural dimensions of nationalism, histories of popular anthropology, transdisciplinary anthropology, as well as the anthropologies of food, art and sport.

Çiğdem Nas is an Associate Professor of International Relations at the Yildiz Technical University in Istanbul. She is a graduate of the Political Science Department, Bosphorous University, and received her Master's degree in European social policy at the London School of Economics and Political Science. She completed her PhD on politics and international relations of the EU at the Marmara University EU Institute and worked at the same institute as a researcher and assistant professor between 1994 and 2007. She has been a lecturer at the Yildiz Technical University since 2007 and has also been working since that date at the Economic Development Foundation, which is an NGO dedicated to Turkey's EU integration. Her research interests cover the European Union, Turkey–EU relations, European integration, European politics, identity and foreign policy.

Devyani Prabhat is a Professor in Law at the University of Bristol Law School, UK, with legal practice experience in constitutional law. She holds an LL.M and a PhD from New York University and is an Attorney at Law, New York. She researches and teaches migration, citizenship and nationality from a socio-legal and comparative perspective. Dr Prabhat's book *Unleashing the Force of Law: Legal Mobilization, National Security, Basic Freedoms* (Palgrave Macmillan Socio-legal Studies Series, 2016) won the Birks Prize for Outstanding Legal Scholarship (Society of Legal Scholars, 2017).

Alina Rzepnikowska is a Senior Lecturer in Sociology and Politics, and a member of the Institute for Social Justice and Crime at the University of Suffolk. Her research and teaching interests include migration, ethnicity, gender and conviviality. Dr Rzepnikowska's book, published in 2020, is titled *Convivial Cultures in Multicultural Cities: Polish Migrant Women in Manchester and Barcelona*, part of the Routledge Studies in Migration and Diaspora series. She has also published work in the *Journal of Ethnic and Migration Studies*, *Gender, Place and Culture*, *Central and Eastern European Migration Review* and *Migration Studies – Polish Diaspora Review*.

Djordje Sredanovic is a Lecturer in sociology in the Division of Social and Political Science, University of Chester, and an associated researcher of the Group for research on Ethnic Relations, Migration and Ethnicity at the Université libre de Bruxelles. He is a specialist in the study of everyday citizenship and comparative citizenship policy, and has worked on the experiences and meanings of naturalisation for different groups in the UK and Belgium in the context of Brexit. He is the author of *Implementing Citizenship, Nationality and Integration Policies* (Bristol University Press, 2022) and the co-editor of *Governing Diversity* and *Migration Control in Practice* (Éditions de l'Université de Bruxelles, respectively 2018 and 2022).

Colin Yeo is a barrister at Garden Court Chambers in London specialising in immigration and asylum law. He is the founder and director of the Free Movement immigration law website and before becoming a barrister worked for two charities, the Immigration Advisory Service and the Refugee Legal Centre. He writes and campaigns extensively on immigration issues and is the author of *Welcome to Britain: Fixing Our Broken Immigration System* (Biteback, 2020) and *Refugee Law* (Bristol University Press, 2022).

Acknowledgements

The origins of this book go back to two workshops, 'Resurgences of national citizenship in Europe? Brexit and other restrictions' and 'Citizens of Brexit: Exploring status, belonging and participation in Brexit times', organised at the University of Manchester. We thank the Manchester Jean Monnet Centre of Excellence and the Centre on Dynamics of Ethnicity for having funded the first workshop, and the British Academy and the Royal Society for having funded the second workshop, as well as the first two years of Sredanovic's project through a Newton International Fellowship.

The workshops were followed by long and rich exchanges between the editors and contributors to the volume. Some of the collaborations for the workshops and during the development of the book did not materialise in a chapter in this published version. We would like to thank Paul Bagguley, Michaela Benson, Anne-Marie Fortier, Yasmin Hussain, Cristina Juverdeanu, Dora Kostakopoulou, Angeliki Kostantinidou, Jean-Michel Lafleur, Martijn Van den Brink and Daniela Vintila for their contributions. We would further like to thank Madeline Abbas, Amy Cross, Natalie-Anne Hall, Hannah Haycox and Konstantinos Kanellopoulos, who acted as discussants in the first workshop.

Shannon Kneis and Laura Swift (and Thomas Dark before them) at Manchester University Press have given us the editorial guidance to bring the research projects, analyses and discussions into this published book, and we would like to thank them and the anonymous reviewers of MUP.

Hannah Jones' chapter is a revised and updated version of an article previously published in the *Open Arts Journal* (issue 8, article 1).

Finally, we would like to thank the participants of the different research projects that have been included as chapters of this book, who have given their time and experiences to help us understand the different impacts of Brexit.

Introduction: Brexit and citizenship in context

Djordje Sredanovic and Bridget Byrne

Since around the beginning of the twenty-first century, there have been significant policy and political developments around the question of immigration, citizenship and citizen rights in both the UK and Europe, culminating in the ongoing phenomenon of Brexit. Citizens' rights are being profoundly redefined by Brexit, with British citizens losing their EU citizenship rights and EU norms losing validity in UK territory. The Brexit referendum has not only created a division between 'Leavers' and 'Remainers' within UK society but, as we show in this book, a number of groups have felt particularly targeted by Brexit and the Conservative UK governments from Cameron to Sunak. Large pro-EU public mobilisations emerged for the first time in the post-referendum years, with citizens' rights one of the guiding issues (see e.g. Brändle et al., 2018; Galpin, 2022; MacClancy, this volume). EU27 citizens in particular have become a new, declassed, category of migrants in the UK,[1] a group that experiences Brexit as an attack against their rights and life choices. Among Britons in the rest of the EU there are also concerns about the loss of rights and feelings of having been abandoned by the UK government. EU institutions have tended to be more popular among these two groups.[2] However, there also has been some dissatisfaction towards EU institutions regarding the lack of will to do more to avoid the consequences of Brexit, such as negotiating citizens' rights separately from other points of the UK–EU relationship, providing an associated EU citizenship status for the Britons deprived of EU citizenship (cf. Kostakopoulou, 2018) or considering the rights of Britons in the EU to move between different member states. Despite the relevance of citizen rights to the groups impacted by Brexit, the issue has often received limited attention in the negotiations between the UK government and the EU institutions, and has at times lost visibility in public discourse.

This book brings together scholars working on Brexit and citizens' rights across a range of disciplines (sociology, law, political science and anthropology) to show both how Brexit impacts extensively on citizens' rights *and* the ways in which Brexit is in continuity with previous developments in citizenship and migration policies both in the UK and EU. The book combines analyses of legislation and policies and studies of the experiences of the groups impacted – UK and EU27 citizens, but also third-country nationals. The book has two main aims. The first is to show the links between the political and legal changes introduced by Brexit that have resulted in a loss of rights, together with the experiences of such loss of rights, in terms of belonging, political participation and mobilisation, and pursuing new legal statuses. The second is to locate the political and legal changes, as well as the experiences of Brexit, in a longer history of transformation of both UK and EU citizenship, migration and mobility regimes.

This Introduction will begin with a discussion of the importance of formal citizens' rights and the ways in which the Brexit process impacts different groups. We will then discuss how Brexit should not be considered an isolated event, showing its links with other processes of reduction of citizens' rights at both the UK and European level. Finally, we will consider the contribution of this edited collection.

Citizens' rights and their relevance

Formal legal rights are one of the expectations of living in a contemporary state with a minimum level of functioning. They are far from absolute, both because they can remain only on paper (particularly for certain groups – see, for example Basok, 2004) and because a lack of formal rights does not exclude the possibility of social recognition (see e.g. Ambrosini, 2016) or of political mobilisation around a claim (Isin and Nielsen, 2008). To the degree that the rule of law functions (ensuring, for example, a functioning administration and judiciary, access to and affordability of legal representation), formal rights can be depended upon, claimed in front of the administration or upheld in court. There are clearly limitations in the power of formal rights, which may fail to protect individuals and groups from significant social, economic and political exclusions. Nonetheless, research has shown how formal rights matter for practical, emotional and symbolic reasons to those holding them (e.g. Brettell, 2006; Ruget and Usmanalieva, 2010; Sredanovic, 2014; Nunn et al., 2016; Della Puppa and Sredanovic, 2017; Prabhat, 2018). In addition, it is clear that economic and social opportunities are differently distributed between residents with different legal statuses (see e.g. Ruhs, 2017; Fellini and Guetto, 2022) and that obtaining a legal status improves one's condition (Gathmann, 2015; Peters et al., 2018, 2020).

The rights deriving from legal residence or permanent residence are linked to the security of living in a country and in not being excluded from social interactions we take for granted, as well as affecting the ability to access welfare, health and other support. Unauthorised/undocumented migrants are still covered by a modicum of human rights and can potentially live for long periods avoiding interaction with immigration enforcement and expulsion, circumventing the obstacles the state poses (see e.g. Bloch et al., 2014). However, they remain in a status of deportability (De Genova, 2002) and face proliferating internal bordering practices (Yuval-Davis et al., 2019) which, in addition to the psychological weight imposed, forces migrants into precarious and marginalised social and economic conditions. National citizenship rights entail voting rights, particularly at the national level (while local voting rights across Europe are often available to residents and especially permanent residents, only a few countries worldwide give access to national elections).[3] Citizenship further offers full access to social rights as well as restricted public jobs, which according to the context can vary from all public jobs to only public jobs with a security dimension. While across Europe citizenship-based property limits mainly relate to strategic industries, in other contexts non-citizens are barred from the ownership of certain assets, such as land. Citizenship is further a factor of mobility, as obtaining a new, often stronger, passport can offer the choice of moving either permanently or temporarily to another country, or facilitate pre-existing movements between different countries (Della Puppa and Sredanovic, 2017; Harpaz and Mateos, 2019). Finally, national citizenship is the highest level of protection against both deportation and migration controls. The possibility of deportation experienced by unauthorised migrants persists in a limited way for residents and permanent residents, who can still be expelled for criminal convictions and for reasons of public order or national interest. Full citizenship not only potentially offers protection from deportation but also interrupts the migration controls that continue even with permanent residence in the territory (requirements for people to renew or update their status) and at the borders (stricter controls on entry).[4] In contexts in which migration controls are expressed as a strong bureaucratic pressure, interrupting such controls can be a sufficient reason to apply for citizenship (Sredanovic, 2014). Finally, holding citizenship is for many a symbolic issue of identity and recognition that can align with a subjective identification with the state and/or the society of residence, or it can remove part of the feeling of othering and exclusion derived from a lesser legal status (see e.g. Brettell, 2006; Byrne, 2014; Prabhat, 2018).

Thus, naturalising has both practical and symbolic consequences. Practically, naturalisations can be protective – they can be started as a reaction to measures depriving non-citizens of rights (Coutin, 2003; Gilbertson and Singer, 2003), and more generally they can follow a certain tactical calculation (Harpaz and Mateos, 2019), although the latter should not be exaggerated (Sredanovic, 2022). Symbolically, the procedure of naturalisation involves procedures that aim to convince candidates of the value of citizenship (Fortier, 2013, 2017, 2021). With the diffusion across Europe of policies that introduce citizenship tests and citizenship ceremonies, candidates are increasingly presented with normative images of the nation and their duties within it (Byrne, 2012, 2014, 2017, 2019; Khan and Blackledge, 2015; Bassel et al., 2018; Fortier, 2018; Khan, 2019; Monforte et al., 2019; Barrios Aquino, this volume).

Certainly, legal national citizenship is still not an absolute guarantee of the protection of rights. National citizenship is often imagined in racialised ways, which serves to compromise the protection of the rights of certain groups of citizens. Many states have kept denaturalisation powers for citizenship acquired by fraud and for extreme cases such as high treason. In the last few years, there has been an increase both in new legislation introducing denaturalisation powers and in actual use of denaturalisation (Mantu, 2015, 2018; Prabhat, this volume; Yeo, this volume). While the overall use of denaturalisation remains relatively small scale, the potential for certain citizens to be denaturalised is a further dimension of uncertainty in the domain of citizenship. It also undermines the idea of the equality of all citizens, as in a number of countries denaturalisation for reasons other than fraud can only be applied to those who are deemed to have a claim to an alternative national citizenship. This places migrants and some descendants of migrants at risk of loss of citizenship, while other citizens by birth with no family history of migration cannot be denaturalised whatever their crimes (Yeo, this volume).

British citizenship is one of the most stratified and complex national citizenships currently existing, with several semi-citizenship statuses deriving from the decolonisation process (Sredanovic, 2017). EU citizenship is not monolithic either. Isin and Saward (2013) suggest a conceptualisation of *European* citizenship that goes beyond EU citizenship, including both claims to rights not enshrined in EU norms and formal rights either deriving indirectly from EU norms (see Nas and Baykal, this volume, on Turkish citizens) or deriving from other cross-European institutions, such as the Council of Europe (see also Sredanovic and Stadlmair, 2018). Having considered the importance of citizen rights in broad terms, the next section examines the particular impact of Brexit on rights within the UK and EU.

The groups impacted by Brexit

The effects of Brexit can be conceptualised as including 'direct' and 'indirect' loss of rights. The 'direct' loss of rights includes the loss of a legal status (e.g., British citizens losing EU citizenship) and the end of validity of a legal status (e.g., EU citizenship) in UK territory; in both cases the main dimension of such loss is linked to nationality and migratory status. The 'indirect' loss of rights is more limited to the UK and can be identified in cases in which UK laws give less protection and rights than EU laws. Workers' rights (Countouris and Ewing, 2021) and gender and LGBT+ related rights (Dustin et al., 2019) are among the domains in which such impact of Brexit has been explored. Along with the issues of family migration, which we also explore, Brexit has a disproportionate impact on women and minors, and endangers specific gender and LGBT+ rights enshrined in EU law, although some analyses look further at the potential for a redefinition of such laws, either at the UK level or in devolved nations (Dustin et al., 2019). Similarly, the workers' rights enshrined in EU law have been only vaguely reaffirmed in the Withdrawal Agreement, leaving substantial space for a worsening of workers' protection in the UK, which is further endangered by the government pursuit of new free trade agreements (Countouris and Ewing, 2021). More directly linked to migration, Brexit entails a reduction of guarantees in terms of asylum (e.g., Xanthopoulou, 2019) and human rights, particularly in reference to deportation (Yong, 2019), as we discuss in more detail below.

In this book, we examine what happens with the complex range of legal statuses impacted by the withdrawal of the UK from the EU, including those with lesser legal status such as temporary or permanent residence.[5] In the UK, these legal statuses have been substituted for EU27 citizens by 'pre-settled' and 'settled' status since 2019. The Brexit process has impacted, and is impacting on, the citizenship rights of several groups in significant ways. While the resulting deprivation of rights raises normative and potentially legal issues (e.g., Mindus, 2017; Kostakopoulou, 2018), the challenges brought in courts against the consequences of Brexit have been largely unsuccessful (More, 2020). British citizens lost their EU citizenship on 31st January 2020, unless they also hold the citizenship of an EU27 member state. The main losses deriving from this development are freedoms to settle, work and access social rights with few limitations in the 27 member states of the EU.

However, the impact of Brexit goes beyond removing EU citizenship from British citizens and potentially making British citizenship less valuable (and at the same time making it more necessary for EU27 citizens in the UK). Brexit also affects the most developed supranational citizenship currently existing – that of the European Union. It has been observed (e.g. Bauböck, 2019) that EU citizenship rights have been most attractive to mobile Europeans, and less so to sedentary ones. Intra-EU mobility is socially stratified, including along the lines of education, class, ethnicity, age and life stage, and EU accession seniority (Kuhn, 2015). This stratification can partly explain the different degrees of attachment in populations to both the EU and freedom of movement, especially in the more affluent EU member states (Vasilopoulou and Talving, 2019).

For the British citizens who settled in an EU27 member state before Brexit, or during the transition period which ended on 31st December 2020 (estimated to be between 1 million and 2.25 million people in Benson, 2019), there are certain guarantees (see More, 2020) deriving from the UK/EU Withdrawal Agreement. EU member states have followed different approaches, in some cases unilaterally attributing a new status to British citizens resident in their territory, and in others requiring them to apply for the new status. As with the pre-settled and settled status for EU27 citizens in the UK, the ramifications of the new status will probably emerge over the next few years. What has been completely absent from the negotiations is the right for British citizens resident in an EU27 member state to move to other EU27 member states. This limitation frustrates migration plans and imaginaries that had incorporated easy intra-EU mobility as part of career strategies, management of transnational family links or aspirations for specific lifestyles (Sredanovic, 2021). In addition to mobility rights, Brexit has deprived British citizens of EU political rights, including passive and active voting rights for the EU Parliament and, for those living in an EU27 member state, of voting rights in local elections.[6]

There has been a limited number of studies on British citizens in the EU27. A stereotype continues to be worryingly popular in journalism, describing most of the group as composed of retirees living in separate British enclaves in tourist areas. Research has shown, however, that, even in countries particularly prone to this stereotype, such as Spain, most Britons in the EU are of working age and reside well beyond the enclaves on the Costa del Sol (O'Reilly, 2020). Research has shown how Britons in Belgium are attached to intra-EU freedom of movement and are willing to protect it not only through naturalisation in the country of residence, but also by obtaining citizenship of other member states through ancestry or marriage (Sredanovic, 2021, 2022, 2023a). Although some individuals have opportunities to obtain more secure citizenship in EU countries, Benson (2020) shows how Britons in France have had their first experience of being othered in the country due to Brexit. However, for Britons of colour, the othering brought about by Brexit continues previous experiences of racism and exclusion (Benson and Lewis, 2019).

EU27 citizens in the UK are perhaps the group that has been most vocal about the loss of rights deriving from Brexit. Originally estimated at 3 million (an estimate that has been chosen as the name of the main group advocating the rights of EU27 citizens in the UK), the 2021 Census found there were 3.6 million EU-born residents, while the EU Settlement Scheme had 6.9 million applications (which, however, includes multiple applications from the same people, third-country relatives of EU citizens and people who have since left the country). Before the start of the Brexit process, EU27 citizens had the right to stay and work in the UK, extensive access to social rights, as well as voting rights in local elections, including those for the Scottish and Welsh Parliaments and the Northern Ireland Assembly. Free movement rights were not absolute even before Brexit. Firstly, EU enlargements have been accompanied with the option for existing member states to temporarily limit the access to work of citizens of the newly acceding member states. The UK government did not opt to limit migration for work during the 2004 accession but introduced limits for citizens of Romania and Bulgaria in 2007 (which expired in 2014) and Croatia in 2013 (which expired in 2018). In both cases the mobile Europeans from these countries had to register for authorisation to work. Secondly, the UK government has been active in making use of EU norms that allow the expulsion of EU citizens in specific cases. While hate crime reports significantly increased after the Brexit referendum, a number of research projects have noted how, for some Central and Eastern Europeans in particular, hostile rhetoric and xenophobia existed well before the referendum (Fox et al., 2012; Rzepnikowska, 2019, 2020; Rzepnikowska, this volume).

Since the Brexit referendum in 2016, EU27 citizens in the UK have lived through a long period of uncertainty (Hall et al., 2022; Sredanovic, this volume). There were no clear indications on their post-Brexit condition until the first tentative agreements between the EU and the May government in 2017. However, the possible agreement was hindered by a stalled UK Parliament during most of 2018 and 2019, with the possibility of a no-deal Brexit or an annulment of Brexit. Following the 2019 UK general election, Brexit was finalised in January 2020, but the hard Brexit line taken by Boris Johnson and continued by Liz Truss and Rishi Sunak offered further uncertainty. While a deal was finally agreed in December 2020, questions remained as to how the UK government will manage the provisions of the deal, and about the potential ramifications of the change in status, especially for the most vulnerable EU27 citizens (O'Brien, 2021). Currently, the rights of EU27 citizens in the UK are regulated by the European Union Settlement Scheme (EUSS – commonly called settled status). EUSS establishes 'settled status' (for those with more than five years of residence) and 'pre-settled status' (for those with shorter residence). EU27 citizens (as well as non-EU citizens whose status depends on the EU citizenship of a relative) who had established themselves in the UK before the end of 2020 were able to apply for these statuses if they did not have a criminal record. The fact that the EUSS involved an application rather than automatic registration has been criticised by those advocating for a more certain status for EU27 citizens, something that indeed was promised by the Leave campaign before the referendum. Further, the EUSS effectively declassed EU27 citizens holding permanent residence who, despite theoretically holding a permanent status, were also required to apply for settled status to continue enjoying their rights. Moreover, the EUSS is not entirely enshrined in primary legislation, leaving it potentially vulnerable to becoming a weakened status without a vote in Parliament (O'Brien, 2021).

The process through which people were required to apply for EUSS, through a self-conducted, smartphone-based procedure, has been criticised for risking data breaches, as well as for excluding significant parts of the population. Research on the experiences with the settled status application has shown hesitancy in complying with a procedure deriving from a withdrawal or rights, shortcomings in the functioning of the system, as well as difficulties of access for several groups, including those with limited competence in English and online procedures and people with atypical working histories (Botterill et al., 2020; Elfving and Marcinkowska, 2021; Barnard et al., 2022). In recognition of the issues with the settled status procedures, the UK government had to allocate some funds to charities working with vulnerable EU27 citizens to assist them in applying for settled status. Finally, settled status is a purely digital status, without any physical document to prove it. The 3million organisation campaigned for the introduction of a physical document, but the UK government decided to make it an experiment in digital-only status, with the potential to expand to other domains (see also Sredanovic, 2023b). Irish citizens have been to a degree protected from some of the consequences of Brexit, as the Common Travel Area between the UK and Ireland pre-exists the UK accession to the EU, which means that freedom of movement continues and Irish citizens have not been required to obtain settled status.

Research on EU27 citizens in the UK has shown how the rise of xenophobia (e.g. Guma and Jones, 2019; Lulle et al., 2019; Rzepnikowska, 2019, 2020; Sime et al., 2020; Moskal and Sime, 2022) and doubts about the right to stay in the UK (e.g. Lulle et al., 2019; Brahic and Lallement, 2020; Genova and Zontini, 2020; Zontini and Però, 2020; Sotkasiira and Gawlewicz, 2021; Hall et al., 2022), mobility rights (Sredanovic, 2021), and social rights and the economy (e.g. Duda-Mikulin, 2019; Sredanovic, 2021) have impacted on this group. Such doubts have brought many to reflect on whether to apply for British citizenship or consider leaving the UK. The naturalise/leave choices appear to have replaced more open-ended plans based on the reliance on freedom of movement (McGhee et al., 2017; Moreh et al., 2020). This choice between naturalising and leaving is mediated by both positive and negative imaginations of the EU and the future of the UK (Sime et al., 2020; Sredanovic, 2021), and complicated by difficulties in anticipating the evolution of the Brexit process (Sredanovic, 2022). Further, the existing research has shown how the confidence in one's capacity to be able to continue to stay in the UK or to move elsewhere is differentiated among citizens of member states according to seniority of EU accession (Lulle et al., 2018, 2022), as well as according to individual access to different forms of social, economic and cultural capital, migratory experience, age and family networks (Lulle et al., 2019; Godin and Sigona, 2022; Sredanovic and Della Puppa, 2023).[7]

In addition to EU27 citizens, other groups of migrants are directly impacted by Brexit. Firstly, specific nationalities have acquired rights from bilateral agreements with EU member states without, however, accessing full EU citizenship rights. One particularly significant case is that of the citizens of Turkey (see Nas and Baykal, this volume). The Ankara Agreement of 1963 not only offers facilitated migration routes to citizens of Turkey but equates, for many purposes, Turkish workers and their families in the EU with EU citizens, making them similar to quasi-EU citizens. Importantly, integration requirements that cannot be imposed on EU citizens cannot be imposed on Turkish citizens either.

Furthermore, before Brexit, third-country national spouses and relatives of EU27 citizens in the UK depended on EU norms on the right to family life for their own right to stay in the UK (cf. Kilkey, 2017). While their legal status already depended on that of the EU27 relative before Brexit, with the disapplication of EU norms their right to stay in the UK has been further endangered. It should be underlined that the third-country relatives of British citizens have been and are subject to more stringent conditions than in EU law, including income requirements on the UK relative. However, two exceptions have emerged. Firstly, the *DeSouza* case in 2020 resulted in British citizens born in Northern Ireland being able to make use of the more favourable EU norms in relation to family migration. This was the combined result of the Good Friday Agreement giving citizens of Northern Ireland the right to apply for either UK or Irish citizenship, and Republic of Ireland citizenship norms applying to people born anywhere on the island of Ireland. Secondly, the 'Surinder Singh' route applied to British citizens who lived with a third-country spouse in an EU27 member state before moving together to the UK – following a 1983 case, the more restrictive UK norms of family migration could not be applied (cf. Wray et al., 2021). Both third-country nationals that are relatives of EU27 citizens and those part of a 'Surinder Singh' couple were able to apply for the settled status, but these applications were among those that encountered more complications and refusals.

Beyond the third-country nationals who have acquired specific rights under EU norms, there are other third-country nationals for whom Brexit limits their potential plans. Third-country nationals often settle and naturalise in one EU member state before moving to another, often the UK. In some cases, the UK was chosen as further destination mainly because of economic considerations, as for Latin Americans leaving Spain after the 2008 global economic crisis (Mas Giralt, 2017; Ramos, 2018; McCarthy, 2019). In other cases, however, the choice is linked to colonial links with the country of origin, the symbolic role of the UK as a former colonial metropole and the presence of well-established communities in the UK, as in the cases of Bangladeshis, Somalis and Nigerians (van Liempt, 2011; Ahrens et al., 2016; Della Puppa and Sredanovic, 2017; Della Puppa and King, 2019; Morad and Sacchetto, 2020, 2021; Hall et al., 2022). In such cases, the UK was not necessarily the original and deliberate destination, but dissatisfaction with, or a lack of successful establishment in, the first destination country led to onward migration. However, Brexit represents a disruption of what was often a strategy at least partially contemplated by many potential onward migrants (Della Puppa and Sredanovic, 2017). Finally, while third-country nationals in the UK are generally not legally affected by Brexit, Brexit has been recognised by many commentators as part of a larger tendency to restrict migration (Bhambra, 2017; Gilmartin et al., 2018). Indeed, the result of the referendum and the anti-immigrant discourse of the Leave campaign reinforced and encouraged forms of racism directed to a range of racialised and migrant-origin groups who were not necessarily EU27 citizens and were often British citizens (Patel and Connolly, 2019).

Brexit within the context of British citizenship and immigration

While Brexit constitutes a clear break with previous UK policy on EU citizens, it should not be seen in isolation from previous citizenship and immigration policy. British citizenship (or, as it was created, 'Citizenship of the UK and colonies') received its first full codification with the British Nationality Act of 1948, an act linked to the process of decolonialisation as it represented a response to the creation of a specific Canadian citizenship in 1946 and aimed to claim continued UK sovereignty over the subjects of the British Empire (Hansen, 1999; Karatani, 2003). However, importantly, these colonial subjects were for the first time subject to immigration controls on entering the UK (Byrne, 2014). In the following decades the relationship with the (former) colonies dominated UK citizenship policies, making British citizenship highly complex and stratified, with several different levels of citizenship rights attributed to different groups of colonial subjects (Sredanovic, 2017; Prabhat, this volume). The process through which the access and rights of (former) colonial subjects were progressively restricted included cases of large-scale loss of rights and increasingly racialised definitions of citizenship and rights to enter the UK (Byrne, 2014). Such a process included the 1968 Commonwealth Immigrants Act, through which the UK government reneged on the right of former British colonial subjects who were being expelled from Kenya to enter UK territory, and the 1971 Immigration Act, through which only former British colonial subjects with ancestry in the UK could enter Britain (Prabhat, 2019, this volume).

In the 2000s, concerns around immigration became interwoven with a discourse of the 'crisis' or 'failure' of multiculturalism and fears that the celebration of difference had undermined national unity, creating separate groups who were insufficiently attached to a narrowly defined set of 'British values'. Muslims and those with dual citizenship became a particular source of anxiety and scrutiny (Byrne, 2017). The 2002 Nationality, Immigration and Asylum Act was introduced expressing this anxiety about the need for migrants to be transformed into 'active citizens'. The Act introduced language and 'life in the UK' tests and citizenship ceremonies to this end, with further (unfulfilled) plans in 2008 to push candidates into volunteering and punishing parents for infractions committed by their children (Kostakopoulou, 2010a). The overall result is a normative approach to citizenship in which candidates are invited to prove adherence to restrictive ideas of Britishness (Kostakopoulou, 2010a; Byrne, 2012, 2014, 2017; Turner, 2014). As mentioned above, EU27 citizens in the UK, and Central and Eastern Europeans in particular, have been subject to stigmatisation for a number of years (Fox et al., 2012; Rzepnikowska, 2019, 2020). The loss of rights deriving from Brexit is therefore only one in a long series of citizens' rights restrictions promoted through restrictive ideas of Britishness.

Further, in the 2010s the UK government introduced an approach defined as the 'hostile environment' (latterly called the 'compliant environment'), with the primary aim of reducing net immigration and making life difficult for those with irregular legal status and those seeking asylum. This included requiring private citizens and organisations to conduct migration checks for activities such as starting a job or renting a flat, in what has become known as 'internal bordering', where the apparatus of the borders reach into everyday life (Yuval-Davis et al., 2019). The Windrush scandal was one of the consequences of the hostile environment and a failure to recognise the rights of former colonial subjects. Colonial subjects who arrived legally in the UK before 1973 encountered problems under the new immigration regulation in proving their status and right to reside and work in the UK. The newly introduced laws requiring a narrow range of documentation to work, rent property and access benefits effectively removed these rights and subjected some to deportation. The government was forced to recognise this injustice and confirm these residents' status and set up a compensation scheme (Bawdon, 2019; Gentleman, 2019; Shankley and Byrne, 2020). Some parallels have been drawn between the Windrush scandal and the potential future of EU27 citizens (and their relatives) in the UK, both because of the possibility that part of the EU27 population might remain not fully aware of the new requirements and because of the lack of physical documents to prove EUSS (e.g. Sredanovic, 2023b).

As mentioned, the Brexit referendum and the overall Brexit process is also impacting other migrants, including third-country nationals. EU27 citizens who arrived in the UK after 2020 are even more affected, since they do not hold EU settled status and have received limited protection from the Withdrawal Agreement. Three linked phenomena contribute to this. Firstly, the Brexit process has legitimated wider anti-immigration positions, both in the general UK population and in government more specifically. Secondly, by leaving the EU, the UK government has also left EU mechanisms of migration governance, such as the Dublin system for the management of asylum and data-sharing procedures about people crossing borders. Third, EU norms gave stronger guarantees than the British ones in terms of access to asylum (Xanthopoulou, 2019) and protection against deportation (Yong, 2019). It is true that the main source of protection in this case are not EU norms but the European Convention on Human Rights (ECHR), to which the UK continues to adhere. However, several Conservative politicians have expressed hostility to the Convention, including Theresa May during her time as Home Secretary and the subsequent Home Secretaries Priti Patel and Suella Braverman.

The European context of Brexit

Just as Brexit should be placed in a longer UK history of restriction of citizenship rights (including most UK governments approaching EU integration with scepticism – Usherwood, 2018), it would be wrong to reduce Brexit to a story of UK exceptionalism. The rest of Europe has been characterised by attempts to limit migration, a backlash against multiculturalism and the reduction of citizenship rights, long before this was expressed most visibly in the Brexit referendum.

Firstly, EU citizenship rights proper were restricted in some cases before Brexit. EU freedom of movement has always been accompanied by limitations to migration from outside the EU, including restrictive Schengen norms, the militarisation of borders through Frontex and limitations to the right of asylum (see e.g. Aas and Gundhus, 2015; Steinhilper and Gruijters, 2018). In addition, internally, freedom of movement has never been absolute. The European Court of Justice (ECJ) has long been an important actor in the enlargement and reinforcement of EU freedom of movement. The

ECJ has extended through a number of cases what was essentially the freedom of movement of workers to something covering most EU citizens (see Kostakopoulou, 2001, 2007). However, since the 2008 global economic crisis, key decisions of the ECJ have gone in the direction of limiting the citizenship rights of mobile EU citizens. With the *Dano* case, the ECJ limited the full social rights of mobile EU citizens who do not match the categories of workers, former workers or jobseekers to three months. In the *Alimanovic* case, member states have been authorised to withdraw financial assistance from the same group (Barbulescu, 2017). The reversal of orientation of the ECJ adds to a long-term tendency of EU member states to limit the access to benefits of mobile EU citizens, creating an uneven situation across the EU (e.g. Heindlmaier and Blauberger, 2017). The UK started introducing limits to access to benefits as early as 1994 (Dwyer et al., 2019; Barbulescu and Favell, 2020), to which one should add further limitations introduced in bureaucratic practice (Dwyer et al., 2019; Guma, 2020).

The limits to freedom of movement also allow EU citizens to be expelled for reasons of fraud, abuse of rights, threats to public policy, security or health or 'undue pressure' on welfare. While there are general limits to the use of expulsions, each of the concepts involved is vaguely defined in EU norms, and has been unevenly defined across the member states (Maslowski, 2015 – cf. Kostakopoulou, 2014). The first large-scale expulsions were carried out in France and targeted Roma with Romanian or Bulgarian citizenship in 2010 (see e.g. Faure Atger, 2013). While the initial French practice was limited by EU intervention, the French government has established bilateral collaboration with the Romanian government to facilitate further expulsions of Romanian citizens (Vrăbiescu, 2021), and Roma have continued to be among the groups most targeted by expulsions. A second target has been economically inactive EU citizens who apply for welfare provisions after three months of residence (Lafleur and Mescoli, 2018). However, specific member states have been also targeting economically *active* EU citizens on subsidised income and homeless EU citizens who do not apply for benefits but are still expelled on the basis of lack of sufficient economic resources (Mantu, 2017). Considered in this context, Brexit appears not so much as British exceptionalism but rather as the highest point of a larger crisis and curtailment of EU citizenship rights.

Thirdly, national citizenship legislation across Europe have been characterised by a wave of integration-focused restrictionism starting in the late 1990s and accelerating after 2001. Such a wave has been concretised in the introduction of formal tests of language and culture, requirements of economic activity (Goodman, 2010; van Oers et al., 2010; Rea et al., 2018) and symbolic measures such as citizenship ceremonies (Byrne, 2014). The tendency has in some cases given a formal and standardised expression to similar pre-existing discretional requirements, and has come alongside other tendencies to make citizenship more accessible, including increased toleration of dual citizenship, the removal of gender asymmetries and increased measures against statelessness (Vink and de Groot, 2010). However, the general tendency is that, in many European countries, candidates for citizenship have to prove that they are conforming both culturally and economically (and sometimes civically) and deserving of becoming citizens. These processes are linked to the othering of migrants in ways which are often racialised (see e.g. Schinkel and Van Houdt, 2010; Byrne, 2014; Larin, 2020). While this 'citizenship turn' has been cross-European, it has not technically been promoted by EU norms, although a number of member states have taken the 2003 EU Directive on third-country nationals who are long-term residents, which includes integration measures, as a basis to introduce new integration requirements (Kostakopoulou, 2010b). While EU citizens are often subject to integration requirements for naturalisation, they are normally exempt from the same requirements for permanent residence and other statuses. In this perspective, Brexit is a way to apply to EU citizens the restrictive notions of integration that have spread across Europe.

Structure of the book

This book offers insight into the impact and aftermath of the 2016 referendum in the UK as revealed through empirical research projects on citizenship and migration. The book gives an account of Brexit and its effects within its larger historical context of immigration law in both the UK and EU. Drawing on a range of disciplinary and methodological approaches – from legal and policy analysis to interviews, participant observation and cultural analysis – the chapters examine the implications of Brexit for different categories of citizens. The chapters discuss the loss of EU citizenship rights, withdrawal of national citizenship, visas and naturalisation. They further discuss fears, conviviality, identity, belonging, othering and political mobilisation.

The book is structured into two parts. The first part, 'History and policy', offers more context and in-depth analysis of the ways in which Brexit intersects with the longer history of citizenship and migration in the UK, such as how it impacts different groups of people. Devyani Prabhat's chapter shows the parallels between the loss of rights linked to Brexit and the historical erosion of the rights of colonial and Commonwealth subjects. Prabhat starts with the establishment of British citizenship in 1948 to show how such citizenship was progressively restricted by withdrawing the right to enter the UK of all subjects without patrilinear ancestry in Britain. Her analysis further shows the parallels between Brexit, family-based mobility and the new powers of individual denaturalisation of British citizens to highlight the ethnicised and racialised definition of citizenship across the different cases. Çiğdem Nas and Sanem Baykal focus on a group of third-country nationals with specific rights within the EU legal framework, that is, Turkish citizens. They show the developments – both in law and in jurisprudence – that followed the 1963 Ankara Agreement between Turkey and the (then) European Economic Community. By establishing a standstill clause that forbids the introduction of new limits to the mobility of Turkish workers and self-employed and their families, the Ankara Agreement and the legal documents based on it resulted in significant freedom of mobility to the UK of Turkish citizens. These were then revoked by the Brexit process, along with most of the EU freedom of movement. Returning to the topic of denaturalisation introduced by Prabhat, Colin Yeo shows the parallels of Brexit and of the withdrawal of rights from colonial and Commonwealth subjects ('imperial denaturalisation') with the more recent individual withdrawals of British citizenship based on behaviour and fraud. By showing how all the UK cases of denaturalisation based on security reasons targeted Muslims, and how British fraud-based denaturalisation disproportionally targets Albanians, Yeo argues that such policies show both the extension of ethnicisation and racialisation to individual denaturalisation and a renationalisation of citizenship policy.

The second part of the book, 'Experience', shows the different ways in which the loss of rights and the larger context of Brexit impacts on the different groups touched by Brexit. This involves (1) the experiences of pursuing citizenship (British or of an EU27 Member State); (2) the issues of belonging in the context of loss of rights and of political hostility linked to Brexit; and (3) the different forms of political mobilisation in the context of Brexit. Alina Rzepnikowska looks at the experiences of Brexit in terms of belonging, othering and conviviality. Having interviewed Polish women in Manchester before and after the 2016 referendum, she shows how Brexit has reinforced the racialisation of Central and Eastern Europeans already ongoing before the referendum. She further shows different cases in which her interviewees manage to find belonging in multi-ethnic neighbourhoods or, on the contrary, feel othered also at a local level. Marianela Barrios Aquino links the experience of Brexit with the transformations of British citizenship linked to the introduction of integration requirements in the 2000s. Using interviews with EU27 citizens living in Brighton and Hove and undergoing the naturalisation process, she shows how Brexit has pushed them to naturalise in order to safeguard their rights, while eroding their sense of belonging and promoting restrictive integration-focused notions about who can be British. Djordje Sredanovic's chapter combines interviews with EU27 citizens in the UK, British citizens in Belgium and British citizens in the UK who explored obtaining another passport as a result of Brexit. His analysis is located within the sociology of risk, and looks at how the people impacted by Brexit anticipated risks linked to the loss of formal rights, xenophobia and a possible crisis in the UK economy, as well as the approaches they took to contain the risks, including protective naturalisation (i.e. naturalisation explicitly motivated by the desire not to lose rights). Focusing on Britons in the EU, in particular in the Alicante area of Spain, Jeremy MacClancy addresses specifically the discourses of Remainers and Leavers. His analysis shows the specular process of othering conducted by the two political sides within the British population in the area, and explores the anti-Brexit mobilisation of Remainers and its links and discontinuities with the pre-existing forms of more locally focused political activism among the British in Alicante. In the final chapter, Hannah Jones returns to the months of the campaign before the 2016 referendum to discuss the different conceptualisation of family across the UK, the EU and the Brexit debates. She discusses how the 'European family' evoked in the Remain mobilisation still tends to be a racialised and heteronormative one. Such a family is discussed through practices of denaturalisation and non-recognition of family-based citizenship in the UK, as well as of her own recovery of the German citizenship her grandfather was stripped of by the Nazi government, concluding with an exploration of more open ideas of family represented by the artist Gillian Wearing.

Notes

1 British citizens were also EU citizens until 31 January 2020, and some have continued to be EU citizens or are returning to hold EU citizenship by holding or obtaining the citizenship of an EU member state. We therefore use 'EU27 citizens' to refer to the citizens of the other, current, 27 EU member states. Irish citizens are exempt from some of the consequences of Brexit because of the Common Travel Area between the UK and Ireland, but are touched by some of the other consequences of Brexit, for example in terms of family migration. Therefore, we include them in the analysis of EU27 citizens, while keeping in mind that their situation is different on a number of points.

2 In particular, EU institutions had better relations both with EU27 citizens' organisations in the UK, such as 3million (see Vathi and Trandafoiu, 2023) and with British citizens' organisations in the EU (see MacClancy, this volume)

3 The UK is one partial example, as Commonwealth citizens have voting rights at the national level.

4 Although recent developments within the UK, most prominently in the case of Shamima Begum, have shown how citizens with dual nationality (or potential dual nationality) may be vulnerable to deportation or the removal of citizenship while they are in a third country – see the chapters of Prabhat and Yeo.

5 In the UK, these legal statuses were defined in specific terms for EU27 citizens before the Brexit process: while most migrants in the UK hold a leave to remain or indefinite leave to remain status, EU citizens had access to a separate residence status called permanent residence.

6 However, the UK has established bilateral agreements on the continuation of local voting rights, including with Spain, Portugal, Ireland and Luxemburg (More, 2020).

7 Ensuring the access to citizenship of one's children has been one of the main aims of naturalisation in the context of Brexit (Zontini and Però, 2020; Godin and Sigona 2022; Sredanovic, 2023a).

References

Aas, Katja Franko and Gundhus, Helene O. I. (2015) 'Policing humanitarian borderlands: Frontex, human rights and the precariousness of life'. *British Journal of Criminology* 55(1): 1–18.

Ahrens, Jill, Kelly, Melisa and van Liempt, Ilse (2016) 'Free movement? The onward migration of EU citizens born in Somalia, Iran, and Nigeria'. *Population, Space and Place* 22(1): 84–98.

Ambrosini, Maurizio (2016) 'From "illegality" to tolerance and beyond: Irregular immigration as a selective and dynamic process'. *International Migration* 54(2): 144–159.

Barbulescu, Roxana (2017) 'From international migration to freedom of movement and back? Southern Europeans moving north in the era of retrenchment of freedom of movement rights'. In Jean-Michel Lafleur and Mikolaj Stanek (eds) *South-North Migration of EU Citizens in Times of Crisis*. Dordrecht: Springer, pp. 15–32.

Barbulescu, Roxana and Favell, Adrian (2020) 'Commentary: A citizenship without social rights? EU freedom of movement and changing access to welfare rights'. *International Migration* 58(1): 151–165.

Barnard, Catherine, Fraser Butlin, Sarah and Costello, Fiona (2022) 'The changing status of European Union nationals in the United Kingdom following Brexit: The lived experience of the European Union Settlement Scheme'. *Social & Legal Studies* 31(3): 365–388.

Basok, Tanya (2004) 'Post-national citizenship, social exclusion and migrants rights: Mexican seasonal workers in Canada'. *Citizenship Studies* 8(1): 47–64.

Bassel, Leah, Monforte, Pierre and Khan, Kamran (2018) 'Making political citizens? Migrants' narratives of naturalization in the United Kingdom'. *Citizenship Studies* 22(3): 225–242.

Bauböck, Rainer (2019) 'The new cleavage between mobile and immobile Europeans'. In Rainer Bauböck (ed.) *Debating European Citizenship*. Cham: Springer, pp. 125–127.

Bawdon, Fiona (2019) 'Remember when "*Windrush*" was still just the name of a ship?' In Devyani Prabhat (ed.) *Citizenship in Times of Turmoil? Theory, Practice and Policy*. Cheltenham: Edward Elgar Publishing, pp. 173–197.

Benson, Michaela (2019) 'The puzzle of how many Brits abroad there really are'. *BBC News*, 12 January. www.bbc.co.uk/news/uk-46632854 (accessed 21 April 2023).

Benson, Michaela (2020) 'Brexit and the classed politics of bordering: The British in France and European belongings'. *Sociology* 54(3): 501–517.
Benson, Michaela and Lewis, Chantelle (2019) 'Brexit, British People of Colour in the EU-27 and everyday racism in Britain and Europe'. *Ethnic and Racial Studies* 42(13): 2211–2228.
Bhambra, Gurminder K. (2017) 'Brexit, Trump, and "methodological whiteness": On the misrecognition of race and class'. *British Journal of Sociology* 68(S1): S214–S232.
Bloch, Alice, Sigona, Nando and Zetter, Roger (2014) *Sans Papiers: The Social and Economic Lives of Young Undocumented Migrants*. London: Pluto Press.
Botterill, Kate, Bogacki, Mariusz, Burrell, Kathy and Hörschelmann, Kathrin (2020) 'Applying for Settled Status: Ambivalent and reluctant compliance of EU citizens in post-Brexit Scotland'. *Scottish Affairs* 29(3): 370–385.
Brahic, Benedicte and Lallement, Maxime (2020) 'From "Expats" to "Migrants": Strategies of resilience among French movers in post-Brexit Manchester'. *Migration and Development* 9(1): 8–24.
Brändle, Verena K., Galpin, Charlotte and Trenz, Hans-Jörg (2018) 'Marching for Europe? Enacting European citizenship as justice during Brexit'. *Citizenship Studies* 22(8): 810–828.
Brettell, Caroline B. (2006) 'Political belonging and cultural belonging: Immigration status, citizenship, and identity among four immigrant populations in a southwestern city'. *American Behavioral Scientist* 50(1): 70–99.
Byrne, Bridget (2012) 'A local welcome? Narrations of citizenship and nation in UK citizenship ceremonies'. *Citizenship Studies* 16(3–4): 531–544.
Byrne, Bridget (2014) *Making Citizens: Public Rituals and Personal Journeys to Citizenship*. Houndmills: Palgrave Macmillan.
Byrne, Bridget (2017) 'Testing times: The place of the citizenship test in the UK immigration regime and new citizens' responses to it'. *Sociology* 51(2): 323–338.
Byrne, Bridget (2019) 'Naturalisation and becoming a citizen in the UK'. In Devyani Prabhat (ed.) *Citizenship in Times of Turmoil? Theory, Practice and Policy*. Cheltenham: Edward Elgar Publishing, pp. 61–78.
Countouris, Nicola and Ewing, Keith (2021) 'Brexit and workers' rights'. *Institute of Employment Rights Journal* 4(1): 7–84.
Coutin, Susan Bibler (2003) 'Cultural logics of belonging and movement: Transnationalism, naturalization, and U.S. immigration politics'. *American Ethnologist* 30(4): 508–526.
De Genova, Nicolas P. (2002) 'Migrant "illegality" and deportability in everyday life'. *Annual Review of Anthropology* 31: 419–447.
Della Puppa, Francesco and King, Russell (2019) 'The new "twice migrants": Motivations, experiences and disillusionments of Italian-Bangladeshis relocating to London'. *Journal of Ethnic and Migration Studies* 45(11): 1936–1952.
Della Puppa, Francesco and Sredanovic, Djordje (2017) 'Citizen to stay or citizen to go? Naturalization, security, and mobility of migrants in Italy'. *Journal of Immigrant & Refugee Studies* 15(4): 366–383.
Duda-Mikulin, Eva A. (2019) *EU Migrant Workers, Brexit and Precarity: Polish Women's Perspectives from Inside the UK*. Bristol: Policy Press.
Dustin, Moira, Ferreira, Nuno and Millns, Susan (eds) (2019) *Gender and Queer Perspectives on Brexit*. Cham: Palgrave Macmillan.
Dwyer, Peter James, Scullion, Lisa, Jones, Katy and Stewart, Alasdair (2019) 'The impact of conditionality on the welfare rights of EU migrants in the UK'. *Policy & Politics* 47(1): 133–150.

Elfving, Sanna and Marcinkowska, Aleksandra (2021) 'Imagining the impossible? Fears of deportation and the barriers to obtaining EU settled status in the UK'. *Central and Eastern European Migration Review* 10(1): 55–73.
Faure Atger, Anaïs (2013) 'European citizenship revealed: Sites, actors and Roma access to justice in the EU'. In Engin F. Isin and Michael Saward (eds) *Enacting European Citizenship*. Cambridge: Cambridge University Press, pp. 178–194.
Fellini, Ivana and Guetto, Raffaele (2022) 'Legal status and immigrants' labour market outcomes: Comparative evidence from a quasi-experiment in Western and Southern Europe'. *Journal of Ethnic and Migration Studies* 48(11): 2740–2761.
Fortier, Anne-Marie (2013) 'What's the big deal? Naturalisation and the politics of desire'. *Citizenship Studies* 17(6–7): 697–711.
Fortier, Anne-Marie (2017) 'The psychic life of policy: Desire, anxiety and "citizenisation" in Britain'. *Critical Social Policy* 37(1): 3–21.
Fortier, Anne-Marie (2018) 'On (not) speaking English: Colonial legacies in language requirements for British citizenship'. *Sociology* 52(6): 1254–1269.
Fortier, Anne-Marie (2021) *Uncertain Citizenship: Life in the Waiting Room*. Manchester: Manchester University Press.
Fox, Jon E., Moroşanu, Laura and Szilassy, Eszter (2012) 'The racialization of the new European migration to the UK'. *Sociology* 46(4): 680–695.
Galpin, Charlotte (2022) 'Contesting Brexit masculinities: Pro-European activists and feminist EU citizenship'. *Journal of Common Market Studies* 60(2): 301–318.
Gathmann, Christina (2015) 'Naturalization and citizenship: Who benefits?' *IZA World of Labor* 125: 1–10.
Genova, Elena and Zontini, Elisabetta (2020) 'Liminal lives: Navigating in-betweenness in the case of Bulgarian and Italian migrants in Brexiting Britain'. *Central and Eastern European Migration Review* 9(1): 47–74.
Gentleman, Amelia (2019) *The Windrush Betrayal: Exposing the Hostile Environment*. London: The Guardian.
Gilbertson, Greta and Singer, Audrey (2003) 'The emergence of protective citizenship in the USA: Naturalization among Dominican immigrants in the post-1996 welfare reform era'. *Ethnic and Racial Studies* 26(1): 25–51.
Gilmartin, Mary, Wood, Patricia and O'Callaghan, Cian (2018) *Borders, Mobility and Belonging in the Era of Brexit and Trump*. Bristol: Policy Press.
Godin, Marie and Sigona, Nando (2022) 'Intergenerational narratives of citizenship among EU citizens in the UK after the Brexit referendum'. *Ethnic and Racial Studies* 45(6): 1135–1154.
Goodman, Sarah (2010) 'Integration requirements for integration's sake? Identifying, categorising and comparing civic integration policies'. *Journal of Ethnic and Migration Studies* 36(5): 753–772.
Guma, Taulant (2020) 'Turning citizens into immigrants: State practices of welfare "cancellations" and document retention among EU nationals living in Glasgow'. *Journal of Ethnic and Migration Studies* 46(13): 2647–2663.
Guma, Taulant and Jones, Rhys (2019) '"Where are we going to go now?" European Union migrants' experiences of hostility, anxiety, and (non-)belonging during Brexit'. *Population, Space and Place* 25(1): e2198.
Hall, Kelly, Phillimore, Jenny, Grzymala-Kazlowska, Aleksandra, Vershinina, Natalia, Ögtem-Young, Özlem and Harris, Catherine (2022) 'Migration uncertainty in the context of Brexit: Resource conservation tactics'. *Journal of Ethnic and Migration Studies* 48(1): 173–191.
Hansen, Randall (1999) 'The politics of citizenship in 1940s Britain: The British Nationality Act'. *Twentieth Century British History* 10(1): 67–95.

Harpaz, Yossi and Mateos, Pablo (2019) 'Strategic citizenship: Negotiating membership in the age of dual nationality'. *Journal of Ethnic and Migration Studies* 45(6): 843–857.
Heindlmaier, Anita and Blauberger, Michael (2017) 'Enter at your own risk: Free movement of EU citizens in practice'. *West European Politics* 40(6): 1198–1217.
Isin, Engin F. and Nielsen, Greg M. (eds) (2008). *Acts of Citizenship*. London: Zed Books.
Isin, Engin F. and Saward, Michael (eds) (2013) *Enacting European Citizenship*. Cambridge: Cambridge University Press.
Karatani, Rieko (2003) *Defining British Citizenship: Empire, Commonwealth and Modern Britain*. London: Frank Cass.
Khan, Kamran (2019) *Becoming a Citizen: Linguistic Trials and Negotiations in the UK*. London: Bloomsbury.
Khan, Kamran and Blackledge, Adrian (2015) '"They look into our lips": Negotiation of the citizenship ceremony as authoritative discourse'. *Journal of Language and Politics* 14(3): 382–405.
Kilkey, Majella (2017) 'Conditioning family-life at the intersection of migration and welfare: The implications for "Brexit families"'. *Journal of Social Policy* 46(4): 797–814.
Kostakopoulou, Dora (2001) *Citizenship, Identity and Immigration in the European Union: Between Past and Future*. Manchester: Manchester University Press.
Kostakopoulou, Dora (2007) 'European Union citizenship: Writing the future'. *European Law Journal* 13(5): 623–646.
Kostakopoulou, Dora (2010a) 'Matters of control: Integration tests, naturalisation reform and probationary citizenship in the United Kingdom'. *Journal of Ethnic and Migration Studies* 36(5): 829–846.
Kostakopoulou, Dora (2010b) 'Introduction'. In Ricky van Oers, Eva Ersbøll and Dora Kostakopoulou (eds) *A Re-definition of Belonging? Language and Integration Tests in Europe*. Leiden: Nijhoff, pp. 1–23.
Kostakopoulou, Dora (2014) 'When EU citizens become foreigners'. *European Law Journal* 20(4): 447–463.
Kostakopoulou, Dora (2018) '*Scala Civium*: Citizenship templates post-Brexit and the European Union's duty to protect EU citizens'. *Journal of Common Market Studies* 56(4): 854–869.
Kuhn, Theresa (2015) *Experiencing European Integration: Transnational Lives & European Identity*. Oxford: Oxford University Press.
Lafleur, Jean-Michel and Mescoli, Elsa (2018) 'Creating undocumented EU migrants through welfare: A conceptualization of undeserving and precarious citizenship'. *Sociology* 52(3): 480–496.
Larin, Stephen J. (2020) 'Is it really about values? Civic nationalism and migrant integration'. *Journal of Ethnic and Migration Studies* 46(1): 127–141.
Lulle, Aija, King, Russell, Dvorakova, Veronika and Szkudlarek, Aleksandra (2019) 'Between disruptions and connections: "New" European Union migrants in the United Kingdom before and after Brexit'. *Population, Space and Place* 25(1): e2200.
Lulle, Aija, Moroşanu, Laura and King, Russell (2018) 'And then came Brexit: Experiences and future plans of young EU migrants in the London region'. *Population, Space and Place* 24(1): e2122.
Lulle, Aija, Moroşanu, Laura and King, Russell (2022) *Young EU Migrants in London in the Transition to Brexit*. Abingdon: Routledge.

Mantu, Sandra (2015) *Contingent Citizenship: The Law and Practice of Citizenship Deprivation in International, European and National Perspectives*. Leiden: Brill Nijhoff.

Mantu, Sandra (ed.) (2017) 'Expulsion and EU citizenship'. *Nijmegen Migration Law Working Paper Series 2017/02*.

Mantu, Sandra (2018) '"Terrorist" citizens and the human right to nationality'. *Journal of Contemporary European Studies* 26(1): 28–41.

Mas Giralt, Rosa (2017) 'Onward migration as a coping strategy? Latin Americans moving from Spain to the UK post-2008'. *Population, Space and Place* 23(3): e2017.

Maslowski, Solange (2015) 'The expulsion of European Union citizens from the host Member State: Legal grounds and practice'. *Central and Eastern European Migration Review* 4(2): 61–85.

McCarthy, Helen N.J. (2019) 'Spanish nationals' future plans in the context of Brexit'. *Population, Space and Place* 25(1): e2202.

McGhee, Derek, Moreh, Chris and Vlachantoni, Athina (2017) 'An "undeliberate determinacy"? The changing migration strategies of Polish migrants in the UK in times of Brexit'. *Journal of Ethnic and Migration Studies* 43(13): 2109–2130.

Mindus, Patricia (2017) *European Citizenship after Brexit: Freedom of Movement and Rights of Residence*. Cham: Palgrave Macmillan.

Monforte, Pierre, Bassel, Leah and Khan, Kamran (2019) 'Deserving citizenship? Exploring migrants' experiences of the 'citizenship test' process in the United Kingdom'. *British Journal of Sociology* 70(1): 24–43.

Morad, Mohammad and Sacchetto, Devi (2020) 'Multiple migration and use of ties: Bangladeshis in Italy and beyond'. *International Migration* 58(4): 154–167.

Morad, Mohammad and Sacchetto, Devi (2021) 'For the future of the children? The onward migration of Italian Bangladeshis in Europe'. *International Migration* 59(6): 142–155.

More, Gillian (2020) 'From Union citizen to third-country national: Brexit, the UK Withdrawal Agreement, No-Deal preparations and Britons living in the European Union'. In Nathan Cambien, Dimitry Kochenov and Elisa Muir (eds) *European Citizenship under Stress: Social Justice, Brexit, and Other Challenges*. Leiden: Brill Nijhoff, pp. 457–481.

Moreh, Chris, McGhee, Derek and Vlachantoni, Athina (2020) 'The return of citizenship? An empirical assessment of legal integration in times of radical sociolegal transformation'. *International Migration Review* 54(1): 147–176.

Moskal, Marta and Sime, Daniela (2022) 'Young Europeans in Brexit Britain: Unsettling identities'. *Global Networks* 22(2): 183–196.

Nunn, Caitlin, McMichael, Cecilia, Gifford, Sandra M. and Correa-Velez, Ignacio (2016) 'Mobility and security: The perceived benefits of citizenship for resettled young people from refugee backgrounds'. *Journal of Ethnic and Migration Studies* 42(3): 382–399.

O'Brien, Charlotte (2021) 'Between the devil and the deep blue sea: Vulnerable EU citizens cast adrift in the UK post-Brexit'. *Common Market Law Review* 58(2): 431–470.

O'Reilly, Karen (2020) *Brexit and the British in Spain*. Final report, Brexit Brits Abroad. https://ukandeu.ac.uk/wp-content/uploads/2020/03/OReilly-2020-Online-min.pdf (accessed 15 June 2024).

Patel, Tina G. and Connelly, Laura (2019) '"Post-race" racisms in the narratives of "Brexit" voters'. *The Sociological Review* 67(5): 968–984.

Peters, Floris, Schmeets, Hans and Vink, Maarten (2020) 'Naturalisation and immigrant earnings: Why and to whom citizenship matters'. *European Journal of Population* 36(3): 511–545.

Peters, Floris, Vink, Maarten and Schmeets, Hans (2018) 'Anticipating the citizenship premium: Before and after effects of immigrant naturalisation on employment'. *Journal of Ethnic and Migration Studies* 44(7): 1051–1080.

Prabhat, Devyani (2018) *Britishness, Belonging and Citizenship: Experiencing Nationality Law*. Bristol: Policy Press.

Prabhat, Devyani (2019) 'The blurred lines of British citizenship and immigration control: The ordinary and the exceptional'. In Devyani Prabhat (ed.) *Citizenship in Times of Turmoil? Theory, Practice and Policy*. Cheltenham: Edward Elgar Publishing, pp. 198–216.

Ramos, Cristina (2018) 'Onward migration from Spain to London in times of crisis: The importance of life-course junctures in secondary migrations'. *Journal of Ethnic and Migration Studies* 44(11): 1841–1857.

Rea, Andrea, Bribosia, Emmanuelle, Rorive, Isabelle and Sredanovic, Djordje (eds) (2018) *Governing Diversity: Migrant Integration and Multiculturalism in North America and Europe*. Brussels: Éditions de l'Université de Bruxelles.

Ruget, Vanessa and Usmanalieva, Burul (2010) 'How much is citizenship worth? The case of Kyrgyzstani migrants in Kazakhstan and Russia'. *Citizenship Studies* 14(4): 445–459.

Ruhs, Martin (2017) 'The impact of acquiring EU status on the earnings of East European migrants in the UK: Evidence from a quasi-natural experiment'. *British Journal of Industrial Relations* 55(4): 716–750.

Rzepnikowska, Alina (2019) 'Racism and xenophobia experienced by Polish migrants in the UK before and after the Brexit vote'. *Journal of Ethnic and Migration Studies* 45(1): 61–77.

Rzepnikowska, Alina (2020) *Convivial Cultures in Multicultural Cities: Polish Migrant Women in Manchester and Barcelona*. Abingdon: Routledge.

Schinkel, Willem and Van Houdt, Friso (2010) 'The double helix of cultural assimilationism and neo-liberalism: Citizenship in contemporary governmentality'. *British Journal of Sociology* 61(4): 696–715.

Shankley, William and Byrne, Bridget (2020) 'Citizen rights and immigration'. In Bridget Byrne, Claire Alexander, Omar Khan, James Nazroo and William Shankley (eds) *Ethnicity, Race and Inequality in the UK: State of the Nation*. Bristol: Policy Press, pp. 35–50.

Sime, Daniela, Moskal, Marta and Tyrrell, Naomi (2020). 'Going back, staying put, moving on: Brexit and the future imaginaries of Central and Eastern European young people in Britain'. *Central and Eastern European Migration Review* 9(1): 85–100.

Sotkasiira, Tiina and Gawlewicz, Anna (2021) 'The politics of embedding and the right to remain in post-Brexit Britain'. *Ethnicities* 21(1): 23–41.

Sredanovic, Djordje (2014) 'Quelle est la valeur de la nationalité/citoyenneté en Italie? Résultats d'une recherche auprès des migrants et des ouvriers italiens à Ferrare'. *Migrations Société* 153–154: 47–61.

Sredanovic, Djordje (2017) 'Was citizenship born with the Enlightenment? Developments of citizenship between Britain and France and "everyday citizenship" implications'. *Miranda* 15.

Sredanovic, Djordje (2021) 'Brexit as a trigger and an obstacle to onwards and return migration'. *International Migration* 59(6): 93–108.
Sredanovic, Djordje (2022) 'The tactics and strategies of naturalisation: UK and EU27 citizens in the context of Brexit'. *Journal of Ethnic and Migration Studies* 48(13): 3095–3112.
Sredanovic, Djordje (2023a) 'Brexit and citizenship by descent: A relational understanding of defensive pragmatism and of the rediscovery of belonging'. *Revue Européenne des Migrations Internationales* 39(2–3): 109–129.
Sredanovic, Djordje (2023b) 'The vulnerability of in-between statuses: ID and migration controls in the cases of the "Windrush generation" scandal and Brexit'. *Identities* 30(5): 625–643.
Sredanovic, Djordje and Della Puppa, Francesco (2023) 'Brexit and the stratified uses of national and European Union citizenship'. *Current Sociology* 71(5): 725–742.
Sredanovic, Djordje and Stadlmair, Jeremias (2018) 'Introduction: Trends towards particularism in European citizenship policies'. *Journal of Contemporary European Studies* 26(1): 1–11.
Steinhilper, Elias and Gruijters, Rob J. (2018) 'A contested crisis: Policy narratives and empirical evidence on border deaths in the Mediterranean'. *Sociology* 52(3): 515–533.
Turner, Joseph (2014) 'Testing the liberal subject: (In)security, responsibility and "self-improvement" in the UK citizenship test'. *Citizenship Studies* 18(3–4): 332–348.
Usherwood, Simon (2018) 'The third era of British Euroscepticism: Brexit as a paradigm shift'. *The Political Quarterly* 89(4): 553–559.
van Liempt, Ilse (2011) '"And then one day they all moved to Leicester": Somalis' relocation from the Netherlands to the United Kingdom'. *Population, Space and Place* 17(3): 254–266.
van Oers, Ricky, Ersbøll, Eva and Kostakopoulou, Dora (eds) (2010) *A Re-definition of Belonging? Language and Integration Tests in Europe*. Leiden: Nijhoff.
Vasilopoulou, Sofia and Talving, Liisa (2019) 'Opportunity or threat? Public attitudes towards EU freedom of movement'. *Journal of European Public Policy* 26(6): 805–823.
Vathi, Zana and Trandafoiu, Ruxandra (2023) 'The politics of EU diaspora in the UK post-Brexit: Civic organisations' multi-scalar lobbying and mobilisation strategies'. *European Political Science* 22(1): 28–43.
Vink, Maarten P. and de Groot, Gerard-René (2010) 'Citizenship attribution in Western Europe: International framework and domestic trends'. *Journal of Ethnic and Migration Studies* 36(5): 713–734.
Vrăbiescu, Ioana (2021) 'Devised to punish: Policing, detaining and deporting Romanians from France'. *European Journal of Criminology* 18(4): 585–602.
Wray, Helena, Kofman, Eleonore and Simic, Agnes (2021) 'Subversive citizens: Using EU free movement law to bypass the UK's rules on marriage migration'. *Journal of Ethnic and Migration Studies* 47(2): 447–463.
Xanthopoulou, Ermioni (2019) 'Legal uncertainty, distrust and injustice in post-Brexit asylum cooperation'. In Tawhida Ahmed and Elaine Fahey (eds) *On Brexit: Law, Justices and Injustices*. Cheltenham: Edward Elgar Publishing, pp. 175–188.
Yong, Adrienne (2019) 'Human rights protection as justice in post-Brexit Britain: A case study of deportation'. In Tawhida Ahmed and Elaine Fahey (eds)

On Brexit: Law, Justices and Injustices. Cheltenham: Edward Elgar Publishing, pp. 128–141.

Yuval-Davis, Nira, Wemyss, Georgie and Cassidy, Kathryn (2019) *Bordering*. Cambridge: Polity Press

Zontini, Elisabetta and Però, Davide (2020) 'EU children in Brexit Britain: Re-negotiating belonging in nationalist times'. *International Migration* 58(1): 90–104.

Part I

History and policy

1

Empire and Brexit: rights, rollback and categorical exclusion

Devyani Prabhat

'If the flap of a butterfly's wings can be instrumental in generating a tornado, it can equally well be instrumental in preventing a tornado.' (Edward N. Lorenz, 1972)

Introduction

The process of Brexit has often been presented as one which advantages the Commonwealth nations and their nationals while depriving European Union nationals of their privileged position in the UK. Yet both kinds of UK residents have experienced heightened racism during and after the Brexit process. Although Brexit has placed Britain at the crossroads of immigration control, it comes only as the latest episode of tightening immigration conditions for many people. Scholars have been analysing the effects of Brexit, but few present Brexit as linked to past immigration measures, apart from some analysis on the colonial origins of the Commonwealth and Brexit being driven by nostalgia for the British Empire.[1] Yet, it is possible to learn much more about the categorical exclusion of people through immigration and nationality frameworks when different instances of such exclusion are examined together. A key comparator for the Brexit-related nationality and immigration changes is that of similar processes of exclusion of Commonwealth nationals in the past.

While every situation has specific contexts in which these processes of exclusion arise, there may be patterns which emerge and surprising elements which can be analysed in greater depth while acknowledging the obvious differences that also operate across instances. It is with this spirit of enquiry that this chapter situates the categorical exclusion of EU citizens from the UK post Brexit at the end of the transition period in December 2020, together with the previous episode of exclusion of Commonwealth citizens from the UK through restrictive immigration legislation in the 1960s and 1970s.

Both sets of people enjoyed rights of free movement and associated rights to reside and gain long-term secure status, but eventually both lost their nearly unconditional membership of British society. The chapter will cover a number of examples, such as welfare rights linked to citizenship and EU membership, derived rights, acquisition of nationality and cancellation of citizenship especially as a multiple nationality holder, to argue that Brexit and subsequent developments indicate a turn towards rebordering along ethnicised national borders. The examples illustrate that sometimes when rights are granted at a supranational level, nation states retaliate with sharp downturns in the rights held by those deemed foreign. Categorical exclusion of foreigners present in their midst is often an indicator of rising national fervour and a return to ethnicised and racialised notions of national belonging.

The rights of different ethnic groupings and economic strata of migrants are often presented as being in conflict, especially in the labour market, yet the intricate web of migration control links all of humanity. Like a flap of a butterfly's wings can change the earth, each measure touches all in contact with a national jurisdiction and the ever-widening jurisdictional ripples affect others. This chapter demonstrates these patterns of inclusion and exclusion by examining the post-2012 document-checking requirements in immigration control which affect all migrants. It then reviews the derived rights framework and how it brings third-country nationals into the membership of EU nations. Finally, it examines how cancellation of citizenship is linked to multiple nationality holding and acts as a convergence point of migration control for various categories of people.

The expansion of national membership

A continuum of legal statuses has emerged at various key stages of evolution of the concepts of citizenship and immigration in the UK. These transition points were fundamental in nature such as the transformation of subjecthood to citizenship (at the time of Empire), the emergence of citizenship linked to the Commonwealth (after the end of the Empire), the national citizenship plus EU rights model of citizenship (after the UK joined the EU) and the conditional citizenship of present times (linked to modern national security). All are linked in terms of the subject of membership in society and each is connected to the right to reside and move freely.

Let us examine more closely the advent of the EU influence on British national membership and then see how the earlier subjecthood model influenced British citizenship. The UK was enthusiastic about a European Community market and joined the Community on 1 January 1973. Since then, through the Treaty of Maastricht of 1992, the Community has evolved into the European Union and the UK was one of the key members. The rights of EU nationals living in the UK did not emerge all at once. These evolved over time especially through judgments of the European Court of Justice (Kostakopoulou, 2013). By contrast, Commonwealth nationals in the UK were granted a status of Citizens of UK and Colonies (CUKC) through a declaration of their status in the 1948 British Nationality Act (BNA).[2] Previously they held the equal legal status of subjecthood wherever they were located in the Empire, but this was now put in statutory form. This meant that Commonwealth nationals within the UK, and those entering to reside in the UK, were for all practical purposes British citizens in law who had the right to enter, reside in an uninterrupted manner and engage in all the usual activities a citizen would. They did not require an incremental validation of their status. Instead, over time what they faced was the reverse; they started losing the security of their status owing to legislative changes.

The story of how citizenship came to be defined in the UK, and how the status of Commonwealth nationals came to be declared in law as equivalent to that of citizens, is part of the history of global geopolitics. Prior to 1948 every British national was treated by law as a British subject. Colonies and dominions had supported the British war efforts during the two world wars. Yet, in the dying days of Empire, subjecthood was challenged and discarded nationally in the former dominions who no longer wanted to let people from colonies enter and settle within their new borders. In different countries, racial and ethnic qualifications to citizenship were eventually removed because of national social and political movements to include minority and Indigenous persons into the fold of national citizenry (see, for instance, Chesterman, 2005). However, discretion often remained regarding racial qualifiers for admission as well as settlement for a long period afterwards, thereby creating discriminatory modes in terms of residence mostly for non-white people.

British politicians had empathy for the dominions and their desire to regulate entry from the colonies. Chamberlain said, for instance:

> We quite sympathise with the determination of the white inhabitants of these colonies which are in comparatively close proximity to millions and hundreds of millions of Asiatics that there shall not be an influx of people alien in civilisation, alien in religion, alien in customs, whose influx, moreover, would most seriously interfere with the legitimate rights of the existing labour population. An immigration of that kind must, I quite understand, in the interests of the Colonies, be prevented at all hazards, and we shall not offer any opposition to the proposals intended with that object.[3]

The driving force behind a continued nationality relationship with people of decolonised nations, including colonies, was the desire of Britain to exert soft power over the former Empire nations and to retain a position as 'first amongst equals' in the Commonwealth. The direct impetus was a piece of Canadian domestic legislation. Canada passed its own citizenship act in 1946 and issued Canadian passports to include its own French-Canadian citizens (Fransman, 2011). Canada's initiative in controlling its own immigration and naturalisation meant that each dominion could now determine its own criteria for entry and residence and regulate subjects from other parts of the Empire. This challenged the common status of British subjecthood, which began to lose its relevance in a post-Empire world.

The British Nationality Act 1948 attempted to preserve the equal status of subjects and permitted former subjects of the Commonwealth and colonies to freely enter and settle in the UK. It changed the focus from having allegiance to the king to just being a citizen of a country in the Commonwealth (Hansen, 2000). Under the British Nationality Act 1948, the concept of a British subject covered, in addition to citizens of the independent Commonwealth countries, 'Citizens of the United Kingdom and Colonies' and 'British subjects without citizenship'. 'British subjects without citizenship' were persons who could potentially become citizens of an emerging independent Commonwealth country on the coming into force of that country's citizenship law. If they did not acquire such citizenship they would, by default, then acquire citizenship of the United Kingdom and Colonies (Dummett, 1986: 143).

Many Commonwealth citizens arrived in the UK in the 1950s. They did not just arrive on their own initiative. British companies actively recruited from the Commonwealth, especially in sectors such as textiles and farm labour where labour was scarce within the UK (for example, see McDowell, 2018). Family members of labourers arrived later, closer to the end of 1950s or early 1960s, when there were strong indications that immigration policies would likely tighten to stem future migration (Turner, 2015). While some EU nationals also migrated for lower-paid jobs, many who exercised free movement were professional workers. However, once the nature of EU migration changed, and people migrated more for lower-paid jobs (Polish plumbers and Eastern European cleaners were often in focus in the media), there was less of a welcome in Britain for EU workers and nationals (Donaghey and Teague, 2006). This pattern of initial warmth, followed by adverse reactions when numbers surged, is also seen for Commonwealth nationals who immediately attracted resentment and racist reactions in the UK when they used their right to enter and reside in larger numbers. Enoch Powell's Rivers of Blood speech, which exhorted a ban on Commonwealth immigration, is a classic example of the political rhetoric of the day. Racial tensions led to hate attacks on Black and Asian people, who were often excluded from jobs and housing (Phillips and Phillips, 1998). Similarly, a pattern of creating or maintaining a common membership and then retracting from it once common membership rights become robust is present for EU nationals too. EU nationals in the UK also likely faced categorical exclusion because they could provide better legal status to connected third-country nationals, who could also then obtain entry and residence rights. For example, third-country national partners of EU nationals were exempt from the minimum-income restrictions for family reunification which are placed on third-country national partners of British citizens, as analysed later in this chapter.

Once EU membership and rights expanded, Britain's membership of the EU became increasingly rancorous as nationalistic fervour and ethnic, linguistic and ancestral conceptions of membership in society resurfaced. Many commentators link nostalgia for Empire with Britain's exit from the EU. Nobel laureate Abdulrazak Gurna said that the British Empire is 'still important in Britain' and may well have played a part in the Brexit vote (Knight, 2022). Aufa Hirsch writes in her book *Brit(ish)* (2018: 270) that 'the ghosts of the British Empire are everywhere in modern Britain, and nowhere more so than in the dream of Brexit'. However, the similar experiences of migrants and categorical inclusion followed by exclusion remain underexplored, with migrant groups often pitted against each other in immigration debates. Eventually, the UK exited the EU after a transition period and categorically excluded EU nationals from the right to enter and reside in the UK, with the exception of those who went through a settlement process.

Although racist incidents were reported much before the Brexit referendum, there is evidence that these increased during the campaign for the referendum and in the aftermath of the Yes vote for Brexit (for example, Rzepnikowska, 2019). Botterill et al. (2019, citing Virdee and McGeever, 2017: 1808) write that racist violence was experienced by many irrespective of their own racial or ethnic backgrounds and irrespective of citizenship or migration status of European, Commonwealth or other residents present in the UK. Professionals who had greater mobility were able to leave in the face of these changes. Many long-term resident EU nationals started leaving the UK in anticipation of rising backlash soon after the referendum (Sumption and Walsh, 2022). Those who stayed faced heightened tensions, arising from both spontaneous racism as well as structurally embedded difficulties, including the evidence documentation asked for under the settlement scheme and the legislation requiring proof of status for work, renting and medical treatment (Sumption and Fernández-Reino, 2020). Arguably, the constitutive system of registration under the European Union Settlement Scheme (EUSS) did not give due consideration to the life situations of the most vulnerable and made them irregular overnight (see Morgan, 2021; Duda-Mikulin, 2023).

Rendering people irregular through automatic operation of law can itself be a manifestation of rising ethnic nationalism. Commonwealth citizens who were settled in East Africa as British subjects had to leave because of the dictatorial regimes of East Africa and the rise of African nationalism there which excluded them from society. It led to the persecution of minorities such as Asian-origin Ugandans and Kenyans who could no longer own businesses or enjoy their family lives (Hansen, 1999). In fear for their lives, in the 1960s and 1970s nearly 70,000 displaced East Asian African British passport holders migrated to the UK.[4] They found that they could not readily enter and settle in the UK because the 1960s and early 1970s saw the end of this Commonwealth free movement era through increasing restrictions on their right to enter and reside in the UK (for instance, based on where their British passports were issued, where their ancestry was and where their close connections remained). The Commonwealth Immigrants Act 1962 ended the right of automatic entry for Commonwealth citizens. They were still 'British subjects' under the British Nationality Act 1948, but that status was detached from any substantive rights. Even if they were ordinarily resident, or had been, they were subject to a new system enabling deportation of those who had committed criminal offences. All of these changes permitted a wide latitude in administrative discretion for determining who could enter and who could stay in the UK. Crucially, the 1962 Act removed the right of entry of Citizens of the United Kingdom and Colonies whose passports had been issued by colonial authorities.

The British government then passed an immigration Act, the Commonwealth Immigrants Act 1968, in just three days, in order to prevent the re-entry of people from countries such as Uganda and Kenya. The 1968 Act further restricted the right of entry of Commonwealth citizens. A citizen could only live and work in the UK if they, or at least one of their parents or grandparents, had been born, adopted, registered or naturalised in the UK, which excluded most non-white people who are more likely to be born overseas or linked to UK through parents or grandparents born overseas. This rule, therefore, without expressly adding race as a direct criterion for inclusion or exclusion, through its racialised operation excluded almost all of the East African Asians who were at that time desperately seeking entry to the UK with their British passports for safety and security.

The British government refused them entry, or detained and deported many of them, stating that their passports were not intended to be used as travel documents. The refusal of entry of several East African Asian British passport holders was challenged at the European Commission of Human Rights. The Commission found in *East African Asians v. United Kingdom* (3 EHRR 76), 15 December 1973, that the UK had participated in the inhumane and degrading treatment of East African Asians in the form of racism and discrimination. In response, the UK government started a voucher system for each head of household (defined as a male member of household) who wanted to resettle in the country.

In 2020, nearly 2.6 million EU citizens lost their right to live and work in the UK automatically; many who were vulnerable could not apply for settlement in time to protect their settlement rights by 30 June 2021, and thereby became irregular (Fernández-Reino and Sumption, 2022). It is likely that the structural discrimination faced by these EU citizens will be contested at length and in various stages in the courts. At the time of writing, the Brexit settlement scheme has been successfully challenged in the High Court (hearings ongoing) by the Independent Monitoring Authority (IMA) because of the loss of free movement rights for all the pre-settled EU people whose rights were not recognised by the settlement scheme.[5] The High Court has held that the settlement scheme is illegal to the extent that the rights of pre-settled EU nationals are not adequately protected.

In the context of Commonwealth citizens, the zenith of the process of their exclusion was realised in the enactment of the Immigration Act 1971, which ended the system of labour vouchers and student entry for Commonwealth citizens altogether. It introduced the concept of 'patriality' as well as 'right of abode' for Citizens of the United Kingdom and Colonies (CUKC) as restrictions on their entry. Patrials had to have a special connection with the country. Patriality depended on close connections (for instance, grandparent or parent born in the UK). A 'patrial' was generally (1) a citizen of the United Kingdom and Colonies who held that citizenship through birth, adoption, naturalisation or registration in the UK or (2) a citizen of the United Kingdom and Colonies who acquired citizenship outside the UK but who had lived in the UK for a continuous five-year period. Only 'patrials' held the right of abode in the United Kingdom.

These new categories carried over the earlier dominion versus colony divide as these continued to give preference to those who were ethnically similar to the white British population. People from former dominions with their white settler populations were more likely to have parents or grandparents born within the United Kingdom because of having ethnic links to the white-majority British population. They could readily establish patriality. Non-patrials resided mainly in the former colonies in Asia and Africa. They were ethnically different and were usually not able to prove such a link. They were excluded from prospective migration to the UK. It should be noted though that the UK-based settled population of Commonwealth citizens were not meant to be affected by the prospective exclusion of newer arrivals, just as the EU nationals with settled status were not supposed to be affected by Brexit and the end of free movement. Yet the documentation-checking regime affects everyone who are rendered precarious under the hostile environment legal framework. Instituted primarily by a series of new pieces of legislation such as Immigration Act 2014 and 2016 but also supported by secondary legislation (for example, regulations governing National Health Service charges), bureaucratic changes (such as embedding of immigration officials at police stations and in local authorities) and data sharing agreements between government departments (such as memorandums of understanding between the Home Office and Department for Education and the Department of Health), the hostile environment makes life extremely difficult for irregular migrants and also affects lawful residents without documentary proof of their status. Among the Windrush generation, many faced immigration action, including deportation, simply because of their inability to prove their British citizenship through paperwork that they were never required to obtain in the first place. Termed the Windrush scandal, many people who had lived all their lives in the UK suddenly found themselves homeless, unemployed, without health care, and were even deported (Bawdon, 2019; Gentleman, 2019). Similarly, post Brexit, vulnerable rough sleepers or poorer EU nationals who did not apply to the European Union Settlement Scheme in a timely manner (by 30 June 2021) suddenly became deportable overnight even if they had resided for a long time in the UK (Radziwinowiczówna and Lewis, 2021).

These new changes have affected all categories of migrants who came to secure status in the UK but due to reversal in laws lost their status or had to re-establish it in light of new legal requirements. EU nationals who arrived prior to 1989 may not have acquired any proof of their status at that time. The Windrush scheme is a special process for people to acquire proof of their legal status so that they can produce documentation of their status at work or wherever required by law,[6] and it provides EU nationals proof of status as well if they arrived before 1989.[7] Later in the chapter we examine cancellation of citizenship as another point of convergence between EU nationals, Commonwealth nationals and indeed any others who may potentially have another nationality. But before proceeding to that point, it is important to understand why EU nationals became subject to immigration control despite their earlier expansive rights. Their exclusion took a different trajectory from the incremental exclusion of Commonwealth nationals.

Welfare rights linked to citizenship and 'foreigners'

Similar to the idea of the British Empire as an area of free movement, the European Economic Area (EEA) created an area of free movement through agreement of member states (treaty law) but this only applied to a limited set of people who were mostly EU nationals.[8] EU nationals could work and travel throughout the territory, while others remained excluded through heavily monitored borders. Indeed, while being lauded as an area of free movement, the same region is often referred to 'fortress Europe' for its harsh migration/asylum policies targeting third-country nationals. Even with its formidable bordering policies, membership of the EU has been widely viewed as a liberal expander of national borders and citizenry. This is because of the changing nature of EU citizenship-linked rights such as substantive thickening of rights linked to worker status and the expansion in number of members of the EU as new member states are admitted and considered for future candidacy. Third-country nationals who are linked to EU nationals as family could acquire derived rights from their status, thereby widening the pool even further. These transformations in the content and scope of rights, as well as membership growth, have triggered a backlash in several member countries who perceive these changes as undermining their individual borders.

During the campaign for Brexit, the increasing rights of resident foreigners and prospective arrival of foreigners who would potentially obtain eligibility were rallying calls for Brexiteers. In terms of expansion of membership of nation states, Bulgaria and Romania joined the EU in 2007. There were rumours of Turkey also being admitted, leading to fears of mass inward migration into the UK. Regarding the thickening of rights in the beginning, originally, rights for residence and movement in the EU were strictly tied to being a worker. This changed in the 1980s when the European Court of Justice started looking broadly at who is a worker. It was not necessary to be in work in order to be a worker but simply to be actively looking for work. Thus, freedom of movement for jobseekers meant that unemployed foreigners from other EU countries could stay for days without earning a means of supporting themselves and potentially becoming welfare dependent. Further, the non-discrimination rule (between nationals of a state and outside jobseekers) levelled the field between EU nationals and British citizens. The tension between the prohibition of discrimination on grounds of member state nationality and the welfare states and social systems in Europe which retained their national links has been palpable. In the UK, the main political fallout of non-discrimination was resentment about loss of the privileged status of British citizens in employment and welfare support.

Derived rights: overlapping categories of EU and others

Perhaps free movement erodes national borders, thereby challenging the nation-state model of social protection because it raises questions about the allocation of national resources. Free movement also highlighted the differing levels of social protection among the member states. EU states may perceive migrants as a drain on the social protection available if their welfare benefits are more generous than elsewhere and attract migrants. Restricting welfare benefits is a means of preventing outsiders from depleting national resources.

One such measure in the UK was the minimum income which a British citizen needs before bringing their foreign family members into the UK. This measure separates thousands of British citizens and residents from family members. It was challenged in a case about access to social welfare and links to family migration. The *MM* case concerned the entry criteria for a non-EU national to join their British citizen (or long-term resident) spouse or partner ('the sponsor') in the United Kingdom. These include a requirement that the sponsor has an income of at least £18,600 per annum or substantial savings, with additional sums needed for dependent non-citizen children ('the minimum income requirement' or MIR). British nationals were placed in a worse-off situation than EU nationals and their third-country family members. Yet the MIR was upheld by the Supreme Court.[9] The primary challenge in the *MM* case was to the level of the MIR. The Court found that there was adequate justification for adopting the MIR and that the limit had also been carefully considered and set. The Supreme Court did not find the MIR incompatible with Article 8 of the European Convention on Human Rights (the right to respect for private and family life). The Court came to this conclusion despite nearly 15,000 children being separated from at least one parent because of the current MIR, with many of these children being British children. The case reconfirms the protectionist stance of national welfare regimes. By contrast, prior to Brexit, EU nationals could bring their third-country family members into the UK with no such restriction. EU nationals and their family members did not have to satisfy the minimum income rules for family reunification inside the UK. Associated third-country nationals could obtain derived immigration status (through their EU family members) and also transmit the status to their children because the free movement rights of EU nationals expanded the rights of their connected third-party nationals. The anomaly in the rights of EU nationals, and their associated third-country nationals, and the situation of British nationals with foreign family members demonstrates the spillover effect of restrictions. Those who are deemed 'foreign' as a category are rarely the only ones affected by the measures. The unevenness of rights holding gives third-country nationals the opportunity to claim European citizenship rights to overcome 'restrictive' member states' provisions. Perceptions of such instrumental advantages (both real and unfounded) have contributed to the 'take back control of our borders' narrative. During the pro-Brexit campaign and post-referendum politics, immigration control has thus been a flashpoint (for example, see HM Government, 2018).

A derived rights framework has also had the unintended consequence of leading to the withdrawal of generous *jus soli* citizenship regimes in other EU member states. For example, children obtaining birth nationality in Ireland via a *jus soli* regime has led to their third-country national parents obtaining nationality of Ireland as well. Rather than welcoming third-country nationals in this manner, countries such as Ireland have preferred to abandon the jus soli model (Ryan, 2004). The *Chen* case, in which a Chinese woman moved to Ireland to give birth, is especially important for understanding the context of derived rights for immigration status and the link to free movement in Europe, as well as the subsequent backlash. The background to this case is the Good Friday Agreement, a 1999 amendment to the Irish constitution which specified that Irish citizenship was the 'birthright of every person born in the island of Ireland', including Northern Ireland.

Ms Chen, a wealthy Chinese businesswoman working in the UK for a firm owned by her husband, travelled to Belfast to give birth to her daughter. She then sought a UK residence permit on the basis of the baby's EU (Irish) citizenship (Kochenov and Lindeboom, 2017). Though the baby's Irish citizenship was established as a matter of fact, UK authorities initially refused to extend a residence permit. The case was referred to the European Court of Justice, where Irish citizenship and EU citizenship were discussed at length. The Advocate General in the case opined that unconditional *jus soli* in Ireland was a problem. The Court, however, allowed the parents to hold derived rights to reside to accompany the citizenship rights of their (Irish-born) child.

The *Zambrano* (C34/09) case thereafter extended the reasoning of Chen and permitted third-country national parents to hold the right of residence and work rather than be deported. This is because their children, born in Belgium, would not be able to enjoy their EU citizenship rights without their parents being able to look after them. Zambrano expanded on Chen because while in Chen the exercise of rights was still connected to free movement, in Zambrano it became a freestanding right independent of cross-border free movement. In Zambrano the situation was not about moving between EU countries but only about residing in Belgium.

The *Chen* case is likely to have informed the process that led to the Twenty-Seventh Amendment of the Constitution of Ireland in March 2004 (Ryan, 2004). It eventually passed with a huge majority and led to a new rule on acquisition of Irish citizenship: a baby born in Ireland 'who does not have, at the time of the birth of that person, at least one parent who is an Irish citizen or entitled to be an Irish citizen is not entitled to Irish citizenship or nationality'.

It is only a matter of historical pre-determination that the UK did not encounter this exact issue; it had already rolled back jus soli in 1983 when it transitioned from being solely a jus soli regime to one which was based on a mixed model of birth connected with blood links. Only children of parents with long-term status such as citizenship, indefinite leave to remain or permanent residence in the UK who were born in the UK could now gain British citizenship at birth. All other children would have to apply for citizenship later in their lives through a process known as registration (available until adulthood at age 18) if they wanted to become British. This shift was ostensibly to curb irregular migration and the transmission of citizenship to the progeny of irregular migrants. The move away from territorial birth citizenship, however, affected all in the UK, whether EU nationals, Commonwealth citizens or from elsewhere, as they could no longer directly transmit citizenship at birth in the UK unless they (at least one parent) also had settled long-term status themselves.

Point of convergence: cancellation of citizenship

While an obvious point of convergence has been changes in manner of acquisition of citizenship which affects all migrants, citizenship stripping or cancellation of citizenship is another point of convergence which particularly affects those with migrant links. Cancellation demonstrates how there is a resurgence of national scrutiny over multiple nationality holders and the creation of aliens out of citizens. Part of the process of being a global citizen has been the capacity to hold multiple nationalities. However, states have the power to recognise or derecognise this capacity and they can strip their own nationals of their citizenship. But here, too, European integration has created situations in which member state nationality law had to adapt to the growth of EU citizenship.

One example is the *Rottmann* case, in which an Austrian citizen who was charged with financial crime fled to Germany and was naturalised. By becoming a German citizen, he lost his Austrian citizenship under Austrian nationality law. When Austrian authorities later asked Germany to extradite Mr Rottmann, German authorities decided that he had obtained German citizenship fraudulently and moved to revoke his German citizenship. But doing so could render him stateless, and thus also result in loss of EU citizenship (which had originally provided him with the right to reside in Germany). The Advocate General's opinion noted that EU citizenship is a 'legal and political status conferred on the nationals of a state beyond their state body politic', in which EU citizenship is 'a citizenship beyond the State'; it is based on the Member States' 'mutual commitment to open their respective bodies politic to other European citizens and to construct a new form of civic and political allegiance on a European scale' (Case C-135/08 [2010] Rottmann, Opinion of Advocate General Poiares Maduro, 30 September 2009, paras 16, 23). Thus, although decisions about the acquisition or loss of Member State (and thereby EU) citizenship are not in themselves governed by EU law, they need to be compatible with the EU Community rules and respect the rights of European citizenship. The judgment concluded that it is not contrary to EU law for a member state to denaturalise one of its citizens 'when that nationality has been obtained by deception, on condition that the decision to withdraw observes the principle of proportionality' (Case C-135/08 [2010] Rottmann, para 59). The idea that member state nationality law must be compatible with EU citizenship and respect the rights of the EU citizen leads in the judgment to the conclusion that, for EU citizens, member state decisions about naturalisation and denaturalisation are 'amenable to judicial review carried out in the light of European Union law' (Case C-135/08 [2010] Rottmann, para 48). It is evident that Rottmann restricts Member State autonomy in the field of citizenship (Kochenov, 2010), and that it is connected with the derived rights cases we have already examined. However, in recent UK practice and case law on cancellation, EU law had little effect even when the UK was a member of the EU.

More recently in instances such as the deprivation of Shamima Begum, *Begum (Respondent) v Secretary of State for the Home Department (Appellant)* [2021] UKSC 7, a person born in the UK and British citizen from birth can still be stripped if it appears they have any connection with any other country (in Begum's case through her parental links with Bangladesh which theoretically gave her eligibility for Bangladeshi citizenship). The link to Bangladesh exists only through Bangladesh's legal framework but it becomes a condition for British citizenship stripping. How is that possible? Earlier, under the British Nationality Act of 1981, the Home Secretary could deprive a person of citizenship if they were satisfied that this would be conducive to the public good (s.40(2)), but not if they were satisfied that the order would make him or her stateless (s.40(4)). There are now new elements in the power. Previously, birth citizens could not have their citizenship taken away, but the reach of the power increased after the 11 September 2001 attacks on the Twin Towers of the World Trade Center in New York City (referred to as 9/11). After 9/11, the Nationality, Immigration and Asylum Act 2002 rendered birth citizens subject to cancellation of citizenship powers for the first time in the UK. However, no one could be rendered stateless through cancellation for their conduct at this point.

From 2015, this scenario changed. An amendment to the British Nationality Act 1981 changed the legal situation and enabled the government to render any naturalised citizen stateless while depriving them of their citizenship. The new subsections to Section 40 of the British Nationality Act (4A) permits cancellation for naturalised persons even at risk of statelessness, so it follows that under Section 40 (4), the Secretary of State may not make an order under subsection (2) if they are satisfied that the order would make a person stateless. However, they can still render a citizen stateless if they are naturalised citizens. The amended provision says:

(4A) ... that does not prevent the Secretary of State from making an order under subsection (2) to deprive a person of a citizenship status if—
(a) the citizenship status results from the person's naturalisation,
(b) the Secretary of State is satisfied that the deprivation is conducive to the public good because the person, while having that citizenship status, has conducted him or herself in a manner which is seriously prejudicial to the vital interests of the United Kingdom, any of the Islands, or any British overseas territory, and
(c) the Secretary of State has reasonable grounds for believing that the person is able, under the law of a country or territory outside the United Kingdom, to become a national of such a country or territory.

Thus, the Home Secretary can now deprive British citizens of their citizenship in a few different scenarios: (1) it would be 'conducive to the public good' to deprive the person of their citizenship and to do so would not leave them stateless; (2) the Home Secretary is satisfied that citizenship was acquired through naturalisation and obtained fraudulently or by false representation; or (3) on 'conducive' grounds where citizenship was acquired through naturalisation and the Home Secretary has reasonable grounds to believe they could acquire another nationality. The Secretary of State can use these powers for all naturalised citizens, irrespective of issues of statelessness if the conduct in question is 'not conducive to the public good' and is 'prejudicial to the vital interests of the country'. All they need is a reasonable belief that another nationality may be acquired.

Why was there a change to specifically target naturalised citizens and render them stateless? A stateless person is defined in Article 1(1) of the 1954 Convention on Statelessness as 'a person who is not considered as a national by any State under the operation of its law'. The 1954 Convention, which is binding on the UK, also establishes minimum standards of treatment for stateless people in respect to a number of rights including, but not limited to, the right to education, employment and housing. A subsequent convention, the 1961 Convention, aims to prevent statelessness and reduce it over time. It requires that states establish safeguards in their nationality laws to prevent statelessness at birth and later in life.

Naturalised citizens are more likely to have some other nationality and thus would be less likely to be rendered stateless, but it can be argued that in that case there is no necessity for specifically mentioning in the legislation that naturalised citizens can be cancelled even when they are at risk of statelessness.

The House of Lords debates on the amendment proposed that the Secretary of State should have reasonable grounds to believe the deprived persons could acquire another nationality so that people would not be rendered stateless without any safeguards in place. Adding a higher standard of conduct ('seriously prejudicial to the vital interests') was also considered an important means of constraining widespread statelessness.[10] Yet, now, under the new Nationality and Borders Act 2022, the government is allowed to strip people of citizenship without giving them notice to appeal against the measure, thereby diluting the earlier protections as people may remain unaware of their loss of nationality while outside the country.[11] In this manner, cancellation powers have morphed into targeted instruments of bordering that are especially effective against naturalised citizens and multiple nationality holders. The Shamima Begum case is as much about the precarity of citizenship as it is about expulsion from the national community.

It appears that the process of safeguarding against statelessness has paradoxically led to a situation where anyone with a potential dual nationality may become more vulnerable to cancellation powers. By the broad parameters used in the *Begum* case, nearly anyone with some sort of ancestry which is ethnically different from white, British, and even a lot of white, British people with links to any other country, become amenable to citizenship stripping for loosely defined reasons of conduct. It appears to be a resurgence of the suspicion of multiple nationality holders and people from 'elsewhere' whose loyalty, often linked to ethnicity, just could not be trusted. Such prejudices predate the current human rights regime but perhaps surprisingly continue to co-exist with various rights frameworks.

The confusion from the application of multiple nationality principles and rules is longstanding but increased with increasing migration and rights of nationality acquired by people in different nation states. The 1930 Hague Convention Concerning Certain Questions Relating to the Conflict of Nationality Law set out a multilateral approach to multiple nationality so that states can still identify their own nationals but also cooperate in terms of recognition of the duties and rights associated with divergent nationalities. Nationality cannot be forced on an unwilling individual, but the Convention does not cover the kind of situations involving loss of citizenship for multiple nationality holders.

Double nationality may cause practical problems which cannot be resolved if the two states adopt a strictly national attitude in the matter. The idea of predominant nationality is of great importance in resolving this problem, involving a hierarchy of the two nationalities of the claimant, whereby the ranking nationality would be the principal or dominant nationality and the next in rank would be the other nationality, seen as the subsidiary nationality. A new legal concept, namely, that of effective and dominant nationality, has emerged as a solution but if this is only about emotive elements of citizenship, such as demonstrating belonging, it can become arbitrary in nature. Given formal legal requirements for naturalisation, it is also unlikely there are any emotive requirements for acquisition of citizenship in the UK. A determination made at the point of cancellation where a person has already held citizenship with all its connections for a long period of time cannot solely be about emotive aspects. Indeed, it is unclear why greater loyalty (or lack of disloyalty) is expected from naturalised citizens or multiple nationality holders.

Targeting multiple nationality holders for cancellation is regressive in a world where the number of people holding at least two citizenships is constantly increasing, both because of increasing mobility and different nationality regimes across countries. Despite the prevalence of assessment of foreign nationality in cancellation cases, and the wider reach of cancellation powers over citizens with dual/multiple nationality, the UK has one of the least restrictive regimes in terms of permitting as many other nationalities as anyone desires. Upon acquiring other nationalities, one does not lose British nationality (Hansen, 2002: 179). The Home Office does not assist other countries in enforcing prevention of double nationality (Hansen, 2002: 182). Historically, this liberal stance towards multiple nationality holding was linked to a soft power strategy for British nationality: it was considered beneficial for British nationality to remain with people even if they subsequently obtained other ones (Hansen, 2002: 186). The converse is now the national approach, as apart from keeping people outside the country, cancellation powers make expressive statements about who does not belong. As Bosniak (1999: 465) writes, racial subordination has distorted formally egalitarian polities to create 'second-class citizens' who enjoy the status of citizenship but are nevertheless denied the enjoyment of citizenship rights or 'equal citizenship'.

Cancellation appears to be a measure that absolves a nation state of its duties towards citizens as well, but this begs the question of who bears responsibility for these people. Provision of diplomatic protection to nationals who are in need in foreign territories is a state responsibility.[12] Under international law, the UK and other nation states can grant diplomatic protection to their citizens if it is shown that another country has committed an intentionally wrongful act against them. In such situations, if a dual/multiple nationality holder is involved, the main enquiry becomes who is the nation state responsible.

The challenging scenario is where a dual national brings a claim against one of their states in their other state of nationality. Article 4 of the 1930 Hague Convention declares that 'a State may not give diplomatic protection to one of its nationals against a state whose nationality that person possesses'. In other words, an individual traditionally cannot invoke the protection of one of their states against the other. In its 2006 *Articles on Diplomatic Protection*, the International Law Commission adopted a more flexible rule, which relied on a test of predominant nationality. Article 7 Articles on Diplomatic Protection thus provides that:

> A State of nationality may not exercise diplomatic protection in respect of a person against a State of which that person is also a national unless the nationality of the former State is predominant, both at the date of injury and at the date of the official presentation of the claim.

Multiple citizenship was a liability for Nazanin Zaghari-Ratcliffe, a dual UK-Iranian national imprisoned in Iran. Zaghari-Ratcliffe was in an Iranian prison from 2016 and was subject to human rights abuses, such as denial of a fair trial and being tortured. All diplomatic remedies had been exhausted. It was then decided that Zaghari-Ratcliffe, although a dual national, was predominantly British,[13] and she was eventually released only in 2022 and flown back to the UK to be reunited with her family (Farrer, 2022). Her situation also serves as a cautionary tale on the challenges of multiple nationality, as well as the scope and limits of diplomatic protection. In January 2023 another British dual-nationality holder in Iran was executed on allegations of spying (McGarvey and Walsh, 2023).

The suspicion with which multiple nationality holders are perceived (despite often being inadvertent nationality holders) is based on the same concerns about loyalty and allegiance as those underlining cancellation cases. The expansive approach to another nationality for purposes of citizenship stripping has brought under its wide umbrella all kinds of citizens who may be of EU, Commonwealth or any other origin, so long as some connection to another country is established. These developments once again demonstrate that borders may indeed target specific groups or categories of people but have widespread effects of exclusion which go beyond those directly targeted.

Conclusion

As already mentioned, a continuum of legal statuses, such as subjecthood to citizenship of UK and its colonies, European Union citizenship and national security linked conditional citizenship, has emerged at various key stages of evolution of the concept of citizenship/immigration in the UK. Each of these stages has created new categories of people through British immigration and nationality laws. Each developed processes of inclusion and exclusion which affected many others beyond those apparently or directly targeted.

The examples of transitions in status in this chapter illustrate that sometimes when rights attach and consolidate at a supranational level, nation states retaliate with new restrictions. It appears that having access to a wider bundle of citizenship rights than just those guaranteed by one nation state is often viewed with renewed suspicion. Brexit has provided the latest instance of loss of status for an entire category of long-term residents as EU nationals lost their automatic right to settle and work in the UK after enjoying these rights blossom over a number of years.

The Brexit political context has led to the precarity of EU long-term residents in the UK, but their true vulnerability comes from legislation designed to target irregular migrants who do not have documents, and which first affected the Windrush arrivals. The hostile environment towards migration has affected all migrants and many settled populations, whether they be the Windrush generation (Caribbean/Commonwealth diasporas) or EU nationals or indeed long-term citizens. National security linked conditionality of British citizenship has rendered naturalised and multiple nationality holder citizens especially vulnerable.

The fates of people, whether migrant communities, settled populations or citizens (or indeed a complicated mix of these), are intertwined. Categories in which people are sorted by law are neither discrete nor self-contained. Pathways to citizenship, and the variety of legal statuses available to others, are part of a membership continuum. Residents are not just insiders or outsiders but may share some attributes of insiders while remaining outsiders and vice versa. Indeed, contemporary developments of the precarity of long-term residents can be understood properly only if the uncertain origins of British citizenship and immigration are evaluated.

There has been a resurgence of the nation state and nation borders as states seek to redefine who they are in this century. Perhaps, at least in the case of the UK, this is a step in the direction of a new post human rights laws era alongside controlling borders. It is likely that this is the new formulation we are observing in developments of national asylum provision which divert from the right to seek asylum framework of the Geneva Convention on Refugees (1951) and focus on seeking permission before crossing national borders. Or perhaps a new critical juncture will arrive to shake up the current statuses, such as with the inward journeys of people from Hong Kong or Ukraine into the UK in greater numbers.

Notes

1 An interesting analysis of these arguments can be found in Saunders (2020).
2 Citizens of UK and Colonies (CUKC) is used interchangeably in this chapter with Commonwealth citizens or Commonwealth nationals.
3 Joseph Chamberlain in a conference in 1896, cited in Huttenback (1973: 117).
4 https://minorityrights.org/minorities/east-african-asians/ (accessed 1 February 2023).
5 https://ima-citizensrights.org.uk/news_events/independent-monitoring-authority-successful-in-landmark-high-court-challenge-against-home-office/ (accessed 11 June 2024).
6 www.gov.uk/windrush-prove-your-right-to-be-in-the-uk (accessed 11 June 2024).
7 For instance, see: https://the3million.org.uk/node/1100849921 (accessed 11 June 2024).
8 The EEA includes EU countries and also Iceland, Liechtenstein and Norway. It allows them to be part of the EU's single market.
9 [2017] UKSC 10.
10 See House of Lords debates on the proposed Clause 60 (House of Lords Hansard Debates, 2014).
11 See Section 10 of the Nationality and Borders Act 2022, www.legislation.gov.uk/ukpga/2022/36/enacted (accessed 11 June 2024); critique of this provision in Prabhat (2021).
12 www.gov.uk/government/collections/support-for-british-nationals-abroad (accessed 11 June 2024).
13 www.gov.uk/government/news/foreign-secretary-affords-nazanin-zaghari-ratcliffe-diplomatic-protection (accessed 11 June 2024).

References

Bawdon, Fiona (2019) 'Remember when "*Windrush*" was still just the name of a ship?' In Devyani Prabhat (ed.) *Citizenship in Times of Turmoil? Theory, Practice and Policy*. Cheltenham: Edward Elgar Publishing, pp. 173–197.

Bosniak, Linda (1999) 'Citizenship denationalized'. *Indiana Journal of Global Legal Studies* 7(2): 447–509.

Botterill, Kate, McCollum, David and Tyrrell, Naomi (2019) 'Negotiating Brexit: Migrant spatialities and identities in a changing Europe'. *Population, Space and Place* 25(1): e2216. https://doi.org/10.1002/psp.2216

Chesterman, John (2005) 'Natural-born subjects? Race and British subjecthood in Australia'. *Australian Journal of Politics and History* 51(1): 30–39.

Donaghey, Jimmy and Teague, Paul (2006) 'The free movement of workers and social Europe: Maintaining the European Ideal'. *Industrial Relations Journal* 37(6): 652–666.

Duda-Mikulin, Eva A. (2023) 'Brexit and precarity: Polish female workers in the UK as second-class citizens?' *Sociology Compass* 17(1): e13038. https://doi.org/10.1111/soc4.13038

Dummett, Ann (1986) 'Nationality and immigration status'. In Ann Dummett (ed.) *Towards a Just Immigration Policy*. London: Cobden Trust, pp. 143–149.

Farrer, Martin (2022) 'Nazanin Zaghari-Ratcliffe returns to the UK after six-year ordeal'. *The Guardian*, 17 March. www.theguardian.com/news/2022/mar/17/nazanin-zaghari-ratcliffe-anoosheh-ashoori-returns-uk-six-years-iran-prison (accessed 11 June 2024).

Fernández-Reino, Mariña and Sumption, Madeleine (2022) *How Secure is Pre-Settled Status for EU Citizens After Brexit?* Oxford: Migration Observatory.

Fransman, Laurie (2011) *Fransman's British Nationality Law*. London: Bloomsbury Professional.

Gentleman, Amelia (2019) *The Windrush Betrayal: Exposing the Hostile Environment*. London: The Guardian.

Hansen, Randall (1999) 'The Kenyan Asians, British politics, and the Commonwealth Immigrants Act, 1968'. *Historical Journal* 42(3): 809–834.

Hansen, Randall (2000) *Citizenship and Immigration in Post-war Britain*. Oxford: Oxford University Press.

Hansen, Randall (2002) 'The dog that didn't bark: Dual nationality in the United Kingdom'. In Randall Hansen and Patrick Weil (eds) *Dual Nationality, Social Rights and Federal Citizenship in the US and Europe: The Reinvention of Citizenship*. New York: Berghahn Books, pp. 179–190.

Hirsch, Aufa (2018) *Brit(ish): On Race, Identity and Belonging*. London: Jonathan Cape.

HM Government (2018) *EU Exit: Taking Back Control of Our Borders, Money and Laws While Protecting Our Economy, Security and union*. Cm 9741. London: HMSO.

House of Lords Hansard Debates (2014) *Debates of 17 March 2014: Column 40*.

Huttenback, Robert A. (1973) 'The British Empire as a "white man's country" – racial attitudes and immigration legislation in the colonies of white settlement'. *Journal of British Studies* 13(1): 108–137.

Knight, Lucy (2022) 'British empire nostalgia played part in Brexit vote, says Nobel laureate'. *The Guardian*, 28 May. www.theguardian.com/books/2022/may/28/british-empire-brexit-vote-nobel-laureate-abdulrazak-gurnah (accessed 11 June 2024).

Kochenov, Dimitry (2010) 'Case C-135/08, Janko Rottmann v. Freistaat Bayern, judgment of the Court (Grand Chamber) of 2 March 2010'. *Common Market Law Review* 47(6): 1831–1846.

Kochenov, Dimitry and Lindeboom, Justin (2017) 'Breaking Chinese law – making European one: The story of Chen, or two winners, two losers, two truths'. In Fernanda Nicola and Bill Davis (eds) *EU Law Stories: Contextual and Critical Histories of European Jurisprudence*. Cambridge: Cambridge University Press, pp. 201–223.

Kostakopoulou, Dora (2013) 'Co-creating European Union citizenship: Institutional process and crescive norms'. *Cambridge Yearbook of European Legal Studies* 15: 255–282. https://doi.org/10.5235/152888713809813459

Lorenz, Edward N. (1972) 'Predictability: Does the flap of a butterfly's wings in Brazil set off a tornado in Texas?' American Association for the Advancement of Science, 29 December 972.

McDowell, Linda (2018) 'How Caribbean migrants helped to rebuild Britain'. www.bl.uk/windrush/articles/how-caribbean-migrants-rebuilt-britain (accessed 11 February 2020).

McGarvey, Emily and Walsh, Aoife (2023) 'Alireza Akbari: Iran executes British-Iranian dual national'. *BBC News*, 14 January. www.bbc.co.uk/news/world-middle-east-64273520 (accessed 2 February 2023).

Morgan, Benjamin (2021) 'Back to the bad old days? Defending the rights of homeless EU citizens'. *The Justice Gap*, 22 October. www.thejusticegap.com/back-to-the-bad-old-days-defending-the-rights-of-homeless-eu-citizens-after-brexit-covid-19/ (accessed 11 June 2024).

Phillips, Mike and Phillips, Trevor (1998) *Windrush: The Irresistible Rise of Multi-Racial Britain*. London: HarperCollins.

Prabhat, Devyani (2021) 'Stripping British citizenship: The government's new bill explained'. *The Conversation*, 14 December. https://theconversation.com/stripping-british-citizenship-the-governments-new-bill-explained-173547 (accessed 11 June 2024).

Radziwinowiczówna, Agnieszka and Lewis, Olayinka (2021) *The Post-Brexit Legal Framework for International Migration in the UK: Differentiated Deportability of Poor Europeans?* CMR Working Papers, No. 126/184. Warsaw: University of Warsaw, Centre of Migration Research.

Ryan, Bernard (2004) 'The Celtic cubs: The controversy over birthright citizenship in Ireland'. *European Journal of Migration and Law* 6(3): 173–193.

Rzepnikowska, Alina (2019) 'Racism and xenophobia experienced by Polish migrants in the UK before and after the Brexit vote'. *Journal of Ethnic and Migration Studies* 45(1): 61–77.

Saunders, Robert (2020) 'Brexit and Empire: "Global Britain" and the myth of imperial nostalgia'. *The Journal of Imperial and Commonwealth History* 48(6): 1140–1174. https://doi.org/10.1080/03086534.2020.1848403

Sumption, Madeleine and Fernández-Reino, Mariña (2020) *Unsettled Status – 2020: Which EU Citizens Are at Risk of Failing to Secure their Rights after Brexit?* Oxford: Migration Observatory.

Sumption, Madeleine and Walsh, Peter William (2022) *EU Migration to and from the UK*. Migration Observatory Briefing. Oxford: Migration Observatory.

Turner, Joe (2015) 'The family migration visa in the history of marriage restrictions: Postcolonial relations and the UK border'. *British Journal of Politics and International Relations* 17(4): 623–643.

Virdee, Satnam and McGeever, Brendan (2017) 'Racism, crisis, Brexit'. *Ethnic and Racial Studies* 41(10): 1802–1819.

2

Brexit and legal status of Turkish nationals in the UK: a case study on the standstill clauses of the Association

Çiğdem Nas and Sanem Baykal

Introduction

One of the implications of Brexit was its impact on certain aspects of the UK's relations with third countries and the legal status of their nationals within the territory of the UK. This chapter aims at analysing an area which has been adversely affected by Brexit: the rights of Turkish nationals deriving from the Turkey–EU Association relationship established by the Ankara Agreement (AA) of 1963. As well as regulating the trade relations between the Parties, the AA also had a social element, since it covered the prospective free movement of workers and service providers between the Parties, adopting a gradual approach. Following the accession of the UK to the EU in 1973, the UK became party to the AA, binding both the EU and its member states under EU legal order, as well as Turkey.[1]

From a wider perspective, many such rights of Turkish nationals deriving from the AA are related to areas such as migration law and policy and the status of third-country nationals in EU member states, issues which are contentious in the European political, economic and social sphere in particular. So much so that 'taking back control of the borders' and restricting regular migration while combatting irregular migration on the basis of the sovereign policies and decisions of the UK became one of the most employed populist discourses of the Leave campaign during the 2016 referendum (see Garavoglia, 2016). In that vein, it is striking to remember that, in fact, the UK had opted out of most of the EU's border management policies such as the Schengen Area, and would only be adversely – to a limited extent – affected by policies relating to the migration of third-country nationals (Costello and Hancox, 2014; Somerville, 2016).

In addition to drawing attention to the movement of Syrian refugees in the Balkan route towards the EU in campaign posters, the issue of Turkey's EU candidacy was also debated during the campaign, with the suggestion that '80 million Turks would come to the UK if it stayed in the EU'.[2] Both the leader of UKIP Nigel Farage and future Prime Minister Boris Johnson warned the electorate that Brussels was negotiating with Turkey an agreement that would give 'all Turks the option of living in Britain' (Perring, 2016). It was argued that the perception of millions of Turks coming to the UK and staying indefinitely was a factor in favour of the Leave campaign (Clarke et al., 2017; Merrick, 2017). The strong anti-immigration stance espoused by certain segments of British society around the time of the Brexit campaign, skilfully manipulated by politicians, laid the foundation for a transition in the UK immigration regime towards skill-based criteria that would 'attract the brightest and best to a United Kingdom that is open for business'.[3] This meant an end to the favourable regime for Turkish nationals which was based on the AA and developed by the case law of the Court of Justice of the EU (CJEU).

With this backdrop in mind, this chapter aims first to provide the legal grounds and illustrative compilation of the rights of the Turkish nationals in the EU and, consequently, in the UK legal order until the official withdrawal of the UK from the EU. Those rights were derived from the legal documents of the Association and the interpretation provided by the CJEU. In this regard, the chapter concentrates on one of the most highlighted aspects of such CJEU case law: the standstill clauses and their impact. This analysis will be instrumental in demonstrating the role of the CJEU in the advancement of the legal status of Turkish nationals in the EU member states, also highlighting the possible gap that might develop between the status of Turkish nationals in the UK and in EU member states following Brexit. The current situation in the UK legal order will then be briefly touched upon and the analysis will conclude by focusing on whether any developments can be expected in that regard.

Since Brexit, many aspects of the trade relations between Turkey and the UK have been resolved by the conclusion of a Free Trade Agreement (FTA) between the Parties.[4] Yet, the expectations and, to a certain extent, the existing rights of Turkish nationals relating to their legal status while living and working in the UK have not been taken up any further. Since the Parties seem politically unwilling or incapable of envisaging any further steps in this area, the situation will likely remain the same in the foreseeable future. This turn of events provides an interesting example of the politically charged nature of the migration issue, as well as the far-reaching and complicated ramifications of entering into and withdrawing from international agreements that envisage some level of integration between the peoples as well as the states.[5]

Turkey–EU Association relationship: objectives and tools

The AA between Turkey and the then European Economic Community (EEC) aimed to integrate Turkey through enhanced trade and economic relations, thereby contributing to improved living standards in the country. Designed according to the model of the European Community common market, the Association would also aim to realise the four freedoms inherent in the Community, including the free movement of workers and services. Hence, the physical movement of Turkish citizens as a result of the AA within the Community territories would elevate the rights of non-EU nationals from Turkey to enjoy the rights of EU citizenship, at least partially. Brexit ended this privileged status for Turkish citizens who enjoyed the privileges of the AA in Britain. Following Brexit, the UK withdrew from the Association regime with Turkey and transformed the bilateral relationship to a more transactional and pragmatic one. This new relationship, mostly based on trade and economic concerns, was portrayed as a relationship that would contribute to the competitiveness of both parties. The new relationship paid little attention to social and cultural concerns and did not include provisions on freedom of movement or freedom to provide services. In the meantime, rights of residence and quasi-citizenship status as a result of the AA framework ended for Turkish nationals, replaced by a new skills-based immigration regime.

The economic and concrete objective of the AA was stipulated in Article 2/1 as follows: '… to promote the continuous and balanced strengthening of trade and economic relations between the Parties, while taking full account of the need to ensure an accelerated development of the Turkish economy and to improve the level of employment and living conditions of the Turkish people'.

The method and tools to achieve this objective were also to be found in Article 2/2: 'In order to attain the objectives set out in paragraph 1, a customs union shall be progressively established in accordance with Article 3, 4 and 5.'[6]

Moreover, the objective of gradual enabling the free movement of workers, services and capital between the parties was also stipulated in the Agreement in Articles 12–20.

The AA referred to a process for abolishing the restrictions on the free movement of workers, freedom of establishment and the freedom to provide services between the contracting parties. These provisions were to be further developed with the Additional Protocol (AP) and with Association Council Decisions.

The three main provisions of the AA concerning so-called migration law and policy were Articles 12, 13 and 14. While Article 12 laid down the aim of 'progressively securing freedom of workers' between the Parties, it also referred to the related articles of the Rome Treaty as a reference point for this freedom.[7] Article 13 focused on 'abolishing restrictions on the freedom of establishment' and similarly referred to the guidance of the related articles of the Treaty. Finally, Article 14 concerned 'abolishing restrictions on freedom to provide services' in the same spirit of being guided by the related articles of the Founding Treaty. Both workers and the self-employed would be considered within the framework of such provisions, aiming for the gradual free movement of all nationals of EU member states and Turkish nationals.

In that context, the right of establishment and the right to provide services enjoyed by Turkish nationals in the territories of the member states as regulated by the AA and on its basis as furthered by the AP and Association Council Decisions, together with the rights of the lawfully employed Turkish workers, have become critical areas which have been constantly developed by the CJEU through its jurisprudence since the mid-1980s. The Association Council Decisions 2/76, 1/80 and 3/80 are the basic legal instruments that provide the legal basis of those rights arising from the Association relationship.

The provisions of the AA were based on, inspired by or referred to the similar provisions of the Rome Treaty. Therefore, the CJEU declared this agreement as an integral part of the EU legal order and as an act of EU institutions on the basis of the powers granted by the Founding Treaties, so that its legal interpretation within the context of EU legal order would belong with the CJEU, taking into consideration the corresponding provisions of the Founding Treaties. Here, of course, the objectives of the AA would also have to be taken into account during such interpretation.

The CJEU has developed a comprehensive body of case law in the area of the rights of Turkish nationals deriving from the AA that would have direct effect and consequently could be invoked before the national courts by Turkish nationals. Such case law comprises a list of rights, including the rights of departure, entry, residence and protection against expulsion and equal treatment in many respects. We will provide certain examples of the body of rights of Turkish nationals in accordance with the case law of the CJEU.

Association Agreement Article 9: non-discrimination on the basis of nationality

According to Article 9 of the AA:

> The Contracting Parties recognize that within the scope of this Agreement and without prejudice to any special provisions which may be laid down pursuant to Article 8, any discrimination on grounds of nationality shall be prohibited in accordance with the principle laid down in Article 7 of the Treaty establishing the Community.

This provision has corollaries in the field of social security regarding remuneration and conditions of work and charges applied to Turkish nationals or to members of their family. In accordance with this principle enshrined in the AA, AP Article 37 also stipulated that Turkish workers would be treated in the same way as the workers of the member states regarding conditions of work and remuneration.

Decision 1/80 of the Association Council in Article 10 elaborated further, stating that member states would make sure that 'Turkish workers duly registered as belonging to their labour forces' would not be discriminated against regarding remuneration and other conditions of work. Article 10 also added that Turkish workers and 'members of their families' would also have the right to receive 'assistance from the employment services in their search for employment'. Similarly, Article 3 of Decision No 3/80 stipulated that the workers already 'resident in the territory of one of the member states' would 'be subject to the same obligations and enjoy the same benefits' as the nationals of that state.

In that context the CJEU case law has underlined certain rights for Turkish nationals. For instance, a Turkish family member should be subjected to the same conditions as the nationals of the member state to obtain a social security benefit, and the member state cannot exclude Turkish workers from eligibility for election to the general assembly of a body representing and defending the interests of workers. Moreover, no new restriction can be imposed on all of the charges for the issuance of or extension of residence permits when these charges are disproportionate in relation to those imposed on nationals of member states. Additionally, a rule which states that clubs are authorised to field only a limited number of players from non-member states in competitions organised at a national level may not apply to a Turkish professional sportsperson.

Turkish workers' and family members' rights deriving from Association Council Decision 1/80

Article 6 of the Decision stipulated the conditions that would be applicable to a Turkish worker 'duly registered as belonging to the labour force of a Member State' as: entitlement to renewal of work permit after one year of legal employment 'for the same employer if a job is available'; entitlement to 'respond to another offer of employment ... for the same occupation' and 'after three years of legal employment and subject to the priority to be given to workers of Member States of the Community', and, finally, the enjoyment of 'free access in that Member State to any paid employment of their choice, after four years of legal employment'.

On the basis of this provision, the CJEU developed case law on the rights of Turkish nationals in the member states, extending as far as possible the application of its case law related to non-discrimination on the basis of nationality for the EU internal market. In that regard, for instance, the residence permit should be treated as a corollary of the right to legal employment. Turkish nationals who enter the member state as an au pair or as a student can acquire worker status after their entry into the EU; any person in the course of vocational training is considered being duly registered as belonging to the labour force; the fact that the Turkish worker was briefly without a valid residence or work permit should not affect the periods of legal employment, and the existence of legal employment can be established without a work permit/residence permit if that employment does not require a specific residence or work permit. Further, after a specified period of legal employment in the member state, the AA grants to Turkish workers access to any paid employment of their choice; this implies the existence of a right of residence. Annual holidays, maternity absences, an accident at work or short periods of sickness are treated as periods of legal employment in calculating the length of the period of legal employment. Periods of unemployment/sickness (long) absences are taken into account only in order to ensure that rights acquired by the worker as the result of preceding periods of employment are preserved. Finally, the renewal of the work permit is not dependent on any condition, such as the circumstances under which the right of entry and residence was obtained; member states may not make conditional or restrict the application of the precise and unconditional rights deriving from Decision No 1/80, and member states may not adopt national legislation which excludes at the outset whole categories of Turkish migrant workers from the rights conferred by Article 6/1.

Article 7 of Decision 1/80, on the other hand, concerned the members of the family of Turkish workers 'who have been authorized to join' the worker in the member state that he or she resides in. Family members are also entitled to 'respond to any offer of employment after they have been legally resident for at least three years', with 'free access to employment' after 'at least five years'. Article 9 stipulated for the children of legally employed Turkish workers admittance to 'courses of general education, apprenticeship and vocational training under the same educational entry qualifications as the children of nationals of that Member State'.

Thus, the rights and entitlements accruing to family members of Turkish workers may be summarised as follows. Family members of Turkish workers, even when not meeting the condition of 'living together for at least three years', may still be entitled to reside in that member state in some cases (existence of a distance between the worker's residence and the place of employment). Holidays, family visits and involuntary stays for less than six months in their country of origin must also be taken into account when calculating that three-year period. The child of a Turkish worker is still entitled to enjoy the rights in cases where that Turkish worker was employed for two and a half years and involuntarily unemployed for six months, irrespective of the fact that that Turkish worker has obtained right of access to the labour market as a political refugee. Even when the worker obtained their refugee status on the basis of false statements, the rights of a family member cannot be called into question if that family member fulfils the relevant conditions. The child has the right to respond to any offer of employment after having completed a course of vocational training, and consequently to be issued with a residence permit when one of his or her parents has in the past been legally employed for at least three years; however, it is not required that the parent should still work or be resident.

Social security rights of Turkish workers

AP Article 39 concerned the social security rights of Turkish workers, stipulating that the Association Council will be responsible for 'social security measures for workers of Turkish nationality moving within the Community and for their families residing in the Community' before the end of the first year after the entry into force of the Protocol. The second paragraph of the Article laid down the intended effect of the provision concerning the social security rights of Turkish workers.[8]

Article 6 of Decision No 3/80 of the Association Council further elaborated on the social security rights of Turkish workers, guaranteeing full coverage of 'invalidity, old-age or survivors' cash benefits and pensions for accidents at work or occupational diseases ... acquired under the legislation of one or more of the Member States'.[9] Accordingly, member states may not withdraw the award of a benefit, such as the supplement to invalidity benefit, from former Turkish migrant workers when they return to Turkey.

Standstill clauses of the Association law

AP Article 41/1 stipulated that 'The Contracting Parties shall refrain from introducing between themselves any new restrictions on the freedom of establishment and the freedom to provide services'. The clause was especially significant due to its scope and impact. The case law of the CJEU established certain rights for Turkish nationals falling under this provision, stating that there were no new restrictions on the exercise of freedom of establishment, including conditions governing the first admission. No new requirement can be introduced that Turkish nationals must have a visa (to enter) in order to provide services on behalf of an undertaking established in Turkey – as from the entry into force of AP (which will be covered in detail below). No new restrictions on all of the charges can be imposed for the issuance of residence permits concerning a first admission/extension of such a permit – when charges are disproportionate in relation to those imposed on nationals of member states. Member states may not enact a new piece of legislation that is more restrictive than previous legislation which, for its part, relaxed earlier legislation concerning the conditions for the exercise of the freedom of establishment of Turkish nationals. No new condition of basic knowledge of the official language can be applied to spouses of Turkish nationals wishing family reunification.

The Association Council Decision 1/80 Article 13, on the other hand, laid down a standstill clause for workers. It was interpreted by the CJEU as covering the prohibition of new restriction to substantive/procedural conditions governing the first admission and new restriction on all of the charges imposed for the issuance of residence permits concerning a first admission/extension of such a permit when charges are disproportionate in relation to those imposed on nationals of member states. Moreover, no new restriction for family reunification (for the child), such as sufficient ties with the member state, could be introduced.

The standstill provisions and the case law of the CJEU: the main area impacted by Association law for Turkish nationals in the UK legal order

The saga triggered by the *Abdülnasır Savaş*[10] and *Tüm and Darı*[11] cases of the CJEU on the framework and reach of the standstill clauses of the Association law provide an example of the significance of such legal provisions for the rights of Turkish nationals in the UK when it was an EU member state. Both cases were based on the rights of Turkish nationals while entering or already present in the UK, claiming the status accruing from the right of establishment provisions of the AA and the AP, in particular standstill provisions of Article 41/1 of the AP.

This case law, including also the Soysal judgment of the CJEU,[12] culminated in a legal, diplomatic and in the end political debate about the legal basis of visa-free travel rights of Turkish citizens in the Schengen Area. It had wide-ranging ramifications,[13] resulting in a specific legal status and a so-called 'Ankara Agreement Visa', a special type of visa for Turkish self-employed persons for leave to enter the UK.

Here we will only deal with aspects of this case law relating to the UK legal order context, regarding the standstill clauses for self-employed

Turkish nationals who would travel to UK with the intention of providing a service or, in particular, establishing a business in the UK.

As mentioned above, Articles 13 and 14 of the AA provided the foundations for freedom of establishment and the freedom to provide services, and they were further developed in Article 41/1 of the AP. However, the Association Council failed to provide for any specific measures in relation to the right of establishment or freedom to provide services in any of its decisions (Rogers, 2002: 507).

Articles 13 and 14 did not have a direct effect. They, however, provided guidance as to the general aims of the contracting parties and to the interpretation of various EU law concepts such as 'conditions of entry into the territory', 'establishment' or 'provision of services' (Ott, 2000b: 500).

Article 41/1 of the AP, on the other hand, furthered the obligations of the Parties regarding the free movement of self-employed persons performing their professions either in a permanent or temporary manner. As mentioned above, according to this provision, the Parties should refrain from introducing between themselves any new restrictions on the freedom of establishment and the freedom to provide services – hence a 'standstill clause'.

A standstill clause, as defined by Nicola Rogers (2002: 27), 'is a provision in an agreement that forbids a party from changing conditions to the detriment of the applicant from how they stand at the time of entry into force of the agreement'. As mentioned above, the version of standstill clause in Association law relating to the free movement of workers is Article 13 of Association Council Decision 1/80.

The interpretation and scope of Article 41/1 of the AP has become a source of litigation before the national courts and the CJEU,[14] and has been an ample source of debate in academic circles,[15] both before and after the first judgment of the Court regarding this provision, that is, the *Savaş* judgment of 2000, a case involving a Turkish national and the UK legal order.

It was stated by the Court in the *Savaş* case that the provisions of Article 41/1 were sufficiently clear, precise and unconditional and pursued aims generally laid down in Articles 13 and 14 of the Agreement.[16] Whereas Article 41/2 provided for the progressive abolition of restrictions on freedom of establishment and on the freedom to provide services under rules to be laid down by the Association Council, no such reference to implementing measures by the Association Council in relation to the standstill clause was made. On the basis of that finding, the Court concluded in its Savaş judgment that Article 41/1 had direct effect but was not itself capable of conferring upon a Turkish national a right of establishment and, as a corollary, a right of residence.

As far as the Court was concerned, the provisions of the AA did not encroach upon the competence retained by the member states to regulate both the entry into their territories of Turkish nationals and the conditions under which they may take up their first employment, but merely regulated the situation of Turkish nationals in lawful self-employment (Ott, 2000a: 448–449).

Turkish nationals might claim certain rights under EU law in relation to exercising self-employed activity and, in relation to residence, only in so far as their position in the member state concerned was regular (Ott, 2000a: 449).

The Court concluded that the standstill clause implies that this provision precludes a member state from adopting any new measures having the object or effect of making the establishment and, as a corollary, the residence of a Turkish national in its territory subject to stricter conditions than those which applied at the time when the AP entered into force with regard to the member state concerned (Ott, 2000a: 449). Therefore, as such, the standstill clause arguably constituted a limitation *ratione temporis* on the exclusive competence of the member states in that field. Consequently, it was established that Article 41/1 is directly effective; that the standstill clause prohibits the introduction of new national restrictions in the domestic legislation regarding the right of establishment and the right to provide services for Turkish nationals in the territory of the member states, and the national court has to determine if the rules applied to the applicant are less favourable than before the time the AP entered into force.

Since the UK acceded to the EU on 1 January 1973, and consequently to the AA and AP on the same date, the law applicable to businesspersons/self-employed persons on that date should be applied in respect of Turkish nationals wishing to establish themselves in the UK today, if those rules are more favourable.[17]

Here, the standstill clause could come into play in favour of Turkish citizens regarding the conditions applied to the entry into the territory of the member states that depended on the interpretation regarding the scope of the standstill requirement: does it cover the first admission of the Turkish nationals to the territory of the member states? If that question could be answered in the affirmative, would the standstill clause specifically cover the visa requirement imposed either individually or jointly, in the EU context, by the member states?

This question has been answered in part by the *Tüm ve Darı*[18] judgment of the CJEU,[19] and has been definitively decided by the *Soysal, Salkım ve Savatlı* case.[20]

In *Tüm and Darı*, a case involving two Turkish nationals seeking leave to enter the UK to perform self-employed activities, the question directed to the CJEU by the national court was whether

> Article 41/1 of the Additional Protocol ... to be interpreted as prohibiting a Member State from introducing new restrictions, as from the date on which that Protocol entered into force in that Member State, on the conditions of and procedure for entry to its territory for a Turkish national seeking to establish himself in business in that Member State?

It is generally accepted that states are free to control the entry and residence of aliens into their territory, and to expel or deport aliens, especially for reasons of public order and national security. Such discretion is limited on the part of the member states as far as the nationals of other member states of the EU are concerned (Meloni, 2006: 7). Such discretion or exclusive competence of the member states might also be limited temporally by the standstill clause of the AP regarding the Turkish nationals who want to establish themselves in the territory of the member states.

In fact, this was the outcome of the judgment of the CJEU in the *Tüm and Darı* case.

As reiterated by the CJEU in its *Tüm and Darı* ruling,

> the 'standstill' clause would not call into question the competence, as a matter of principle, of the Member States to conduct their national immigration policy. The mere fact that, as from its entry into force, such a clause imposes on those States a duty not to act which has the effect of limiting, to some extent, their room for manœuvre on such matters does not mean that the very substance of their sovereign competence in respect of aliens should be regarded as having been undermined.

The Court, however, rejected the argument of the UK government, since the provision of Article 41/1 did not restrict the obligation in any way. In respect to first admission, standstill applied both to substantive and procedural requirements for setting up a business as a self-employed person. This meant that the member states could not make it any more difficult procedurally or substantively by adding new requirements than were applicable at the time of coming into force of the AP (Kabaalioğlu et al., 2008: 13–14).

The Court also pointed to the aims and objectives of AA and the AP in order to strengthen its arguments. The Court admitted the fact that the Association Council had not adopted any measure on the basis of Article 41/2 of the Additional Protocol with a view to the actual removal by the Contracting Parties of existing restrictions on freedom of establishment, in accordance with the principles set out in Article 13 of the AA, and that it was apparent from the case law of the Court that neither of those two provisions had direct effect. It stated, however, that Article 41/1 of the AP was intended to create conditions conducive to the progressive establishment of freedom of establishment by way of an absolute prohibition on national authorities from creating any new obstacle to the exercise of that freedom by making more stringent the conditions which exist at a given time, so as not to render more difficult the gradual securing of that freedom between the member states and Turkey.

Situation in the UK legal order before and in the aftermath of Brexit

Following the above-mentioned judgments of the CJEU, the UK government started to take the necessary steps to incorporate them into its national legal order. The UK Border Agency announced that it had opened a visa route for Turkish nationals applying to establish themselves in business under the European Community Association Agreement (ECAA). The decision follows the judgment in Tüm and Darı.

The CJEU had found that the agreement applied as much to those Turkish nationals who wished to enter the UK to establish themselves in business as it did to those already in the UK. Under the standstill clause of the AP, when the UK joined the EU in 1973 it became bound not to impose any more stringent requirements than those required to be met by people wishing to establish themselves in business in the UK under the 1973 Immigration Rules.

As would be expected, the 1973 Immigration Rules were far less demanding that their modern equivalent – the Tier 1 (Entrepreneur) migrant route of the points-based system.[21] This paved the way for a visa track under the AA, giving Turkish citizens a preferential status to non-EU nationals, who were required to invest at least £200,000 in the UK in order to acquire a comparable 'Tier 1 (Entrepreneur)' visa. In comparison, AA applicants were only required to show that the profits of their business would be sufficient to support them and their dependents, effectively allowing them to work as self-employed contractors or run small businesses.[22]

Such a visa would entail the right to start a new business in the UK, to come to the UK to help run an established business, switch into this visa from another visa category, extend their stay if they are already in this visa category and bring their family with them.

The self-employed Turkish nationals within the scope of this provision would have the right to apply to the Home Office for the extension of their visa for a three-year period, free of charge – if the business activities are deemed to be financially successful after a year – and for indefinite leave to remain (ILR) in the UK after four years of successful or satisfactory business activity. A Turkish businessperson could apply for a visa, allowing a 12-month stay with possibility of extension for up to three years, up to three months before the date of travel to the UK and get a decision on the visa within 12 weeks when the application was from outside the UK. All in all, Turkish nationals falling into this category enjoyed an advantageous status compared to many other nationalities, thanks to the Turkey–EU Association Agreement and its interpretation by the CJEU.

However, following the Brexit referendum of 2016, the British government increasingly sought to constrain the implications of the AA. The move to limit the right of Turkish citizens under the AA appeared to be politically driven. Prior to suspension, a growing number of ILR applications under the AA had been turned down through the implementation of a more stringent reading of the necessary criteria. This peaked after the Brexit vote, when migration from Turkey in particular was demonised.

The first restrictive move from the UK government following Brexit came after the Aydoğdu ruling of the CJEU,[23] and the UK courts and the British government substantially impeded Turkish citizens from securing indefinite leave to remain in the UK.[24]

The British government indicated that it would no longer accept ILR applications from Turkish nationals under the provisions of the ECAA. The decision was announced via an update to the relevant guidance page of the British government's website on 16 March 2018, which stated that ECAA ILR applications made after this date would no longer be processed.

Following the Aydoğdu judgment, a new appendix called 'Appendix ECAA' to the Immigration Rules was introduced which provided a route to ILR for Turkish businesspersons, workers and their family members from 6 July 2018.[25]

Until these recent changes, as mentioned above, the AA had enabled Turkish passport holders to apply for a visa to establish their own business in the UK on relatively attainable terms, subsequently making them eligible for ILR after a period of four years. Following the changes, in order for eligible Turkish businesspersons to qualify, several requirements must be met, including a minimum residency period of five years, adequate UK language skills and cultural knowledge and the ability to pay the application fee of £2,389. The new terms applicable to Turkish nationals also allow for children to settle in the UK at the same time as the main applicant, which includes children over 21 years of age with specific dependency requirements. There is also a new option for spouses of Turkish businesspersons operating in the UK to qualify for additional limited leave to remain, in order to subsequently accrue the five years of continuous residency needed to apply for indefinite leave to remain. Following the withdrawal of the UK from the EU, such privileged legal status for Turkish nationals arising from the AA has been terminated as expected, since the UK would no longer be a party to AA.

There was first a 'transition period', which lasted from 1 February 2020 until 31 December 2020. Throughout the transition period, the UK was still obliged to comply with EU rules, which meant that the CJEU continued to have jurisdiction over the UK. Consequently, the AA remained in force until the completion of the transition period, on the basis that the UK was still obligated to comply with EU rules until 31 December 2020. In other words, Turkish citizens were still able to apply for work visas or for so-called AA visas for the right of establishment until that date and the applications of those who had already made their applications were evaluated under the current laws in effect. In regard to immigration rules, the AA also came to an end for Turkish businesspersons who intended to set up a business in the UK once the transition period was completed.

Consequently, those who had successfully acquired status under the AA were allowed to extend their leave in the UK and apply for settlement if they met the requirements, even after the AA no longer applied to the UK as this would constitute an acquired status and acquired right. In that vein, the UK government preserved the rights of Turkish businesspersons already settled and doing business in the country while extending rights of settlement to resident ECAA workers and ECAA businesspersons and their family members, and consequently safeguarded the acquired rights of such persons.

The last development in that regard came with the introduction of the new UK immigration rules, which are based on a talent and ability scoring system and not where the applicant is coming from. The new legal system, introduced by a White Paper in December 2018, stated that a new, skills-based immigration system, where it is workers' skills that matter, not which country they come from, would be introduced. Consequently, it would be a single system that:

> welcomes talent, hard work, and the skills we need as a country. It will attract the brightest and best to a United Kingdom that is open for business. Migrants have made a huge contribution to our country over our history – and they will continue to in the future. But it will also be an immigration system that is fair to working people here at home. It will mean we can reduce the number of people coming to this country, as we promised, and it will give British business an incentive to train our own young people.[26]

As migration not only from outside but also from within the EU was one of most sensitive and controversial issues debated before the Brexit referendum, it was to be expected that the Brexit process also entailed a revision of the UK's approach to migration. This new skills-based immigration system may also be viewed in relation to the new motto of 'global Britain' whereby the post-Brexit Britain is to be imagined as both a European and global actor and consequently as the most 'globalised' part of the old continent of Europe. Brexit also implied a move to escape from the strong ties that bound the UK to the Continental Europeans and break free from the norms, standards, legislation and bureaucratic frameworks of the EU. In the process, the Association framework between Turkey and the EU was also transformed into merely a trade framework embodied in the FTA between Turkey and the UK, excluding the idea of gradual integration and the realisation of the four freedoms of the Common Market. As the Turkey–UK relationship was taken out of a regional integration context, it was transformed into a more transactional and pragmatic context, hampering the rights of Turkish nationals in the UK. Turkish nationals can no long benefit from the AA-related rights of residence in the UK based on country of origin. They now have to compete in the global job marketplace based on their skills and the needs of the UK job market, which will also determine their value as future residents of the UK.

Conclusion

This chapter analysed the implications of Brexit for the existing international commitments of the UK arising from the Association relationship of the EU with the UK. It focused on a very specific, yet tangible, issue: the transition in the legal status of Turkish nationals moving to the UK who enjoyed freedom of establishment within the framework of the ECAA visa status. In order to demonstrate the legal background to this, a brief summary has been provided of the rights deriving from the AA and the approach of the CJEU, in particular the standstill provisions of the legal documents of the Association relationship. Brexit resulted in the termination of the favourable immigration regime for Turkish nationals which was based on the AA, AP and the case law of the CJEU. As the UK left the EU, it also withdrew from the AA and the regime for Turkish nationals within the context of the AA drastically changed.

The Free Trade Agreement signed on 29 December 2020 regulated the new relationship between the parties, aiming to maintain preferential trade conditions. This Agreement, however, did not contain any references to the movement of persons or freedom of establishment. Conditions of immigration to the UK for Turkish nationals would be governed under the UK's new skills-based immigration system. Hence, a system that discriminated in favour of nationals of one or several countries was not in line with the new thinking and approach to migration and movement of persons that was reminiscent of the Brexit era. The Parties agreed to start a new round of negotiations on an updated FTA on 18 July 2023. This new agreement when concluded will replace the current FTA between the UK and Turkey, possibly extending the remit of the relationship by including new areas such as services, digital trade and data transfers. It remains to be seen whether the inclusion of services to the trade relationship will also impact on issues of free movement and freedom to provide services for natural persons. It can be inferred that as the second largest services provider in the world, the UK's expectation would be to provide more services trade to Turkey rather than vice versa. However, due to the reciprocity inherent in such agreements, a new and more restrained version of the Ankara Agreement's approach to freedom to provide services and freedom of establishment may also be included as part of the new extended trade deal between the parties. Due to repercussions on the right of residence and citizenship, such developments may trigger sensitivities about issues of migration in the future.

CJEU's ever evolving case law and its progressive interpretation has been the main push factor behind the rights of Turkish nationals arising from EU law. In the aftermath of Brexit, the loss of such a progressive influence might have an increasingly adverse effect on the plethora of rights briefly documented in this chapter, compared to the rights of Turkish nationals still enjoyed in EU member states. On the other hand, it might also be interesting to follow whether the gap will actually increase, considering the political, social and economic environment becoming increasingly inconducive to progressive judicial interpretation as far as issues related to migration are concerned within European countries and beyond. This also necessitates looking into possible means and methods between Turkey and UK to improve, or at least prevent the deterioration of, the legal situation for Turkish nationals that existed before Brexit. This would pave the way for better understanding and building further trust between the parties, which would also lead to more fruitful cooperation in other fields of common interest.

Notes

1 See Article 216/2, Treaty on the Functioning of the EU (TFEU).
2 See BBC News (2016); for the (then) Foreign Secretary Boris Johnson refuting the allegation of making such a statement, see Kartal (2019). See also Dennison and Geddes (2018), who also point out how Leave.EU claimed that 'EU proposals to allow visa-free travel to Turkish citizens had been tabled by the Commission in relation to a deal with Turkey on accommodating people displaced by the conflict in Syria, warning citizens to 'brace yourself for another influx' (Dennison and Geddes 2018, p. 1147).
3 British High Commission New Delhi (2020); for the former Prime Minister Theresa May's approach, see Reuters (2018).
4 The FTA was signed on 29 December 2020 between the UK and Turkey.
5 For the uncertainty created by Brexit for migrants in the UK in general, see Hall et al. (2022).
6 The political and long-term objective was to prepare the ground for Turkey's prospective membership, as stipulated in Article 28 of the AA: 'As soon as the

operation of this Agreement has advanced far enough to justify envisaging full acceptance by Turkey of the obligations arising out of the Treaty establishing the Community, the Contracting Parties shall examine the possibility of the accession of Turkey to the Community.' This is not a legal obligation, but a conditional political commitment for both parties.

7 The TFEU following the Lisbon Treaty amendments.

8 'These provisions must enable workers of Turkish nationality, in accordance with arrangements to be laid down, to aggregate periods of insurance or employment completed in individual Member States in respect of old-age pensions, death benefits and invalidity pensions, and also as regards the provision of health services for workers and their families residing in the Community. These measures shall create no obligation on Member States to take into account periods completed in Turkey.'

9 'Save as otherwise provided in this Decision, acquired under the legislation of one or more Member States, shall not be subject to any reduction, modification, suspension, withdrawal or confiscation by reason of the fact that the recipient resides in Turkey or in the territory of a Member State other than that in which the institution responsible for payment is situated. The provisions of the first subparagraph shall also apply to lump-sum benefits granted in the case of the remarriage of a surviving spouse who was entitled to a survivor's pension.' Article 14 of Decision No 3/80 stipulated limitations 'on grounds of public policy, public security or public health'.

10 C-37/98, *The Queen & Secretary of State for the Home Department, ex parte Abdülnasır Savaş* [2000] ECR I-2927.

11 C-16/05, *The Queen & Secretary of State for the Home Department, ex parte Veli Tüm and Mehmet Darı* [2007] ECR I-07415.

12 C-228/06, *Mehmet Soysal, Cengiz Salkım, İbrahim Savatlı v. Bendesrepublik Deutschland; Joined party: Bundesagentur für Arbeit.* The case deals with Turkish lorry drivers and their employers' rights related to the provision of services and right of establishment as stipulated in Articles 13–14 of the AA and the standstill clause of Article 41/1 of AP.

13 See Visa Liberalisation Dialogue and Readmission Agreement as separate documents signed on 16 December 2013 in Ankara.

14 C-37/98, *The Queen & Secretary of State for the Home Department, ex parte Abdülnasır Savaş* [2000] ECR I-2927; C-317/01 and C-369/01, *Eran Abatay and Others and Nadi Şahin v. Bundesanstalt für Arbeit* and C-16/05, *The Queen & Secretary of State for the Home Department, ex parte Veli Tüm and Mehmet Darı* 20 September 2007.

15 Guild (2007); according to Guild, Turkey's Association agreement and the standstill clauses contained thereof are *sui generis* in nature (p. 20). Nicola Rogers (2002: 30–31) also states that this would be the correct interpretation of the standstill clause contained in the AP during the period preceding the *Savaş* judgment of the CJEU.

16 C-37/98, *The Queen & Secretary of State for the Home Department, ex parte Abdülnasır Savaş* [2000] ECR I-2927.

17 Such rules were inter alia about the minimum amount of investment, the requirement that the investment had to create new paid employment for persons already settled there and the requirement to obtain entry clearance for the purpose. There was no general rule to prevent persons admitted as visitors from setting up in business obtaining an appropriate extension of stay. See Rogers (2000: 30–31).

18 Judgment of the CJEU, 20 September 2007 in Case C-16/05, *Reference for a Preliminary Ruling by the House of Lords, by order of that court dated 2 December 2004, in the case of The Queen on the application of 1) Veli Tüm and 2) Mehmet Darı against Secretary of State for the Home Department.*

19 See the unfavourable Opinion of the Advocate General Geelhoed in *Tüm and Darı*, dated 12 September 2006, which was almost ignored by the court during its ruling.

20 C-228/06, *Mehmet Soysal, Cengiz Salkım, İbrahim Savatlı v. Bendesrepublik Deutschland; Joined party: Bundesagentur für Arbeit.*

21 Since the UK's withdrawal from the EU, Immigration Rules Appendix ECAA: Extension of Stay pp. 568–588 have been archived. See Immigration Rules archive: 31 December 2020 – 30 January 2021 at https://assets.publishing.service.gov.uk/government/uploads/system/uploads/attachment_data/file/957520/Immigration_Rules_-_Archive_31-12-20.pdf (accessed 18 June 2024).

22 Such eligibility conditions were as follows: a genuine intention to set up a viable business; bringing sufficient funds to establish your business; being able to pay your share of the costs of running the business; your share of the profits should be enough to support you and your family without your needing to have another job; in order to join an existing partnership or company you must show that you would have an active part in running the business and there would be a genuine need for your services and investment

23 In the 2017 Upper Tribunal case of *Aydoğdu v SSHD* [JR/15737/2015] the Upper Tribunal confirmed that the ECAA does not apply to ILR for Turkish businesspersons. As a consequence, the previous policy on ILR for ECAA businesspersons was withdrawn and new rules were introduced as of 16 March 2018.

24 The leave to remain application period was increased from four to five years; within those five years the period spent outside UK should not exceed 180 days within 12 months; applicants were required to pass a language and life in the UK test and to pay a residence application fee of £2,389 fee per application.

25 For indefinite leave to remain (ILR) and further leave to remain (FLR) guidance, please see version 1.0 published on 6 July 2018. See also the latest version as published for Home Office staff on 6 November 2022, Appendix ECAA indefinite leave to remain (ILR) and further leave to remain (FLR) guidance, version 4.0 at https://assets.publishing.service.gov.uk/government/uploads/system/uploads/attachment_data/file/1115092/Turkish_ECAA_indefinite_leave_to_remain.pdf (accessed 18 June 2024).

26 https://assets.publishing.service.gov.uk/government/uploads/system/uploads/attachment_data/file/766672/The-UKs-future-skills-based-immigration-system-accessible-version.pdf (accessed 18 June 2024).

References

BBC News (2016) 'EU referendum: Nigel Farage tells Leave campaigners to focus on migration'. *BBC News*, 29 April. www.bbc.com/news/uk-politics-eu-referendum-36167329 (accessed 18 June 2024).

British High Commission New Delhi (2020) 'UK announces new points-based immigration system' www.gov.uk/government/news/uk-announces-new-points-based-immigration-system (accessed 18 June 2024).

Clarke, Harold D., Goodwin, Matthew and Whiteley, Paul (2017) 'Why Britain voted for Brexit: An individual-level analysis of the 2016 referendum vote'. *Parliamentary Affairs* 70(3): 439–464.

Costello, Cathryn and Hancox, Emily (2014) *The UK, the Common European Asylum System and EU Immigration Law*. Migration Observatory Policy Primer. Oxford: Migration Observatory.

Dennison, James and Geddes, Andrew (2018) 'Brexit and the perils of "Europeanised" migration'. *Journal of European Public Policy* 25(8): 1137–1153.

Garavoglia, Matteo (2016) 'What Brexit means for migration policy'. Brookings Institution, 26 September. www.brookings.edu/blog/order-from-chaos/2016/09/26/what-brexit-means-for-migration-policy (accessed 18 June 2024).

Guild, Elspeth (2007) *European Union and Third-Party Service Trades: Four Essays on EU Services*. Global Economic Issues Publications. Geneva: Quaker United Nations Office.

Hall, Kelly, Phillimore, Jenny, Grzymala-Kazlowska, Aleksandra, Vershinina, Natalia, Ögtem-Young, Özlem and Harris, Catherine (2022) 'Migration uncertainty in the context of Brexit: Resource conservation tactics'. *Journal of Ethnic and Migration Studies* 48(1): 173–191.

Kabaalioğlu, Haluk, Rogers, Nicola, Abdulkuddus, Mohammed and Baykal, Sanem (2008) *Avrupa Toplulukları Adalet Divanı ve İngiltere Mahkemelerinin Türk Vatandaşlarının Ülkeye Giriş Koşullarına İlişkin Son Kararları (The Recent Judgments of the European Court of Justice and UK Courts on the Admission Conditions of Turkish Nationals)*. İstanbul: İktisadi Kalkınma Vakfı (İKV) Yayınları (Economic Development Foundation Publications), No. 215.

Kartal, Ahmet Gurhan (2019) 'Johnson distances self from anti-Turkish Brexit slogan'. *Anadolu Ajansi*, 18 January. www.aa.com.tr/en/europe/johnson-distances-self-from-anti-turkish-brexit-slogan/1368522 (accessed 18 June 2024).

Meloni, Annalisa (2006) *Visa Policy within the European Structure*. Berlin-Heidelberg: Springer.

Merrick, Rob (2017) 'Brexit: People voted Leave over fears of "80 million Turks coming to live in their village", says Vince Cable'. *The Independent*, 11 July. www.independent.co.uk/news/uk/politics/brexit-vince-cable-vote-leave-turks-live-village-80-million-liberal-democrat-leader-church-halls-turkey-eu-membership-a7835891.html (accessed 18 June 2024).

Ott, Andrea (2000a) 'The Savaş case – analogies between Turkish self-employed and workers?' *European Journal of Migration and Law* 2(3–4): 445–458.

Ott, Andrea (2000b) 'The rights of self-employed CEEC citizens in the Member States under the Europe agreements'. *The European Legal Forum* 1(8): 497–596.

Perring, Rebecca (2016) 'EU loophole could see 77 MILLION Turks head to Britain, warn Farage and Johnson'. *Daily Express*, 18 April. www.express.co.uk/news/uk/661387/Migrant-crisis-Nigel-Farage-Turkey-EU-visa-free-travel (accessed 18 June 2024).

Reuters (2018) 'PM May says post-Brexit immigration system will attract brightest to UK'. *Reuters*, 26 September. www.reuters.com/article/uk-britain-eu-may-immigration-idUSKCN1M61TC (accessed 18 June 2024).

Rogers, Nicola (2002) 'Movement of persons (Association agreements with Turkey)'. In Andrea Ott and Kirstyn Inglis (eds), *Handbook on European Enlargement: A Commentary on the Enlargement Process*. The Hague: T.M.C. Asser Press, pp. 495–508.

Somerville, William (2016) 'Brexit: The role of migration in the upcoming EU referendum'. Migration Policy Institute. www.migrationpolicy.org/article/brexit-role-migration-upcoming-eu-referendum (accessed 18 June 2024).

3

Understanding and explaining the practice of denaturalisation in the United Kingdom

Colin Yeo

Introduction

The universally acknowledged gap between what politicians say and what politicians do is particularly wide when it comes to matters of immigration, nationality and race. In the case of denaturalisation, the gap becomes a chasm. Analysis of legislative reform or administrative practice by reference to the explanations advanced by ministers may be revealing in some respects but it cannot offer a complete account (see, for example, Gibney, 2013). The norms of parliamentary discourse in a liberal democracy constrain what policymakers can say in public because piloting a reform through Parliament always carries a risk of unexpected media and public engagement and therefore an attendant political risk. Relatively very minor reforms to citizenship deprivation law in 2022, discussed later, led to far more media coverage of issues around citizenship deprivation than ever before, for example (see van der Merwe, 2021).

In the United Kingdom, denaturalisation was first introduced for fraud in 1914 and expanded to behaviour in 1918. Following the denaturalisation of several hundred German and former enemy aliens after the First World War, exercise of the power fell into abeyance in the second half of the twentieth century. The orthodox view is that a recent surge in behaviour-based denaturalisation is therefore a novel departure for the British state which requires explanation (see, for example, Gibney, 2013; Fargues, 2017). On this understanding, the ideology of universal human rights that emerged in the aftermath of the Second World War acted as an effective constraint on the power – or at least willingness – of the state to strip citizens of their status. A series of legal reforms from 2002 onwards have been attributed with encouraging and facilitating a new policy of active denaturalisation. There has certainly been a remarkable increase in behaviour-based denaturalisation from 2010 onwards. However, I argue in this chapter that it is a mistake to regard denaturalisation as absent from British state practice in the decades following the Second World War, that government statements as to why the law was changed cannot be taken at face value and that it is just as necessary to explain the increase in fraud-based denaturalisation as the increase in behaviour-based denaturalisation. The real change in British state policy on denaturalisation occurred around 2010 and was only enabled by, not caused by or reflected in, the earlier legal reforms.

Three major forms of denaturalisation have been practised by the British government: imperial denaturalisation of racialised colonial peoples, fraud-based denaturalisation and behaviour-based denaturalisation. It is behaviour-based denaturalisation that has attracted the most attention in the literature on denaturalisation (Fargues, 2019 is a notable exception), but imperial denaturalisation and fraud-based denaturalisation have both been pursued with more vigour by the British state. These under-studied forms of denaturalisation may well therefore tell us more about the meaning of citizenship to policymakers. Figure 3.1 represents fraud and behaviour-based denaturalisation over the last decade, compiled from various sources.[1] Very small numbers of denaturalisations occurred in some of the years between 2003 and 2012. No attempt is made here to quantify imperial denaturalisation, which was massive in scale.

Imperial denaturalisation involved the large-scale withdrawal by the imperial state of rights of entry into and residence within the United Kingdom from colonial subjects in the 1960s and 1970s.[2] This involuntary loss of rights should be regarded as conceptually distinct from the voluntary

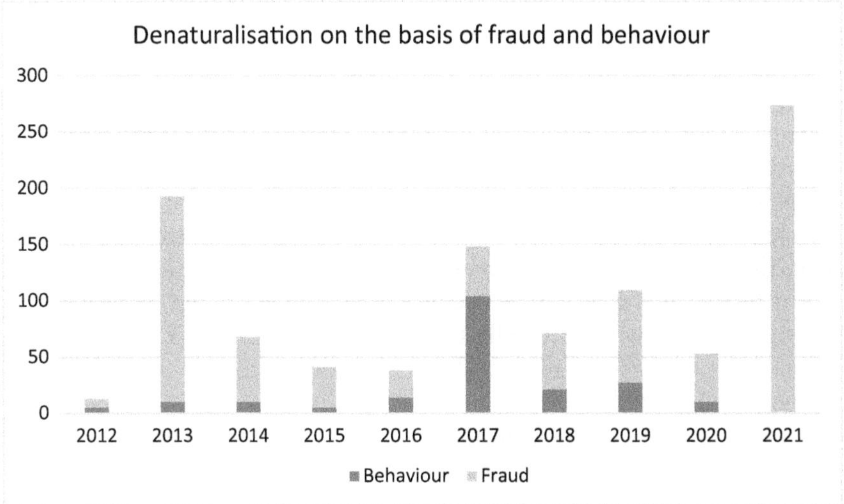

Figure 3.1 Denaturalisations on the basis of fraud and behaviour in the UK, 2012–21. Own elaboration based on several sources (see note 1).

withdrawal from imperial citizenship by those who gained a new and effective citizenship on gaining independence. I argue here that this prolonged and ongoing episode can and should be seen as *de facto* then *de jure* denaturalisation.[3] Parallels can be drawn with Brexit. The removal of automatically conferred, citizenship-like and inherent free movement rights from EU citizens resident in the United Kingdom and the replacement of those rights with a formal and more readily revocable domestic immigration status is essentially a rerun of the imperial denaturalisation process (see further Prabhat, this volume; Yeo et al., 2019).

Denaturalisation based on fraud may take two forms. One is statutory citizenship deprivation and the other is a process called 'nullification', whereby the government simply declares that a previous grant of citizenship to a naturalised person is null, in the sense that it was never in truth effective.[4] At the very end of 2017 the Supreme Court held that this latter form of fraud-based denaturalisation had been deployed inappropriately in a considerable number of cases, leading to a virtual abandonment of its use.[5] When these two forms of fraud-based denaturalisation are combined, we can see that there have been around four times as many denaturalisations based on fraud compared to behaviour over the last decade.[6]

Finally, I argue that amendments to the law of behaviour-based denaturalisation in Britain were not brought about by changing theories of the social contract between citizen and state or by 'thick' or 'thin' visions of the nature of citizenship (Joppke, 2010). Nor did the changes in the law lead to a change in policy on the part of the British state, at least directly. The legal reforms were driven principally by the short-term political imperative to denaturalise specific, high-profile individuals: Abu Hamza, David Hicks, Hilal Al Jedda and an anonymous individual known only as D4, who acted as a proxy for the better-known Shamima Begum. Officials and ministers were no doubt also mindful that individual cases might highlight what they regarded as systemic problems with the prevailing state of the law. The management of risk to public safety has played a role in at least some cases of individual denaturalisation but is irrelevant in many others. Seen in this light, the changes appear largely unplanned, reactive and pragmatic rather than strategic and doctrinal. It is considered poor form and bad legislative practice to pass laws specifically to address the situation of individuals. If this motivation was a significant driver of policy change, it therefore could not be stated in public.

The absence of a chronological correlation between the enabling reforms and the incidence of denaturalisation reinforces this thesis. The principal reforms intended to widen the power of denaturalisation based on behaviour occurred in 2002, 2004 and 2006, yet the surge in public interest denaturalisation does not occur until around 2010 and beyond. The legal changes really were about denaturalising a handful of individuals. Further, changes in the legal regime cannot explain the dramatic increase in denaturalisation based on fraud and nor do such changes explain the mass denaturalisation of colonial peoples between the 1960s and 1980s. It is more accurate to say that the legislative changes between 2002 and 2006 enabled the later surge in the use of denaturalisation powers rather than causing it. This begs the question of what really did bring about the various incidents and escalations of denaturalisation, a question to which I return at the end of this chapter.

Imperial denaturalisation

Denial of residence in the imperial heartland of the United Kingdom to colonial subjects was characterised as immigration control by those who enacted it. The very titles of the Acts of Parliament responsible make this point: the Commonwealth Immigrants Acts 1962 and 1968 and the Immigration Act 1971. That the restrictions imposed on racialised colonial people were immigration controls rather than denaturalisation may appear a plausible analysis if one's starting points are that the world is divided into nation states and racialised people ought to stay where they are. In the same vein, it might be argued that imperial denaturalisation did not deny those affected a right of residence in their 'normal' country of residence. This understanding is fundamentally misaligned with the imperial nature of British subject status, however, and it ignores the reality faced by many former subjects.

Historically, British subject status arose from the relationship between the individual and the Crown. A British subject held that status because of their relationship of ligeance with the king. At its core, the concept of ligeance was a feudal one centred on ownership and the land on which a person was born. This continued to be the case through the prolonged expansionist imperial period beginning in the seventeenth century, initially as a matter of common law and then embedded in statute law from 1914 (see, for example, Jones, 1948; Fransman, 2011). All those born within the Crown's dominions were the Crown's subjects. The logic of this imperial doctrine of ownership meant that British subjects were all in theory equal in their relationship with the Crown. Also in theory, it therefore seemed to follow that any subject would be able to move anywhere in the Crown's dominions. Neither of these logical propositions was true in practice, of course, as a considerable volume of literature has definitively shown.[7] Nevertheless, the logic and power of the doctrine meant that restrictions and discrimination were usually indirect or enacted by means of camouflaged administrative practices rather than open legislation. The British Nationality Act 1948 entirely changed the constitutive basis of British subjecthood, but it perpetuated the imperial doctrine and maintained British subject status as the primary form of British nationality.[8] As Sredanovic (2017) has observed, this was attributable more to path dependency and institutional inertia than the strength of ideas; any change to the status quo would have involved a revolution in the conception of British nationality.

It was only later that the sub-statuses of citizenship of the United Kingdom and Colonies and citizenship of independent Commonwealth countries came to the fore. Legislation characterised as concerning immigration law in effect locked British subject status away in the attic by detaching from it the right to enter and reside in Britain itself. It was rarely talked of again; the legal synonym for British subject status, Commonwealth citizen, was used instead.[9] In British political discourse 'Commonwealth citizen' came to be understood to mean 'Commonwealth citizens who are not British' despite in law being a term that encompassed citizens of the United Kingdom and Colonies. Eventually, the status was despatched with a final *coup de grâce* by the British Nationality Act 1981.

It might be thought that stripping a colonial subject of their right of entry into and residence within the imperial heartland does not deny them the right of residence in the colony in which they reside, unlike a conventionally understood act of individual denaturalisation. They are not exiled from their habitual home in that sense. But this overlooks important features of both forms of denaturalisation, which overlap far more than might first be appreciated.

Firstly, those colonial subjects who had already moved from their original colony of residence were routinely denied the right to re-enter or reside – or at least reside with dignity and rights of citizenship – in their new country of residence. The East African Asians are one such group, for example. They were denied the right to live as full and active citizens in their country of residence; some were denied formal citizenship as well and some were forcibly expelled. Many of those British subjects who moved from colonies to the United Kingdom, later dubbed 'the Windrush generation', form another such group. It is thought that a very considerable (but unknowable) number were later denied re-entry to the United Kingdom following temporary absences abroad, for example. Some recent examples have been documented in the reporting on what has become known as the Windrush scandal, but in historical terms these cases probably represent the tip of an iceberg. Most such exclusions would have occurred decades earlier. Others were later excluded from formal British citizenship status by complex and paid-for registration requirements when nationality law was later reformed. Later, some were denied de facto citizenship rights by the suite of hostile environment laws (Griffiths and Yeo, 2021). For those affected this felt a lot like denaturalisation, and with good reason. 'I don't feel British. I am

British. I've been raised here, all I know is Britain,' Paulette Wilson told journalist Amelia Gentleman in 2017. 'What the hell can I call myself except British? I'm still angry that I have to prove it. I feel angry that I have to go through this' (Gentleman, 2019: 40). Wilson was not in fact a British citizen according to law, although she was able very belatedly to obtain leave to remain as a foreign national before she died in 2020. This was not before she had been rendered homeless, denied welfare benefits and health care and even detained for deportation at the notorious Yarl's Wood detention centre. Her situation and her feelings of betrayal and estrangement were very far from unique (Gentleman, 2019).

Secondly, individually targeted acts of denaturalisation often leave the person concerned resident in their country in any event. Removal of formal citizenship may well in the short term leave the person concerned with no immigration status and no legal right to remain. If the person is in the United Kingdom at the time of the deprivation – which is by no means always the case, as discussed later – then it may well prove difficult to remove them elsewhere. Such a person will normally retain a second nationality after all. The British government recognised this in 2002, stating in the White Paper proposing reform that it was 'not always possible in such cases to take subsequent action to remove an individual from the UK' but that 'deprivation action would at least mark the UK's abhorrence of their crimes and make it clear that the UK is not prepared to welcome such people as its citizens'.[10] As discussed in the following section, a change to the law in 2004 led to many of those citizens who were denaturalised being excluded from the country as well, but they were not expelled or removed as such; rather, the state waited until they were abroad and then denaturalised them, preventing their return. In particular, citizenship deprivation on the basis of fraud will routinely leave the person concerned resident in their country of former citizenship, as becomes evident from the case-law reports in which the gap between termination of citizenship and grant of temporary immigration status is discussed.[11]

Denaturalisation based on behaviour

The power to denaturalise a British subject on the basis of their behaviour was first introduced by legislation in 1918.[12] With some adjustments, the power remained broadly the same until as late as 2002.[13] Essentially, only a person who had naturalised as British could be stripped of their citizenship and the main grounds for doing so involved disloyalty or disaffection to the Crown, assisting an enemy or proven criminal conduct. These powers were exercised against some German and allied nationals who had naturalised as British but fell into abeyance. The last denaturalisation under this legal regime occurred in 1973.

In 2002, reforms for the first time enabled denaturalisation of those born as British citizens, as long as they were not thus rendered stateless, and introduced a new test of doing anything 'seriously prejudicial to the vital interests of the United Kingdom'.[14] However, the old test would continue to apply to past events and actions; it was only matters arising after the commencement of the new test to which the new test would apply.[15] This was to become relevant in the case of David Hicks, discussed in a moment. These reforms were presaged by a White Paper, albeit only in scant outline, and appeared in the original draft legislation that was presented to Parliament. The new test for denaturalisation was derived from international conventions on statelessness and nationality.[16]

Three days after the new powers came into effect, the notorious cleric Abu Hamza was served with a notice of intention to strip him of his British citizenship. Hamza held Egyptian citizenship and had naturalised as British, making him a dual national. He could therefore potentially be removed to Egypt and was potentially subject to denaturalisation under the old legal regime. However, he had been convicted of no offences and disloyalty or disaffection might well have been considered too ephemeral a mental state to use as a basis for such a draconian and controversial act. It is plausible to suggest that the 2002 reform was conceived specifically to target Hamza. He was certainly in the public eye from at least 2001 onwards.[17] Shortly before the reform came into effect, then Home Secretary David Blunkett stated, referring specifically to Hamza, that 'every word and every action is being monitored, and we need to do so in a way that secures the confidence of people who are sick and tired of individuals like him abusing our hospitality'.[18] Without doubt, the change certainly enabled his denaturalisation and it was intended for use against other perceived supporters of radical political Islam (Ansari, 2021). However, denaturalisation did not take immediate effect because Hamza appealed and the law provided that his status was protected until the conclusion of the appeal. While the appeal was ongoing, the Egyptian government then stripped Hamza of his Egyptian citizenship.[19] This meant that the only nationality held by Hamza was his British citizenship. He could therefore no longer be denaturalised by the British government because to do so would render him stateless. His appeal succeeded and Abu Hamza remains a British citizen to this day. As Audrey Jacklin has put it, there is a 'race to see which country can strip citizenship first. To the loser goes the citizen' (Macklin, 2014: 52). The British government, eager to avoid losing any similar races in future, changed the law again in 2004.

The legal provision continuing citizenship during any appeal was quietly repealed by a new piece of legislation not otherwise addressing nationality law at all.[20] A person's citizenship would be immediately withdrawn on receipt of a decision, irrespective of whether the person pursued an appeal or not. If the appeal were to succeed, the person's citizenship would be restored. The change had a significant side-effect. If a British citizen was denaturalised while outside the country, this meant they would be unable to return, even to contest any appeal they might lodge. It would also become harder to resource and contest any appeal, or even to get an appeal lodged in the first place given the strict and inflexible time limits imposed. In a process led by the security services, denaturalisation decisions were henceforth served as soon as a person was outside the country, in effect exiling the recipients (Chief Inspector of Borders and Immigration, 2018: paragraphs 3.14 and 8.6 to 8.7).

Further legal changes were wrought in 2006. The 'seriously prejudicial to the vital interests of the United Kingdom' test was replaced with one of merely whether denaturalisation was considered by the Home Secretary to be 'conducive to the public good'. The new test was on the face of it unrelated to issues of state-level or civic harm or questions of loyalty. If a decision was challenged, the question for a judge would not be whether conduct was 'seriously prejudicial' and affecting the state's 'vital interests' but simply whether the person concerned had in fact conducted themselves as asserted by the Home Secretary and, if so, whether the Home Secretary's opinion of the public good was a rational one. The threshold of conduct was potentially far lower, and it was far harder to challenge in court. Indeed, the new test for denaturalisation was equivalent to the test for deporting foreign nationals on the basis of criminal or merely undesirable behaviour.

Unlike the reforms of 2002 and 2004, though, this change was not seemingly one that was pre-planned. There was no White Paper and the original Bill presented to Parliament was silent on the issue of citizenship deprivation.[21] The relevant clause was only introduced by the government at the scrutiny stage of the legislative process, in October 2005.[22] The minister responsible claimed that the purpose was to enable denaturalisation in the event that a British citizen engaged in 'certain unacceptable behaviours' in breach of the government's 'wider counter-terrorism initiative'. Admitting that the existing powers introduced in 2002 had not led to any actual denaturalisations (although notably silent on the failed attempt to denaturalise Abu Hamza), the minister justified the change by asserting '[w]e think that things have moved on and it is appropriate to have the power that we are discussing in the locker, if nothing else, given the way circumstances are'. Past behaviour by a British citizen would not be the only factor in denaturalisation decisions under the new test. Ministers would also consider 'potential threat' and 'a particular threat now from which the public need protection'. Finally, the minister all but admitted that the changes were not compatible with the international treaties from which the 'seriously prejudicial' test had been drawn. A seemingly unrelated amendment was introduced at the same time, which imposed for the first time the good character test on registrations as British nationals.

The saga of eligibility for British citizenship of David Hicks was running in parallel with these developments. Hicks was an Australian citizen who had ended up detained by the United States government at Guantanamo Bay on suspicion of involvement with Islamist terrorist groups prior to his capture in Afghanistan in 2001. He reportedly became aware he was eligible for registration as a British citizen in September 2005 and submitted an application soon afterwards in the hope this might prompt his release from detention. The application was rejected by the Home Office in November 2005. Eventually, after a series of court defeats for the British government, Hicks was briefly to be registered as British. Because the 'seriously prejudicial' test only applied to events after it came into force in 2003, it was actually the original test for citizenship deprivation set out in the 1981 legislation that was considered by the courts in Hicks' case. The Court of Appeal held that Hicks could have shown neither disloyalty nor disaffection because both require 'an attitude of mind towards an entity to which allegiance is owed, or at least to which the person belongs or is attached'.[23] He had not been British at the time so had owed no allegiance. In the meantime, the British government introduced the two amendments discussed above to the Bill then passing through Parliament. These amendments would have empowered the government to refuse Hicks' registration on good character grounds and, because this came too late, also enabled the government to denaturalise Hicks as soon as his registration had eventually been granted in July 2006.

The correlation between legal change and individual cases does not end there. In 2014, the law was changed so that a British citizen could in some circumstances be denaturalised even if this rendered them stateless. Once again, the relevant clause was not included in the Bill originally presented to Parliament. It was only after the handing down of the Supreme Court decision in *Al Jedda v Secretary of State for the Home Department* that the Bill was amended to include this provision.[24] The accompanying explanatory notes to the amendment made the link absolutely explicit, specifically citing the *Al Jedda* case.[25] The government minister presenting the amendment in the House of Lords was more circumspect, arguing the new power was needed 'to allow a small number of naturalised citizens who have taken up arms against British forces overseas or acted in some other manner seriously prejudicial to the vital interests of the UK to be deprived of their citizenship, regardless of whether it leaves them stateless'.[26]

The pattern was repeated in the parliamentary session of 2021–22. The legislation initially introduced to Parliament on 6 July 2021 did not touch on denaturalisation. On 30 July 2021, the High Court held that notice had to be given in writing in order for a denaturalisation decision to take effect.[27] It did not take the government long to respond. An amendment was introduced at the committee stage in November 2021 to abolish this requirement.

Behaviour-based denaturalisations peaked in 2017 at around the time that the territorial area in Iraq and Syria controlled by ISIS or the Islamic State group was collapsing. British citizens who had associated with the group may well have been looking to escape and return home at around that time. The Home Secretary at the time was Amber Rudd, but it was her successor, Sajid Javid, who provided the most detailed public justification for denaturalisation action. Speaking on breakfast television about Shamima Begum, he claimed that '[i]f you did know what I knew, as I say because you are sensible, responsible people, you would have made exactly the same decision, of that I have no doubt' (Newman, 2021). Javid framed the decision as one involving risk to the British public, essentially. He also, however, stated a very different justification for denaturalisation action. At a party conference speech he boasted of expanding use of citizenship deprivation powers to 'those who are convicted of the most grave criminal offences. This applies to some of the despicable men involved in gang-based child sexual exploitation.'[28] There is a clear moral dimension to this statement. A few months later he discussed the denaturalisation of a group of dual-national Pakistani-British men convicted of sexual offences. Pressed on the risk to citizens of Pakistan once they were removed there, Javid reverted to suggesting it was all a matter of risk, albeit only of risk to the British public: '[m]y job is to protect the British public and to do what I think is right to protect the British public' (Weaver, 2018). More recently, lawyers have reported that denaturalisation action is now being pursued against individuals convicted of human trafficking offences. It is hard to see how removing a person to a country from which they have previously trafficked others reduces risk to either the citizens of that country or the United Kingdom.

The expansion in the use of denaturalisation powers from threats to national security to very serious crimes would have been impossible without the reforms to citizenship deprivation law enacted in 2006 in response to the case of David Hicks. It is not realistically possible to argue that serious sexual offences or human trafficking amount to acts seriously prejudicial to the vital interests of the United Kingdom, but it clearly is possible to successfully argue that such conduct is sufficient for the Home Secretary to be satisfied that denaturalisation is conducive to the public good.[29] There is a significant chronological gap between enactment of the powers and their expanded use, though, which suggests that this was not what was originally envisaged. The reasons for the more extensive use of the power against a wider range of individuals lie in an ideological shift that comes after, not before, the legal reforms.

Denaturalisation based on fraud

The statutory power to deprive a British citizen of their status on the basis of fraud was introduced in 1914.[30] It is unknown how frequently this statutory power was exercised in previous years but it is thought to be seldom. A further form of fraud-based denaturalisation emerged through case law. In the 1978 case of *Sultan Mahmood*, a man had adopted the identity of his dead cousin and later purported to register as a British citizen in that identity.[31] The Court held that the purported registration was a nullity because of the man's fraudulent adoption of the identity of a real person. Later cases expanded the circumstances in which a previous recognition or grant of citizenship might be simply disregarded in this fashion. Statistics for both these forms of fraud-based denaturalisation are available for the period since 2012, and they show a significant subsequent expansion in exercise of the power. This coincides with an increased use of behaviour-based denaturalisation, as discussed previously.

From an administrative perspective, the state found it convenient to rely on simple declarations of nullity, challengeable only by way of an application for judicial review, rather than the statutory power, which carried procedural safeguards and a full right of appeal. The number of nullity declarations soared in 2013 from a very low base to 176 cases in a single year before subsiding again. In 2018, the Supreme Court held that cases subsequent to *Sultan Mahmood* had taken a 'wrong turning' and therefore that many of the subsequent nullity declarations had been unlawful. The statutory power should have been exercised instead.[32] The number of statutory fraud-based deprivations then began to rise and then increased sharply to 273 cases in 2021. It may well be the case that a proportion of the more recent statutory deprivation decisions have been made in respect of individuals whose citizenship was previously unlawfully nullified and then in effect restored by the Supreme Court judgment.

In contrast to the considerable literature addressing behaviour-based denaturalisation, fraud-based denaturalisation has attracted little analysis (an important exception is Fargues, 2019). It could potentially be argued that there is little to explain, in that there has been no change of state policy as such, merely a change in the propensity of would-be citizens to deploy fraud. If more grants of citizenship had been made in the relevant period, that might explain the increase in denaturalisation, or it might be the case that deception has been practised more frequently in recent years compared to the past. The first of these propositions is not borne out by the available statistics. While there was an increase in grants of citizenship in the period of 1980 to 1999 (average 63,000 per year) and 2000 to 2021 (average 150,000 per year), this does on the face of it explain the sharp increase in fraud-based denaturalisation since 2012.[33] Whether modern migrants have deployed fraud more than historical migrants is unknowable but it seems unlikely as an explanation. It is more plausible to suggest either or both that more effort is made to detect fraud – which would represent a change in state policy – and perhaps that fraud is easier to detect in the modern world, given the proliferation of databases against which checks can be made.

Fargues (2019) argues convincingly that the British government made the need to tackle fraud one of its priorities in the field of migration, particularly but not exclusively in the context of asylum and marriage migration. The equation of migration with deception is hardly new, but there is evidence to suggest that additional priority and resources have been dedicated to the issue in the context of citizenship. The Home Office team responsible for denaturalisation at the time of writing, the Status Review Unit, was created in 2012. Prior to that, no fraud-based denaturalisations at all had been processed in the years 2008 to 2012 (Chief Inspector of Borders and Immigration, 2014: 33). The entire unit consisted of 25 staff in 2017 (Chief Inspector of Borders and Immigration, 2018: 11), of whom five were found by Fargues (2019) to be dedicated to denaturalisation. In March 2017, the unit was reported to have a backlog of 1,338 deprivation cases and to be processing between 12 and 23 such cases per month (Chief Inspector of Borders and Immigration, 2018: 14). The delays caused by persistent backlogs, the opportunistic, non-systematic way in which cases are referred to the team within the Home Office, the internal system of prioritisation and the availability of only snapshots of statistics on the work in progress render it impossible to link any prior migration trends with the number of denaturalisations occurring in a given year. Meanwhile, at some point between July 2014 and December 2014, a pragmatic policy to the effect that denaturalisation would not be pursued against a person who had resided in the United Kingdom for 14 years was abolished.[34] The abolition of this policy opened the doors to pursuit of denaturalisation of long-term residents, some of whom had been British citizens for well over a decade by the time deprivation action was taken. This was despite the Home Office being aware of the underlying fraud for substantial periods of time. In one reported case, for example, an Albanian man had entered the United Kingdom in 1999, been naturalised as British in 2005, was warned of possible denaturalisation action in 2009 and then formal action was only pursued in 2018.[35] In another, an Albanian man entered the country in 1996, was naturalised as British in 2003, issued with a nullity decision in 2013 (which was then itself effectively invalidated by a Supreme Court judgment, as discussed earlier) and statutory deprivation action was taken in 2018.[36]

A high proportion of fraud-based denaturalisations since 2012 involve Albanian citizens. This is reflected in the inspection reports addressing denaturalisation and in the reported cases on fraud-based denaturalisation. In short, some Albanians arrived in the United Kingdom in the late 1990s and early 2000s and claimed to be from Kosovo in order to benefit from a Home Office policy of granting asylum to Kosovars. Some were granted asylum and some were not. Where asylum was refused, it was often because the asylum claimant was disbelieved. Nevertheless, many continued to use their fabricated details in their various dealings with the Home Office and were eventually granted limited leave, indefinite leave to remain and then sometimes British citizenship. The earlier fraud became evident in many cases after the person concerned sponsored the entry of family members from Albania. Denaturalisation action sometimes followed relatively swiftly but was often delayed. It later emerged that one explanation for the delay was simply that officials deciding immigration and citizenship applications within the United Kingdom did not have access to the database used by officials deciding applications for entry from abroad.

The purpose of fraud-based denaturalisation appears to be a moral one. Fargues (2019) suggests the officials responsible justify their work as threatening the purpose of naturalisation, namely to celebrate citizenship as a prize available only to those deemed sufficiently worthy. Contrary to Fargues' findings, however, it is thought that in practice very few fraud-based deprivation decisions lead to removal action. Those concerned almost invariably have partners and children in the United Kingdom, who are often themselves British by birth or naturalisation. Indeed, the original deception is often detected only by means of the sponsoring of a family member to come to the United Kingdom. This lack of real consequence calls into question the purpose of the denaturalisation action. In short, why devote resources to this issue – there are many arguably more pressing issues facing the contemporary Home Office – when the deception is so historical and denaturalisation will not lead to removal in any event?

Understanding British denaturalisation policy

Competing and overlapping concepts of citizenship have been proposed to explain the increase in behaviour-based denaturalisation across the Global North since the turn of the millennium. Denaturalisation can be regarded as one dimension of citizenship 'thickening', a process by which citizenship is invested with more significance, becoming both harder to obtain and also easier to lose by one's conduct.[37] More recently, Joppke (2021) identifies the rise of the idea of neoliberal 'earned citizenship', in which citizenship is regarded as a conditional, earned privilege rather than an inalienable right. Fargues (2017) argues that denaturalisation is better understood as part of a 'renationalising' of citizenship in which not only is citizenship regarded as more significant but also the national community is conceptualised as a homogenous entity. These lenses are useful when considering the case of the United Kingdom but they do not fully explain how law and practice have evolved.

The idea of the 'renationalisation' of citizenship can certainly contribute to understanding imperial denaturalisation in the context of the United Kingdom, although it would be better stated as simple nationalisation given there was no national citizenship prior to the advent of the British Nationality Act 1981. There was an important racial dimension: the process was very much one of white nationalisation (see, for example, Paul, 1997). Those who were white were regarded as belonging to the national community, and immigration legislation was therefore adopted to modify nationality laws that were considered too broad and inclusive, yet also too difficult to change at that point in time (Hansen, 2000). The form of quasi-citizenship to emerge from the process ('patrials' were the closest analogue to citizens prior to legal reforms in 1981) was an exceedingly 'thin' one, based on place of birth or on length of residence. After the 1981 reforms, it was relatively straightforward for a long-term resident of the United Kingdom to acquire full British citizenship, subject to a small fee, a fairly cursory good character test and the swearing in private of a loyalty oath. Until the introduction of hostile environment laws, there seemed little advantage to moving from the status of long-term resident to that of citizen, however (Griffiths and Yeo, 2021). It was not much of an upgrade and the benefits of doing so were few, particularly as Commonwealth citizens enjoyed the right to vote in elections and long-term resident Commonwealth citizens enjoyed the right of abode, could sponsor family members on the same basis as citizens and were in theory immune from deportation.[38]

Reforms in the 2000s without doubt represent actual and attempted thickening of British citizenship. A citizenship test was introduced in 2002 along with public citizenship ceremonies and, as discussed earlier, the radical widening of the criteria for denaturalisation to include those born British.[39] Reforms in 2004 and 2006, also discussed earlier, focused on widening yet further the criteria for denaturalisation. Further changes to the way in which citizenship would be acquired intended to 'enhance the bond of citizenship' and introduce 'earned citizenship' were passed by Parliament in 2009.[40] These were, however, never implemented following a change of government in 2010. At this stage, even the reforms that were enacted were rarely deployed in practice. Neither is it really clear how taking citizenship away from one person 'thickens' the concept or value of citizenship for others, even if it is carried out as an act of communal opprobrium. The reforms in 2004 and 2006 appear opportunistic when seen in context and were certainly deployed in an opportunistic fashion against a limited number of individuals once enacted. Those who executed these denaturalisations may well, as Sajid Javid did later, have seen these as acts of risk reduction intended to protect the British public from harm. The risk of discrimination was always high, though. As Gibney (2020: 2566) observes, 'the imaginative leap required to justify turning a citizen into an alien still requires that the individual in question be part of a group already viewed as less than full citizens'.

The fact that every known case of behaviour-based denaturalisation involves a Muslim has not gone without comment. There is undoubtedly a serious threat to public safety from some individuals who are Muslim, but it would be entirely unrealistic to suggest that the threat is uniquely posed by Muslims. Denaturalisation has never been pursued against Irish nationalists, adherents of right-wing terror groups, anarchists or other dual foreign nationals representing a threat to national security. It is possible that no such individuals were identified who held dual citizenship and were thus eligible for denaturalisation but this seems inherently unlikely. The discrimination becomes even more stark when the case of the Rochdale sex offenders is considered. The men who were denaturalised were all Muslim men of Pakistani origin. It seems highly likely that there have been many, many other dual nationals who committed sexual and other offences of similar or worse gravity – where seriousness is measured by the length of sentence rather than media judgement – who were never considered for denaturalisation.

A similar issue of discrimination arises in fraud-based denaturalisation. Albanians have, seemingly overwhelmingly, been the principal target. Albania is a majority-Muslim country, albeit Albanians are often not perceived as Muslim. Albanians have undoubtedly become a racialised group in the United Kingdom, though, and are heavily overrepresented in immigration detention and in enforced removals as well as in denaturalisation decisions (see, for example, Fox et al, 2012; De Noronha, 2021: 75–79). It is improbable that Albanian migrants are uniquely liable to have used deception at some point in order to secure status in the United Kingdom. A plausible case could perhaps be made for arguing that Albanians are uniquely unfortunate in being more liable to be caught; their government has been unusually cooperative in checking identity details on request by British immigration officials. Similar identity checks cannot be so readily carried out on those who claimed asylum from Iraq in the late 1990s and early 2000s claiming to be from the Kurdish autonomous area, for example. The fact remains that the British government has chosen to devote considerable resources to this exercise since 2010 and overwhelmingly targeted a particular national group, whereas potential deception within other migrant groups has been tacitly tolerated. Fargues (2019) argues that the obsession with fraud-based denaturalisation suggests a new focus on migrant morality. This is surely so, but it is a very narrowly targeted focus.

The politics of race has therefore played an important role not just in imperial denaturalisation but in behaviour-based denaturalisation and in fraud-based denaturalisation. Racism in immigration and citizenship policy is hardly new, though, and cannot alone explain the increase in behaviour and fraud-based denaturalisation from 2010 onwards. Some incidents of denaturalisation are attributable to opportunistic but also discriminatory targeting of individuals considered to pose a risk to public safety. This is particularly so where a person was denaturalised while abroad to prevent their return home. The public discourse on denaturalisation has gone further, though, and denaturalisation clearly also performs a function of expressing public opprobrium. Again, this has been done selectively and in a discriminatory fashion. This thread runs through the high-profile cases of Abu Hamza, David Hicks, Al Jedda, Shamima Begum and the Rochdale sexual offenders. It also connects the fraud-based denaturalisations. The resources directed to fraud-based denaturalisations, which are likely to result in no removal from the United Kingdom, are impossible to explain other than as the belated imposition of punishment for past violations of a moral code. Political expediency should not be discounted as a driver in many of these cases: politicians have felt compelled to respond to media coverage and demonstrate that they are not powerless. Underlying all of this is a change to the way in which value is attributed to citizenship. The once-controversial statement that citizenship is a 'privilege not a right' first appears in parliamentary debates on the abortive earned citizenship legislation of 2008 and 2009.[41] For some, the high value of citizenship means it should only be removed in exceptional circumstances, if ever. For others, the value of citizenship is enhanced by fragility. If citizenship can be broken or lost, those who hold it will cherish it all the more. This moral dimension to citizenship is rarely stated explicitly in public but has become increasingly prevalent. It is likely to lead to ever wider use of denaturalisation powers, albeit primarily and disproportionately against perceived out groups.

Notes

1 Home Office response to Freedom of Information request, FOI 38734; HM Government transparency reports CM 9609 (July 2018), CP 212 (March 2020) and CP 621 (March 2022); Immigration and protection transparency data, table RCM_01 (February 2022).

2 Commonwealth Immigrants Acts 1962 and 1968 and the Immigration Act 1971.
3 Literature on the practice of 'bordering' argues that the process continues. See, for example, El-Enany (2020).
4 Statutory citizenship deprivation is enabled by the British Nationality Act, section 40. The key case establishing the practice of nullification is *R v Secretary of State for the Home Department, ex p. Mahmood (Sultan)* [1981] QB 58n.
5 *R (Hysaj & Ors) v Secretary of State for the Home Department* [2017] UKSC 82.
6 There were a total of 801 fraud-based denaturalisations by means of deprivation or nullification in the years 2012 to 2021 compared to a total of 206 behaviour-based denaturalisations between 2012 and 2020 (figures for 2021 unavailable at the time of writing).
7 The so-called 'common code' of British nationality law was in truth never effective, particularly in facilitating horizontal movement between colonies; see Parry (1957).
8 British Nationality Act 1948, section 1.
9 British Nationality Act 1948, section 1: 'Any person having [the status of a British subject] may be known either as a British subject or as a Commonwealth citizen; and accordingly in this Act and in any other enactment or instrument whatever, whether passed, or made before or after the commencement of this Act, the expression "British subject" and the expression "Commonwealth citizen" shall have the same meaning.'
10 'Secure Borders, Safe Haven: Integration with diversity in modern Britain', CM 5387, February 2002.
11 See for example *Laci v Secretary of State for the Home Department* [2021] EWCA Civ 769 at paragraphs 14–15 and 56–57.
12 British Nationality and Status of Aliens Act 1918, section 1.
13 British Nationality Act 1948, section 20(3) and British Nationality Act 1981, section 40(3).
14 Nationality, Immigration and Asylum Act 2002, section 4. Came into effect on 1 April 2003.
15 See Nationality, Immigration and Asylum Act 2002, section 4(4).
16 Article 8 of the 1961 UN convention on the reduction of statelessness and Article 7 of the 1997 European Convention on Nationality.
17 See, for example, *Hansard* HC Deb vol. 372, col. 1085–1088, 16 October 2001 (Andrew Dismore).
18 *Hansard*, HC Deb vol. 397, col. 691, 15 January 2003.
19 The precise date is unknown. See judgment of Mitting J in *Abu Hamza v Secretary of State for the Home Department* (SC/23/2003), 5 November 2010 at paragraph 21.
20 Asylum and Immigration (Treatment of Claimants, etc) Act 2004, Schedule 2, paragraph 4. See Weston (2011).
21 Immigration, Asylum and Nationality Bill, as introduced in the House of Commons on 22 June 2005.

22 Laid on 25 October 2005 and formally introduced and debated on 27 October 2005. Immigration, Asylum and Nationality Bill Deb (Bill 13) 27 October 2005, col. 253.
23 *Secretary of State for the Home Department v Hicks* [2006] EWCA Civ 400, Pill LJ, paragraph 32.
24 [2013] UKSC 62, [2014] 1 AC 253.
25 HL Bill 84-EN 2013–14, Explanatory notes to the Bill, 3 February 2014, paragraph 32.
26 HL Deb 10 February 2014 cols 416–417.
27 *R (On the Application of D4) v Secretary of State for the Home Department* [2021] EWHC 2179 (Admin). Later confirmed by the Court of Appeal at citation [2022] EWCA Civ 33.
28 Sajid Javid, speech to Conservative Party conference, 2 October 2018.
29 The Rochdale sex offenders lost their legal challenge: *Aziz & Ors v Secretary of State for the Home Department* [2018] EWCA Civ 1884.
30 British Nationality and Status of Aliens Act 1914, section 7.
31 *R v Secretary of State for the Home Department, ex p. Mahmood (Sultan)* [1981] QB 58.
32 *R (on the application of Hysaj) v Secretary of State for the Home Department* [2017] UKSC 82.
33 Home Office quarterly immigration statistics published 25 August 2022, table Cit_02.
34 Dates ascertained by comparing captures of the relevant policy document in the National Archive at https://webarchive.nationalarchives.gov.uk/ukgwa/*/https://www.gov.uk/government/publications/chapter-55-deprivation-section-40-and-nullity-nationality-instructions (accessed 11 June 2024).
35 *Laci v Secretary of State for the Home Department* [2021] EWCA Civ 769.
36 *Ciceri (deprivation of citizenship appeals: principles) Albania* [2021] UKUT 238 (IAC).
37 The opposite of the 'lightening' Joppke (2010) proposed.
38 Representation of the People Act 1983, sections 1(1) and 4; Immigration Act 1971, sections 2 and 7.
39 Nationality, Immigration and Asylum Act 2002.
40 Borders, Citizenship and Immigration Act 2009, the citizenship elements of which were based in part on the 'Goldsmith Review' of 2008 entitled *Citizenship: Our Common Bond.*
41 David Davis HC Deb vol. 472, col. 354, 20 February 2008; Chris Grayling HC Deb vol. 493, col. 182, 2 June 2008; Damien Green HC Deb vol. 496, col. 223, 14 July 2009.

References

Ansari, Fahad (2021) 'Citizenship deprivation: The legacy of Tony Blair's desperation to deport one British man'. www.cage.ngo/citizenship-deprivation-the-legacy-of-tony-blairs-desperation-to-deport-one-british-man (accessed 10 October 2022).

Chief Inspector of Borders and Immigration (2014) *An Inspection of Nationality Casework*. London: HMSO.

Chief Inspector of Borders and Immigration (2018) *Report on the Review and Removal of Immigration, Refugee and Citizenship "Status"*. London: HMSO.

De Noronha, Luke (2021) *Deporting Black Britons: Portraits of Deportation to Jamaica*. Manchester: Manchester University Press.

El-Enany, Nadine (2020) *(B)ordering Britain: Law, Race and Empire*. Manchester: Manchester University Press.

Fargues, Émilien (2017) 'The revival of citizenship deprivation in France and the UK as an instance of citizenship renationalisation'. *Citizenship Studies* 21(8): 984–998.

Fargues, Émilien (2019) 'Simply a matter of compliance with the rules? The moralising and responsibilising function of fraud-based citizenship deprivation in France and the UK'. *Citizenship Studies* 23(4): 356–371.

Fox, Jon E., Moroşanu, Laura and Szilassy, Eszter (2012) 'The racialization of the new European migration to the UK'. *Sociology* 46(4): 680–695.

Fransman, Laurie (2011) *Fransman's British Nationality Law* (3rd ed.). London: Bloomsbury.

Gentleman, Amelia (2019) *The Windrush Betrayal: Exposing the Hostile Environment*. London: The Guardian.

Gibney, Matthew J. (2013) '"A very transcendental power": Denaturalisation and the liberalisation of citizenship in the United Kingdom'. *Political Studies* 61(3): 637–655.

Gibney, Matthew J. (2020) 'Denationalisation and discrimination'. *Journal of Ethnic and Migration Studies* 46(12): 2551–2568.

Griffiths, Melanie and Yeo, Colin (2021) 'The UK's hostile environment: Deputising immigration control'. *Critical Social Policy* 41(4): 521–544.

Hansen, Randall (2000) *Citizenship and Immigration in Post-war Britain*. Oxford: Oxford University Press.

Jones, James Mervyn (1948) *British Nationality Law*. Oxford: Clarendon Press.

Joppke, Christian (2010) 'The inevitable lightening of citizenship'. *European Journal of Sociology* 51(1): 9–32.

Joppke, Christian (2021) 'Earned citizenship'. *European Journal of Sociology* 62(1): 1–35.

Macklin, Audrey (2014) 'Citizenship revocation, the privilege to have rights and the production of aliens'. *Queen's Law Journal* 40(1): 1–54.

Newman, Vicki (2021) 'Sajid Javid says no one would let Shamima Begum return if they knew what he does'. *The Mirror*, 15 September. www.mirror.co.uk/tv/tv-news/sajid-javid-says-no-one-24987905 (accessed 11 June 2024).

Parry, Clive (1957) *Nationality and Citizenship Laws of The Commonwealth and of The Republic of Ireland*. London: Stevens and Sons.

Paul, Kathleen (1997) *Whitewashing Britain: Race and Citizenship in the Post War Era*. New York: Cornell University Press.

Sredanovic, Djordje (2017) 'Was citizenship born with the Enlightenment? Developments of citizenship between Britain and France and "everyday citizenship" implications'. *Miranda* 15.

van der Merwe, Ben (2021) 'Exclusive: British citizenship of six million people could be jeopardised by Home Office plans'. *New Statesman*, 1 December 2021. www.newstatesman.com/politics/2021/12/exclusive-british-citizenship-of-six-million-people-could-be-jeopardised-by-home-office-plans

Weaver, Matthew (2018) 'Sajid Javid defends deportation of grooming gang members'. *The Guardian*, 26 December. www.theguardian.com/politics/2018/dec/26/sajid-javid-defends-deportation-of-grooming-gang-members

Weston, Amanda (2011) 'Deprivation of citizenship – by stealth'. Institute for Race Relations. https://irr.org.uk/article/deprivation-of-citizenship-by-stealth/

Yeo, Colin, Sigona, Nando and Godin, Marie (2019) *Parallels and Differences Between Ending Commonwealth and EU Citizen Free Movement*. Eurochildren Research Brief Series, No. 4.

Part II

Experience

4

Citizenship and belonging in the times of Brexit: the case of Polish migrants in Manchester

Alina Rzepnikowska

Introduction

The question of belonging is one of the most controversial issues raised by Brexit. This is particularly important since 'Brexit made a definite change to everyday understandings of inclusion as now there is a felt imperative to decide who is a rightful autochthonous member of society' (Cassidy et al., 2018: 191) – who belongs and should have rights and who should not. These questions cannot be answered without reference to race and migration (Bhambra, 2017). Populist politics contributed to anxiety, fears and resentment of those who are seen as different and not belonging. Anti-immigration Leave campaigns have been linked with xenophobic and racist attacks on migrants and ethnic minorities (Rzepnikowska, 2019, 2020). Black, Brown or white migrants and ethnic minorities were all at risk of being targeted by xenophobic racists, as they all were seen as a threat to Englishness (Virdee and McGeever, 2018).

As it is emphasised in the Introduction to this volume and the existing literature (Bhambra, 2017), Brexit is not an isolated event, and the links with other processes of limiting citizens' rights in the UK should not be overlooked. The imperial citizenship regime in the early post-war years restricted the ability of the British government to control immigration from the colonies (Hampshire, 2005). The introduction of Citizenship of the United Kingdom and Colonies (supposedly open multinational and multiracial citizenship based on the rhetoric of *Civis Britannicus sum*) by the Labour government in 1948 meant that those arriving from the colonies could enjoy the same citizenship rights as British people born in the UK. The immigration legislation passed by the British government from the 1960s gradually took rights away from Black and Brown citizens. A distinction between 'belonging' and 'non-belonging' citizens had to be developed to justify this restrictive immigration legislation (Hampshire, 2005: 16). The main concern at that time was about limiting the freedom of movement of less desirable racialised British colonial and Commonwealth citizens (Hampshire, 2005; Bhambra, 2017). The defining of British citizenship has been based on racialising citizens as non-belonging Others and making them immigrants based on a racial hierarchy (Karatani, 2003; Hampshire, 2005; Bhambra, 2017). In contrast, Poles who fled to Britain after Germany's invasion of Poland, as well as their families joining them in the post-war period, were categorised as white. This categorisation rendered them desirable immigrants in the eyes of the government and employees (McDowell, 2009), although their working conditions and conditional immigration status marked them as the Other.

Hampshire (2005: 16) highlights the tension between citizenship and belonging which continued to influence immigration policy until 'British citizenship was redefined in narrow, post-imperial terms'. The Windrush scandal in 2017/2018, having its origin in racist legislation since the 1950s, including more recent 'hostile environment' policy announced in 2012 by the former Home Secretary Theresa May, further highlights this tension. A significant number of Commonwealth citizens had been wrongly detained, deported and denied legal rights, affecting the lives of many Black British people.[1] The tension between citizenship and belonging could also be observed at the time of the EU referendum followed by Brexit, when European Union citizens' rights to live and work in the UK changed.

The distinction between who belongs and who does not has played an important role in the politicisation and racialisation of Central and Eastern European migration.[2] Nevertheless, it is important to point out the difference between the Windrush arrivals and migrants from Europe in more recent times (many of whom are advantaged by white privilege), since the former 'belonged' to the British Empire (Cassidy et al., 2018), and the magnitude of racialisation of people of colour over decades in the UK.

In terms of the right to live and settle in the UK, Polish, among other migrants from Central and Eastern Europe (CEE), were initially privileged by assumptions of whiteness and Europeanness. As Poland joined the EU in 2004, a substantial number decided to exercise their newly won rights to free movement as EU citizens by migrating to the UK (Duda-Mikulin, 2019; Rzepnikowska, 2020; ONS, 2011a). Polish migrants were able to enjoy access to the British labour market and social rights in the UK by virtue of being European citizens. Nevertheless, despite their access to EU citizenship they were not necessarily seen as belonging to the 'British we' – the idea of belonging based on lineage and descent, prominent in use from the 1960s (Hampshire, 2005). Both imperial and multinational citizenship (in the post-war period) and later European citizenship in recent years were incompatible with the right-wing and populist construction of national identity in Britain and the notion of who really and truly belongs, despite previous efforts to diversify the idea of belonging and Britishness.

Despite the initial open-door policy by the Labour government and successful integration of EU citizens into the British labour market, as mentioned above, migration and migrants from Central and Eastern Europe have been gradually politicised and racialised (Fox et al., 2012; Rzepnikowska, 2019, 2023) (although not to the same extent as the dehumanising racialisation of Black people and other visible minorities in the UK), resulting in the Brexit vote redefining non-UK-born EU citizens' rights (Sredanovic and Byrne's Introduction, this volume).

Yuval-Davis (2006: 197) emphasises the distinction between belonging and the politics of belonging, defining the former as 'emotional attachment, about feeling "at home" and ... about feeling "safe"'. The main focus in this chapter is on 'the dimension of how subjects feel about their location in the social world which is generated partly through experiences of exclusion rather than about inclusion per se' (Yuval-Davis et al., 2005: 526). In turn, the politics of belonging 'comprises specific political projects aimed at constructing belonging in particular ways to particular collectivities that are, at the same time, themselves being constructed by these projects in very particular ways' (Yuval-Davis et al., 2005: 526). The Leave campaign and Brexit can be seen as such projects which (re)constructed the 'British we' as distinct from racialised Black, Brown and East European Others, and to some extent also Western Europeans. While it is important to distinguish politics of belonging and (a sense of) belonging, there is a need to acknowledge how politics of belonging influence the sense of attachment, feeling at home and feeling safe, as discussed in this chapter.

Recent research literature shows that Brexit has affected non-UK-born EU migrants' sense of belonging and further contributed to the existing hierarchies along the lines of race,[3] class and gender in the UK (Botterill and Hancock, 2018; Guma and Jones, 2018; Blachnicka-Ciacek et al., 2021; Sotkasiira and Gawlewicz, 2021; Rzepnikowska, 2019, 2023). This chapter contributes to the existing literature on migration and Brexit exploring the impact of Brexit vote, offering a more nuanced discussion on citizenship and belonging from the perspectives of Polish migrant women (Duda-Mikulin, 2023).

I begin this chapter by outlining the context of Polish migration in the UK. Following this, I summarise the methodology. The following analytical sections explore narratives of citizenship and belonging which prompt critical questions about the consequences of Brexit and its divisive rhetoric about immigration on the experiences of living together with attention to locality, race, ethnicity, class, age, gender and other categories which often intersect. This chapter draws on my research in Manchester and the wider area of Greater Manchester. While Manchester had the strongest Remain vote in the northwest, the majority of Greater Manchester boroughs were characterised by a majority Leave vote.

Polish migrants in the UK

The accession of eight member states (A8 – Lithuania, Latvia, Estonia, Poland, Czech Republic, Slovakia, Slovenia and Hungary) to the European Union on 1 May 2004 resulted in significant migration within Europe in the following decade. The UK, as well as Ireland and Sweden, granted A8 nationals free access to the labour market immediately after the EU enlargement due to severe labour market shortages, mainly in low-wage and low-skill occupations in construction, hospitality, transport sectors and public services (Anderson et al., 2006; Drinkwater et al., 2006). Freedom of movement attracted many Polish people, especially the young, affected by high rates of unemployment, low wages and lack of opportunities in Poland (White, 2010). These newly arrived migrants constituted the largest group from the A8 countries entering Britain. Between 2003 and 2010, the Polish-born population of the UK increased from 75,000 to 532,000 (ONS, 2011a). It was estimated that in 2015 the most common non-British nationality was Polish, with 916,000 residents (16.5 per cent of the total non-British national population resident in the UK) (ONS, 2015). According to 2011 census data, Polish migrants had the highest birth rate amongst other migrant groups (ONS, 2011b) and Polish was the most spoken non-native language in England and Wales (ONS, 2011c). According to ONS data on population of the UK by country of birth and nationality from 2020, Polish nationals were the largest group of non-UK-born EU citizens in Britain (ONS, 2021).

In the post-2004 period, Manchester witnessed the arrival of Polish migrants, amongst other A8 nationals, who contributed to greater diversity in the city. The official statistics on the numbers and distribution of Polish migrants in Manchester are very limited. According to Manchester City Council (2015: 29) data, Polish migrants constituted 1.2 per cent of the Manchester population and 0.8 per cent of the Greater Manchester population (based on self-descriptions). Polish residents are dispersed across Manchester and the area of Greater Manchester, although the city centre ward and Cheetham have been described as popular with the Polish community (Manchester City Council, 2015). Many of my research participants arrived in less advantaged areas with cheaper rent and poor housing. However, as a result of an improved socio-economic situation, some moved to more affluent residential neighbourhoods. It is important to highlight a strong Remain vote in Manchester (60.4 per cent), while most Greater Manchester boroughs voted to leave. The Leave vote was reported as being associated with a longstanding frustration over immigration in more deprived parts of Greater Manchester (BBC News, 2016).

Methods

This chapter draws on my ethnographic research carried out in Manchester in 2012 and 2013 and including participant observation, 21 narrative interviews and a focus group, as well as repeat qualitative interviews conducted in 2017 and 2018. The sample in the initial research aimed to capture the heterogeneity of Polish women in terms of age, socio-economic status, marital status, migration history and length of stay. It included Polish migrant women who entered Britain just before or after Poland joined the EU.

The research stressed the importance of migrant women's everyday encounters with the local population in multicultural cities. It follows the idea of research recognising the complex interactions between racialised, gendered and class identities and positions (Phizacklea, 2003; Sumi et al., 2013). The interviewees were mainly recruited through the groups with which I conducted the participant observation, and subsequently snowball sampling was applied. I maintained contact with most of the interviewees in Manchester (15 out of 21) and contacted them in 2017 about their experiences after the EU referendum, and six agreed to take part in the follow-up research. The focus on migrant women stresses the importance of gendered experiences of migration (Duda-Mikulin, 2023; Lutz, 2010), citizenship and belonging.

Initially, my research was not designed as longitudinal. As Ryan et al. (2016) point out, it would have been difficult to plan a longitudinal study considering the temporariness and uncertainty of Polish migrants' trajectories.

The interviews in both studies were transcribed, summarised and coded manually to identify the main themes and subsequently analysed as narratives (Riessman, 2002). All participants have been given pseudonyms. Both research projects were approved by the University of Manchester ethics committee. I adhered to the ethical principles regarding confidentiality, anonymity and data protection.

In this chapter, I mainly focus on the narratives of four research participants and their complex experiences of belonging in the context of Brexit which have been influenced by the areas where they live, the people they interact with, their economic and cultural capital, their age and the stage of their life.

Research findings

All my research participants told me how shocked they were about the Brexit vote and how anxious and uncertain it made them feel. They were aware of anti-migrant sentiment in the run-up to the EU referendum and in the aftermath. Several felt fearful of post-Brexit xeno-racism (Rzepnikowska, 2019). Nevertheless, going back to Poland was not considered a good option because they all felt their home was in the UK, and several felt discouraged by the political situation in their home country, as discussed below. Uncertainty about the future in the light of Brexit has bred further anxiety and distress. I mainly focus on the narratives of Renia, Oliwia, Nikola and Krysia. I use a person and case-centred approach and concentrate on how these interviewees made sense of their experiences of citizenship and belonging at the time of Brexit. This is with attention to interconnections between race, ethnicity, class, gender, age and locality. While qualitative research is not statistically representative of a population, these cases illustrate the main themes which emerged in this research in the context of Brexit. These include a sense of becoming foreigners; a sense of fear and uncertainty about the future in the UK, and, at the same time, concerns about going back to Poland because of growing hostility towards ethno-religious difference; and for others, a stronger sense of belonging reflected through neighbourly and motherly conviviality. While Oliwia and Nikola are mothers caring for younger children, Krysia and Renia are older migrant women with lower social and economic capital and with disabilities, which contribute to the difficulties with complying with the requirements of permanent residency, settled status and British citizenship (Migration Observatory, 2017; Sumption and Fernández-Reino, 2020).

Becoming foreigners

Renia was in her late fifties when I interviewed her first in 2012. She arrived in the UK in 2005. She had worked as a warehouse operator, below her qualifications and work experience. In Poland, she was an office worker. At the time of the second interview, she was not working due to health issues. She had been living in a former mill town in Greater Manchester, where 11.5 per cent of the local population are from an ethnic minority group. 61.1 per cent of the population in her town voted Leave. In fact, all the wards, including Renia's, had a majority Leave vote.

Over the period of the research, Renia's sense of belonging was particularly affected by deteriorating relations with her neighbours. As Devine (2021) argues, political events like referendums can play a significant role in changes in prejudicial behaviour. This is particularly relevant to the Brexit referendum, given the substantial focus on questions of immigration and national identity (Virdee and McGeever, 2018). While Renia and her husband experienced anti-migrant hostility before and after Brexit by local youth, she felt her immediate neighbours of a similar age used to be friendly and made her feel welcome. However, Renia claimed they started to change their attitudes: 'Because of Brexit, something bad has happened to people. The idea of organising the referendum was unfortunate, and now we have to suffer the consequences. Hostility to foreigners is growing.'

This was the first time Renia used the word 'foreigners', which reflects the shift from the idea of the UK as a home by many EU citizens to becoming foreigners who are seen and feel as no longer belonging. It was not the EU referendum and the Brexit vote itself but the increasingly hostile climate that affected Renia, her husband and many other EU citizens, and made them feel a sense of foreignness. As discussed in my earlier work, media and political discourses blamed EU migrants for economic and social problems long before the EU referendum (Rzepnikowska, 2019). This contributed to an 'us' versus 'them' attitude among some sections of the British population. Anti-immigrant rhetoric and xenophobic attitudes in the UK reached a peak during the referendum and following the Brexit vote. In addition, according to Devine's (2021) findings, the EU referendum resulted in a 19–23 per cent increase in racial and religious hate crimes, which is historically significant, although it did not lead to a longer-term increase. Xenophobic references to 'going back to your country' by Renia's husband's co-workers in a meat processing factory further contributed to a feeling that they no longer belong. The imagined British 'we' now appeared to exclude non-UK EU citizens, who earlier had been seen as those who potentially could belong to the 'British we', as indicated in the *Daily Mail* article 'The new Britons' (2006). Shared whiteness between migrants from CEE and the white British majority had not exempted the former from racialisation (Fox et al., 2012; Rzepnikowska, 2019, 2023). The Brexit vote contributed to the construction of an imaginary boundary line of the nation. In this example, EU workers were homogenised and rendered as non-belonging, even though they still had the right to remain in the UK (at the time of the research).

It is important to point out that Renia, as with many other CEE migrants arriving after the EU expansion, moved to an inner-city neighbourhood characterised by high levels of social deprivation. Based on their study in a northern English city, Cook et al. (2012) explored the ways in which established communities experience and make sense of the local impact of new migration within their neighbourhoods. Their research shows that CEE migrants are in competition with established communities for local jobs and welfare resources, and this is central to the concerns of longstanding communities. The 'proactive engagement' with citizenship status among CEE migrants triggers a more 'defensive engagement' among members of local host communities (Cook et al., 2012: 329). Valentine (2008) explains how in areas of relative social and economic deprivation, community-based narratives of injustice and victimhood are prevalent, and migrants are blamed for 'stealing' jobs, undercutting wages and taking benefits.

Renia stressed that her son, a young professional working for a large corporation and living in a more affluent area, did not experience discrimination at work or in his neighbourhood. Renia was aware that that those who were particularly vulnerable to discrimination and xeno-racism were Polish migrants from the lower echelons with limited English-language skills, and those living in deprived areas. The intersection of migration, ethnicity and class is significant in the process of racialisation of Polish migrants. While the British white working class has frequently been blamed for racist and xenophobic attitudes, Khan and Shaheen (2017) argue that working-class communities in the UK have been exploited by politicians telling them that the newcomers are to be blamed for their problems, encouraging resentment of migrants, while the wider socio-economic inequalities in British society are overlooked. And this is nothing new. The interests of the white working class have often been pitched by the media and politicians against those of ethnic minorities and migrants (Skeggs, 2009).

Another key contributing factor to the sense of foreignness was uncertainty about their legal status, the right to reside in the UK and the entitlement to access social rights after Brexit. With gradual removal of welfare rights, 'free movers' had gradually become 'immigrants' (Barbulescu and Favell, 2020), which also contributed to the sense of foreignness and not belonging.

Following Brexit, EU citizens' rights to live and work in the UK changed and they had to make an application by 30 June 2021 under the European Union Settlement Scheme, which was established under the terms of the Withdrawal Agreement, to enable them to continue to live in the UK lawfully (Barnard et al., 2022). At the time of my research there was very little clarity about the documents and evidence required by EU nationals when applying for 'settled status'. This also contributed to the recognition that belonging is conditional, and shows how the impacts of Brexit were unevenly felt and experienced by different individuals (Barnard et al., 2022), with attention to their economic position, occupation, language skills, dis/ability, and so on.

> I applied for Permanent Residence. I submitted the online application 2 months ago. But my children didn't. They think that there is no need, but I feel that I have to. And this is the difference. My daughter and her husband bought a house. My younger daughter bought a flat. But my husband and I live in social housing, and we actually don't have anything here and we hardly speak any English. I feel very insecure [zagrożona], and they don't. And here you have a different way of thinking. It depends on the company and the people you work with. My husband comes back very distressed because he started to feel unwanted for the first time in the last 12 years, as if he was no longer needed, but he is a really good and skilled worker.

In the case of Brexit, the pressure arises on non-UK EU nationals to prove that they have the right to live in the UK. Some of my research participants applied for British citizenship to be safe, even though they would not consider it if it was not for Brexit, as they felt secure enough with their EU citizenship. Sredanovic and Della Puppa (2023) explore how migratory experience, class and age influence the decision on whether to apply for citizenship in the Brexit context based on in-depth interviews with Britons in Belgium, non-UK-born EU27 citizens in the UK, and Bangladeshis who naturalised in Italy before moving to the UK. Renia felt insecure because her rights deriving from legal residence might be affected due to Brexit. She was aware she was in a more precarious position because of her limited English-language skills and not working due to poor health, a very different situation to her economically embedded children. To obtain permanent residence, non-UK EU citizens were required to meet criteria including involvement in economic activity and self-sufficiency (Ryan, 2017). Polish and Finnish research participants in the studies conducted by Sotkasiira and Gawlewicz (2021) thought that economic embedding, for instance through permanent employment, was the most useful type of embedding in terms of improving their chances of obtaining the right to remain. Furthermore, existing research highlights shortcomings in the functioning of the settled status system, as well as difficulties of access for several groups, including those with limited English language proficiency and knowledge of online procedures, as well as those in more precarious economic situations (Botterill et al., 2020; Barnard et al., 2022). Duda-Mikulin (2023: 8) employs the notion of precarity to better understand the experiences of Polish migrant women living in 'a state of unpredictability characterised by insecure employment or income which has been worsened by the Brexit referendum whereby many EU migrants' legal and social rights remain unprotected'.

Renia's narrative stressed the importance of economic and cultural capital (using a Bourdieu-based approach) in understanding the impact of Brexit on migrants. Possession of economic (property ownership) and cultural (speaking English) capital determines people's power position in the context of Brexit. These forms of capital, and the interplay between them, can be considered as important in building a sense of security and belonging. Low economic capital can cause feelings of insecurity and powerlessness, of losing the right to live in the UK – therefore, Renia applied for permanent residency to secure that right. This can particularly affect women migrants who might not be engaged in the paid labour market but are homemakers or carers (Duda-Mikulin, 2019; Sotkasiira and Gawlewicz, 2021), those who are in unregulated work and disabled migrants (Duda-Mikulin and Głowacka, 2024).

Erel (2010: 644) points out that 'Migrants actively constitute their cultural capital to fit in with the ethnically dominant culture of the society of residence'. Resources and assets such as language knowledge, accent or light skin can be converted into 'national capital' to legitimise belonging (Hage, 1998: 53). Renia was concerned that she could not apply for British citizenship because her English-language skills were very limited, and she was afraid she would fail the English-language test. She wanted to learn English not only to apply for British citizenship but because she needed it for practical reasons. She added that her husband did not need to pass the English-language test to apply for citizenship because he was 65. Renia's sense of belonging intersects with her age, the availability of economic resources, access to citizenship, access to housing and disability.

In reference to Renia's last sentence, migrants have experienced a devaluation or non-recognition of their skills, particularly in the context of Brexit and Theresa May's emphasis on highly skilled migrants being favoured as free movement ended. Renia was aware of the undervaluing of the contribution of low-skilled migrant workers and therefore felt she needed to emphasise that her husband is a skilled and hard worker – a good deserving migrant worker, and therefore having a right to belong. This should be placed in the context of political discourses on immigration and the politics of austerity which construct different types of migrants based on oppositions between deserving (hardworking migrants) and undeserving (often referred to as 'benefit scroungers') (Blachnicka-Ciacek et al., 2021). Renia was aware that, due to her disability and relying on welfare benefits, she is the type of migrant that is largely considered as unwanted and undeserving. This is despite the economic contribution she, her husband and her children have made over the years. Blachnicka-Ciacek et al. (2021: 3805) argue that 'the prominence of the deservingness discourse – which has gained momentum in Brexit Britain – entraps migrants in the constant process of boundary making and may prevent them from ever feeling part of the "community of value" '. Furthermore, the authors argue that 'deserving' does not always mean being accepted into the 'community of value'. This reinforces the feeling of not belonging, further magnified by both material and emotional insecurities (see also Duda-Mikulin, 2023), which are influenced by the intersecting dynamics of ethnicity, migrant status, gender, age, disability and class.

Renia's sense of belonging was not only affected by the socio-political situation in the UK, but also in Poland, making her feel stuck in limbo:

> I can't escape to Poland because when I look at Kaczyński [PiS leader] ... I get angry and I am scared to go to Poland to sort out things. I'm scared of those people. I'm scared of those hooligans. I'm scared of ONR [Obóz Narodowo-Radykalny – English translation: The National Radical Camp, a far-right

> movement in Poland]. I'm scared of this mad house over there. Neither in Poland, nor here, because they don't want me here.

While there is evidence that many migrants have returned to Poland, several research participants, especially those with school-aged children in the UK, found it very difficult to decide whether to leave the UK. This includes Oliwia, whose narrative is discussed in the next section.

Post-Brexit choices: stay in the UK or move on?

At the time of the interview, Oliwia (in her thirties) lived in one of the most ethnically diverse areas of Manchester. One of her children was born in the UK. Despite some fear of anti-migrant hostility, Oliwia felt safe from xeno-racism in her multi-ethnic neighbourhood which she called a 'migrant neighbourhood'.

Oliwia, as with other participants, frequently mentioned a sense of uncertainty about her future in the UK:

> When the results were announced I was a bit afraid, and I started to feel uncertain ... I started to think what would change and how quickly changes would happen. For the first few days I had to get used to this new and uncertain situation. I was wondering if the welcoming England would change for the worse.

As a result of the Brexit vote, many EU citizens started to rethink their future of living in the UK (Botterill et al., 2019; Duda-Mikulin, 2018, 2023; Guma and Jones 2018; Lulle et al., 2019; Sotkasiira and Gawlewicz, 2021).

> For about two months we were seriously wondering whether we should return to Poland ... In the end, I decided that we would spend one more year in England. There were various reasons ... now is not a good moment to live in Poland for people like me. Besides, there wasn't enough time to find a good school for children and to move, so I thought it would be better to live in Manchester ... We haven't applied for permanent residency because we didn't have time, but we think about it all the time and we want to do it. We want to apply for passport for our daughter because she was born in England, so there is a chance that she will get it.

Even though several interviewees started to consider going back to Poland or another country, it is not so straightforward because some of their children were born in, growing up and going to school in the UK, and mothers are often reluctant to disrupt these attachments. In any eventuality, Oliwia wanted to make sure her daughter had a British passport and the rest of the family would secure permanent residency in case they decide to return to the UK in the future. This sense of security and protection of rights is particularly important in the context of Brexit and the loss of freedom of movement (Sredanovic and Byrne's Introduction in this volume).

Oliwia and Renia's narratives also highlight the rise of right-wing populism and far-right movements beyond the context of the UK and Brexit. While several other research participants were affected by anti-immigrant rhetoric and hostility in the run-up to the EU referendum and in the aftermath, Oliwia felt safe in her multi-ethnic neighbourhood. In contrast, she was more concerned about going back to Poland because of growing hostility towards those who are considered as foreign looking, meaning less white and deemed as the Other. The growth of racists and xenophobic attitudes was sparked in 2015, when the right-wing populist and nationalist Law and Justice (PiS) obtained a majority in the Polish Parliament alongside the presidency for the first time since 2007. Furthermore, in recent years, racist and anti-immigrant rhetoric at the Polish Independence Day marches involved a combination of nationalist, anti-immigrant, anti-LGBT and Christian/Catholic slogans. In the October 2019 parliamentary elections, the Confederation Liberty and Independence party (Konfederacja Wolność i Niepodległość), a far-right political party in Poland, entered the Parliament of Poland, influencing politics and attitudes. While the issues of race and racism are often assumed to be absent in Poland (Pędziwiatr and Balogun, 2018), racialisation has always been part of the configuration of Polish society (Leszczyński, 2020; Balogun and Pędziwiatr, 2023). Omeni (2016) highlights the feeling of standing out due to visible ethnic difference in Poland (and the threat of racial violence), and this was confirmed by my research participants, who look visibly different due to ethno-religious difference (as not all Poles are and identify as white Christians) and those with mixed-race children and Black partners (Rzepnikowska, 2020). After moving to and settling in a multi-ethnic society, Oliwia did not feel like moving back to Poland would be safe in the current political climate. Being able to blend into multi-ethnic areas of Manchester offers Oliwia and several other research participants a sense of safety and familiarity.

There are also interviewees who get this sense of familiarity, attachment and belonging in their immediate neighbourhoods and through social network formation beyond ethno-national lines, which can lead to longer or permanent settlement (see also Ryan, 2018), as evidenced in Krysia and Nikola's case.

Neighbourly and motherly conviviality and belonging

Several accounts highlight the importance of the neighbourhood and social network formation, which can lead to a stronger sense of belonging. Neighbourly and motherly conviviality, as discussed in my earlier work (Rzepnikowska, 2020), constitute important resources with which to establish anchors (Grzymala-Kazlowska, 2018).

Krysia was 51 when I interviewed her in 2013. She arrived in Manchester in 2006. At the time of the first interview, she lived in a privately rented house near one of the most ethnically diverse areas in the north of Manchester with a steady arrival of migrants from Central and Eastern Europe in the post-2004 period due to more affordable housing. Krysia had mainly worked as a cleaner. However, as her health deteriorated, like Renia, she was unable to work.

Krysia's narrative in the first interview showed how convivial interaction in her neighbourhood developed over time from adaptation practices involving observing and following certain norms, through instances of cooperation and interdependence, to more meaningful forms of contact involving gift giving considered as a gesture of care and maintaining ties (Rzepnikowska, 2020).

When I contacted Krysia in 2018, she lived in the same place. In contrast to Renia's experience, Krysia's relations with neighbours were not negatively affected by the Brexit vote, although she was aware of anti-Polish sentiment at the time of the EU referendum in 2016. In fact, she felt that these relations had become even stronger in recent years. According to Krysia, her neighbours were among those who voted 'Remain'. She made a connection between the unchanged attitudes of her friendly neighbours and their Remain vote.

> Nothing much changed in our neighbourhood. God, I would wish everyone to have neighbours like ours. We are closer than before, and I can count on them ... They aren't happy with Brexit, at least those who live next to us. They don't approve of it. They voted against it. We have been living here for nearly 12 years, and we can talk about everything. We like each other. They like us ... We saw stuff about Poles on the Internet, in the newspapers. We heard about it [anti-Polish sentiment]. We were saying all the time with my [Polish] friend [living with Krysia], 'Jesus, thank God we live in this neighbourhood which is different to what you hear', it's a neighbour-friendly area. Even a bit further away in the shops [people are friendly]. We don't feel discriminated. We didn't experience it at the time when the anti-Polish sentiment was more intense.

Over time, Krysia developed an affectionate relationship with her immediate neighbours. Her neighbourhood offered her a safe haven and a strong sense of local belonging, despite her limited English-language skills.

Krysia's everyday lived experience of neighbourly conviviality encouraged a reflection on the conditions supporting living together despite the challenges posed by the Brexit vote discussed earlier in this chapter. In this example, stronger bonds were formed in response to the challenges of Brexit. Embeddedness, which reflects migrants' attachments and connections with people and places contributing to the sense of belonging (also explored by

Korinek et al., 2005; Ryan and Mulholland, 2015; Erel and Ryan, 2019; Sotkasiira and Gawlewicz, 2021), plays an important part. While Sotkasiira and Gawlewicz (2021) stress that it would not be correct to assume that at times of political upheaval following the Brexit referendum embedding would remain unchanged and secure, Krysia's case shows that sustained conviviality over time has the potential of strengthening the process of embedding and a sense of belonging, despite the circumstances surrounding Brexit.

Similarly, Nikola, an office worker and a mother of two in her late thirties, also experienced an alternative mode of belonging in the context of Brexit. She arrived in the UK as a tourist in 2005, but she decided to stay longer and learn English. She then pursued further studies, obtained a more stable office job, got married to a British man, bought a house and gave birth to two children. Unlike Renia, who lived on a council estate characterised by local tensions and socio-economic inequality, Nikola felt that she became more attached to her neighbourhood, especially after buying her own property and having children. This contributed to an increased sense of security and stability. Because of this, she was also not concerned about her legal status in the light of Brexit. Home ownership binds people both financially and emotionally, and this contributes to belonging claims (Blachnicka-Ciacek et al., 2021). However, Nikola's sense of belonging should not be understood solely in reference to economic capital. While material security is important for Nikola, it is her new family that offers her a real sense of home and belonging.

In the first interview in 2012, Nikola recounted a gruesome experience of becoming a victim of xeno-racist violence which left her traumatised for a long period of time. In 2018, she shared her experiences of living in the UK in the context of Brexit, with an emphasis on living in a suburban area of Manchester which she described as a bohemian neighbourhood. Nikola was aware of the negative sentiments towards Polish migrants at the time and after the EU referendum in the UK. However, she thought that the attitudes of people living in her area did not change for the worse. This, again, stresses the importance of place and class dynamics. Several participants at both stages of my research noticed the absence of negative discourse about Polish migrants in more affluent areas characterised by the absence of competition for jobs and resources. Despite her previous experiences of xeno-racism, Nikola felt safe in her local area. The narratives of the research participants in this chapter show how different local contexts, ethnicity, class dynamics and spatially distinct inequalities may influence the experiences of migrants, their relations with the local population and their sense of safety and belonging.

Nikola's case also highlights the importance of social network formation, which can lead to a more permanent settlement (Ryan, 2018). Nikola had lived in different parts of Manchester and established long-lasting friendships with people from various ethnic and religious backgrounds. Close friendships with other migrants and ethnic minorities enable building a sense of belonging beyond ethnic, national and religious boundaries. This is particularly the case for other interviewees who are mothers engaging in convivial interaction with other mothers from various ethnic backgrounds. Nikola's acquaintances in the local area expanded further after meeting other mums-to-be through antenatal classes, and later mother and toddler groups and activities. As discussed in my earlier work (Rzepnikowska, 2018), motherly conviviality, based on shared experiences of being mothers engaging in cross-cultural interaction, highlights a connection between motherly activities and spaces for mothers such as nurseries, schools and children's centres. These expanding connections and activities in the local area contribute to establishing anchors (Grzymala-Kazlowska, 2018) and a deeper sense of belonging.

Conclusion

I began this chapter by stressing the importance of divisive and anti-immigrant British politics, starting with racialised discourses defining the non-belonging of post-colonial arrivals in post-war Britain, who were subsequently stripped of their British citizenship. I drew some parallels between the politics of belonging in the post-war era and, in more recent times, the hostile environment and Brexit with reference to limiting citizens' rights in the UK. The divisive rhetoric evokes 'the dirty work of boundary maintenance' (Crowley, 1999: 30), which contributes to the feeling of not belonging of migrants and ethnic minorities. While the politics of citizenship and belonging are important in influencing people's sense of belonging, this chapter also explored the actual experiences of migrant women with reference to citizenship and belonging.

The chapter contributes to the literature on citizenship and belonging in the context of Brexit. This concerns not only the questions prominent in populist politics and debates about 'who is a rightful autochthonous member of society' (Cassidy et al., 2018: 191) linked to race and migration (Bhambra, 2017), but also emerging academic research on the sense of belonging in relation to the experiences of CEE migrants in the UK. Blachnicka-Ciacek et al. (2021) argue that these migrants have become victimised by the belonging debates, and at the same time, they reproduce these discourses through social practices of 'othering' and reproducing ethnic and racial hierarchy. This chapter offered a more nuanced discussion focused on belonging and citizenship from the perspective of Polish migrant women, based on interview data collected before and after the Brexit vote, and with attention to often intersecting categories of ethnicity, migration, class, age, gender, dis/ability and location. It offered a longitudinal perspective which is helpful in identifying longer-term patterns, for instance a more sustained form of neighbourly conviviality or persistent forms of xeno-racist harassment, as well as changes in migrants' lives influencing the decision of whether to settle more permanently in the UK or move to another country.

Renia's story shows the negative impact of the divisive rhetoric affecting migrants in their neighbourhoods and workplaces marked by socio-economic deprivation, which contributes to the sense of non-belonging, foreignness and being stuck in a limbo. This has a clear implication for policymaking and further research into deconstructing the idea of the 'British we' as distinct from racialised Black, Brown and East European Others. Policymakers should acknowledge how politics of belonging influence the sense of attachment, feeling at home and feeling safe of migrants and new citizens settling in the UK. Furthermore, the feelings of insecurity and powerlessness regarding losing the right to live in the UK, particularly affecting women migrants who might not be engaged in the paid labour market but are homemakers, carers or disabled, should also be addressed by policymakers and researchers.

Oliwia's account shows the sense of inclusion in a multi-ethnic neighbourhood, accompanied by a dilemma faced by many migrants of whether to stay in the UK or move to another country. Additionally, it highlights the concerns regarding returning to Poland, which is also affected by racialising rhetoric, highlighting the spread of populism, nationalism and racism across Europe and beyond.

In contrast, the narratives by Krysia and Nikola offer examples of alternative modes of being and belonging enabling residents to go beyond borders and differences based on more caring and respectful ways of relating to each other over a longer period. Conviviality does not solve the issue of the loss of rights and precarious conditions some migrants are facing because of Brexit, but it offers a lens through which we can see processes rooted in everyday life at a local level. The examples of multi-ethnic relationships, motherly conviviality and neighbourly conviviality show how stronger bonds are formed in response to the challenges of Brexit.

Notes

1 Many people from the Windrush generation arrived as children on their parents' passports, and the Home Office destroyed a significant number of landing cards and other records. As a result, many lacked the documentation to prove their right to remain in the UK.

2 Racialisation is understood here as a process of ascribing a set of characteristics viewed as inherent to a group because of physical or cultural traits, not always limited to skin colour. These may include language, clothing and religious practices (Garner and Selod, 2015: 12).
3 Race is not an essential characteristic of migrants, but a social construction based on processes and practices of exclusion (Fox et al., 2012).

References

Anderson, Bridget, Ruhs, Martin, Rogaly, Ben and Spencer, Sarah (2006) *Fair Enough? Central and East European Migrants in Low-Wage Employment in the UK*. London: Joseph Rowntree Foundation.

Balogun, Bolaji and Pędziwiatr, Konrad (2023) '"Stop calling me *Murzyn*" – how BlackLives Matter in Poland'. *Journal of Ethnic and Migration Studies* 49(6): 1552–1569.

Barbulescu, Roxana and Favell, Adrian (2020) 'Commentary: A citizenship without social rights? EU freedom of movement and changing access to welfare rights'. *International Migration* 58(1): 151–165.

Barnard, Catherine, Fraser Butlin, Sarah and Costello, Fiona (2022) 'The changing status of European Union nationals in the United Kingdom following Brexit: The lived experience of the European Union Settlement Scheme'. *Social & Legal Studies* 31(3): 365–388.

Bhambra, Gurminder K. (2017) 'Locating Brexit in the pragmatics of race, citizenship and empire'. In William Outhwaite (ed.) *Brexit: Sociological Responses*. London: Anthem Press, pp. 91–100.

Blachnicka-Ciacek, Dominika, Trąbka, Agnieszka, Budginaite-Mackine, Irma, Parutis, Violetta and Pustulka, Paula (2021) 'Do I deserve to belong? Migrants' perspectives on the debate of deservingness and belonging'. *Journal of Ethnic and Migration Studies* 47(17): 3805–3821. https://doi.org/10.1080/1369183X.2021.1932444

Botterill, Kate and Hancock, Jonathan (2018) 'Rescaling belonging in "Brexit Britain": Spatial identities and practices of Polish nationals in Scotland after the U.K. Referendum on European Union membership'. *Population, Space and Place* 25(1): e2217.

Botterill, Kate, McCollum, David and Tyrrell, Naomi (2019) 'Negotiating Brexit: Migrant spatialities and identities in a changing Europe'. *Population, Space and Place* 25(1): e2216.

Cassidy, Kathryn, Innocenti, Perla and Bürkner, Hans-Joachim (2018) 'Brexit and new autochthonic politics of belonging'. *Space and Polity* 22(2): 188–204.

Cook, Joanne, Dwyer, Peter and Waite, Louise (2012) 'Accession 8 migration and the proactive and defensive engagement of social citizenship'. *Journal of Social Policy* 41 (2): 329–347.

Crowley, John (1999) 'The politics of belonging: Some theoretical considerations'. In Andrew Geddes and Adrian Favell (eds) *The Politics of Belonging: Migrants and Minorities in Contemporary Europe*. Aldershot: Ashgate, pp. 15–41.

Devine, Daniel (2021) 'Discrete events and hate crimes: The causal role of the Brexit referendum'. *Social Science Quarterly* 102: 374–386.

Drinkwater, Stephen, Eade, John and Garapich, Michal (2006) 'Poles apart? EU enlargement and the labour market outcomes of immigrants in the UK'.

Discussion Papers in Economics 17/06. www.surrey.ac.uk/sites/default/files/2006_DP17-06.pdf (accessed 25 June 2024).

Duda-Mikulin, Eva A. (2018) '*Should I stay or should I go now?* Exploring Polish women's returns "home"'. *International Migration* 56(4):140–153 https://doi.org/10.1111/imig.12420

Duda-Mikulin. Eva A. (2019) *EU Migrant Workers, Brexit and Precarity: Polish Women's Perspectives from Inside the UK*. Bristol: Policy Press.

Duda-Mikulin. Eva A. (2023) 'Brexit and precarity: Polish female workers in the UK as second-class citizens?' *Sociology Compass* 17(1): e13038. https://doi.org/10.1111/soc4.13038

Duda-Mikulin, Eva A. and Głowacka, Marta (2024) '*"I haven't met one"*: Disabled EU migrants in the UK: Intersections between migration and disability post-Brexit'. *Journal of Ethnic and Migration Studies* 50(6): 1530–1548.

Erel, Umut (2010) 'Migrating cultural capital: Bourdieu in migration studies'. *Sociology* 44(4): 642–660.

Fox, Jon E., Moroşanu, Laura and Szilassy, Eszter (2012) 'The racialization of the new European migration to the UK'. *Sociology* 46(4): 680–695.

Garner, Steve and Selod, Saher (2015) 'The racialization of Muslims: Empirical studies of Islamophobia'. *Critical Sociology* 41(1): 9–19.

Grzymala-Kazlowska, Aleksandra (2018) 'From connecting to social anchoring: Adaptation and "settlement" of Polish migrants in the UK'. *Journal of Ethnic and Migration Studies* 44(2): 252–269.

Guma, Taulant and Jones, Rhys Dafydd (2018) '"Where are we going to go now?" European Union migrants' experiences of hostility, anxiety, and (non-)belonging during Brexit'. *Population, Space and Place* 25(1). https://doi.org/10.1002/psp.2198

Hage, Ghassan (1998) *White Nation: Fantasies of White Supremacy in a Multicultural Society*. Annandale, NSW: Pluto Press.

Hampshire, James (2005) *Citizenship and Belonging: Immigration and the Politics of Demographic Governance in Postwar Britain*. Basingstoke: Palgrave.

Karatani, Rieko (2003) *Defining British Citizenship: Empire, Commonwealth and Modern Britain*. London: Frank Cass.

Korinek, Kim, Entwisle, Barbara and Jampalaky, Aree (2005) 'Through thick and thin: Layers of social ties and urban settlement among Thai migrants'. *American Sociological Review* 70(5): 779–800.

Leszczyński, Adam (2020) *Ludowa historia Polski. Historia wyzysku i oporu. Mitologia panowania*. Warsaw: WAB.

Lulle, Aija, King, Russell, Dvorakova, Veronika and Szkudlarek, Aleksandra (2019) 'Between disruptions and connections: "New" European Union migrants in the United Kingdom before and after Brexit'. *Population, Space and Place* 25(1): e2200.

Lutz, Helma (2010) 'Gender in the migratory process'. *Journal of Ethnic and Migration Studies* 36(10): 1647–1663.

Manchester City Council (2015) *Manchester Migration: A Profile of Manchester's Migration Patterns*. www.manchester.gov.uk/download/downloads/id/22894/a05_profile_of_migration_in_manchester_2015.pdf (accessed 24 June 2024).

McDowell, Linda (2009) 'Old and new European economic migrants: Whiteness and managed migration policies'. *Journal of Ethnic and Migration Studies* 35(1): 19–36.

Office for National Statistics (ONS) (2011a) *Polish People in the UK – Half a Million Polish Residents*. www.ons.gov.uk/ons/rel/migration1/migration-statistics-quarterly-report/august-2011/polish-people-in-the-uk.html (accessed 24 June 2024).
Office for National Statistics (ONS) (2011b) *Statistical Bulletin: Births in England and Wales by Parents' Country of Birth*. www.ons.gov.uk/peoplepopulationandcommunity/birthsdeathsandmarriages/livebirths/bulletins/parentscountryofbirthenglandandwales/2012-08-30 (accessed 25 June 2024).
Office for National Statistics (ONS) (2011c) *Language in England and Wales*. www.ons.gov.uk/peoplepopulationandcommunity/culturalidentity/language/articles/languageinenglandandwales/2013-03-04 (accessed 25 June 2024).
Office for National Statistics (ONS) (2015) *Population of the UK by Country of Birth and Nationality: 2015. Statistical Bulletin*. www.ons.gov.uk/peoplepopulationandcommunity/populationandmigration/internationalmigration/bulletins/ukpopulationbycountryofbirthandnationality/august2016 (accessed 25 June 2024).
Office for National Statistics (ONS) (2021) *Population of the UK by Country of Birth and Nationality: 2020*. www.ons.gov.uk/peoplepopulationandcommunity/populationandmigration/internationalmigration/bulletins/ukpopulationbycountryofbirthandnationality/2020 (accessed 25 June 2024).
Omeni, Edward (2016) 'Troubling encounters: Exclusion, racism and responses of male African students in Poland'. *Cogent Social Sciences* 2(1): 1212637.
Pędziwiatr, Konrad and Balogun, Bolaji (2018) 'Poland: Sub-Saharan Africans and the struggle for acceptance'. In Peter Grant (ed.) *Minority and Indigenous Trends 2018: Focus on Migration and Displacement*. London: Minority Rights Group International, pp. 85–88.
Phizacklea, Annie (2003) 'Transnationalism, gender and global workers'. In Mirjana Morokvasic, Umut Erel and Kyoko Shinozaki (eds) *Crossing Borders and Shifting Boundaries: Gender on the Move*. Opladen: Leske and Budrich, pp. 79–100.
Riessman, Catherine Kohler (2002) 'Narrative analysis'. In A. Michael Huberman and Matthew B. Miles (eds) *The Qualitative Research Companion*. London: Sage, pp. 271–270.
Ryan, Bernard (2017) 'Negotiating the right to remain after Brexit'. *Journal of Immigration, Asylum and Nationality Law* 31(3): 197–226.
Ryan, Louise (2018) 'Differentiated embedding: Polish migrants in London negotiating belonging over time'. *Journal of Ethnic and Migration Studies* 44(2): 233–251.
Ryan, Louise and Mulholland, Jon (2015) 'Embedding in motion: Analysing relational, spatial and temporal dynamics among highly skilled migrants'. In Louise Ryan, Umut Erel and Alessio D'Angelo (eds) *Migrant Capital: Networks, Identities and Strategies*. London: Palgrave Macmillan, pp. 135–153.
Ryan, Louise, Lopez Rodriguez, Magdalena and Trevena, Paulina (2016) 'Opportunities and challenges of unplanned follow-up interviews: Experiences with Polish migrants in London'. *Forum Qualitative Sozialforschung* 17(2): Art. 26.
Rzepnikowska, Alina (2018) 'Polish migrant women's narratives about language, raced and gendered difference in Barcelona'. *Gender, Place and Culture* 25(6): 850–865.
Rzepnikowska, Alina (2019) 'Racism and xenophobia experienced by Polish migrants in the UK before and after Brexit vote'. *Journal of Ethnic and Migration Studies* 45(1): 61–77.

Rzepnikowska, Alina (2020) *Convivial Cultures in Multicultural Cities: Polish Migrant Women in Manchester and Barcelona*. Abingdon: Routledge.

Rzepnikowska, Alina (2023) 'Racialisation of Polish migrants in the UK and in Spain (Catalonia)'. *Journal of Ethnic and Migration Studies* 49(6): 1517–1533. https://doi.org/10.1080/1369183X.2022.2154912

Skeggs, Beverley (2009) 'Haunted by the spectre of judgement: Respectability, value and affect in class relations'. In Kjartan Páll Sveinsson (ed.) *Who Cares about the White Working Class?* London: Runnymede, pp. 36–45.

Sotkasiira, Tiina and Gawlewicz, Anna (2021) 'The politics of embedding and the right to remain in post-Brexit Britain'. *Ethnicities* 21(1): 23–41.

Sredanovic, Djordje and Della Puppa, Francesco (2023) 'Brexit and the stratified uses of national and European Union citizenship'. *Current Sociology* 71(5): 725–742. https://doi.org/10.1177/00113921211048523

Sumi, Cho, Crenshaw, Kimberlé Williams and McCall, Leslie (2013) 'Toward a field of intersectionality studies: Theory, applications, and praxis'. *Signs: Journal of Women in Culture and Society* 38(4): 785–810.

Sumption, Madeleine and Fernández-Reino, Mariña (2020) *Unsettled Status – 2020: Which EU Citizens are at Risk of Failing to Secure Their Rights after Brexit?* https://migrationobservatory.ox.ac.uk/resources/reports/unsettled-status-2020/ (accessed 25 June 2024).

Valentine, Gill (2008) 'Living with difference: Reflection on geographies of encounter'. *Progress in Human Geography* 32(3): 323–337.

Virdee, Satnam and McGeever, Brendan (2018) 'Racism, crisis, Brexit'. *Ethnic and Racial Studies* 41(10): 1802–1819.

White, Anne (2010) 'Young people and migration from contemporary Poland'. *Journal of Youth Studies* 13(5): 565–580

Yuval-Davis, Nira (2006) 'Belonging and the politics of belonging'. *Patterns of Prejudice* 40(3): 197–214. https://doi.org/10.1080/00313220600769331

Yuval-Davis, Nira, Anthias, Floya and Kofman, Eleonore (2005) 'Secure borders and safe haven and the gendered politics of belonging: Beyond social cohesion'. *Ethnic and Racial Studies* 28(3): 513–535.

5

'I will never be British': EU citizens and the illusion of belonging

Marianela Barrios Aquino

Introduction

The historical moment that followed the referendum to leave the European Union in Britain in 2016 was one of political fervour and instability. It is difficult, if not impossible, to isolate the impact of such a context from the experiences of naturalisation that are the focus of this chapter. The guiding research question behind this chapter examines how EU citizens in the southeast of England experienced naturalisation after Brexit; the answers to such a question reveal a great deal about official definitions of citizenship and their impact on non-citizens' experiences of belonging.

The literature on the intersection of migration and citizenship has grown in the light of recent political events in British political history, particularly Brexit. Importantly, studies have focused on how non-citizens experienced the socio-political structures and regulations resulting from Brexit (Guma, 2020; Moss et al., 2020; Blachnicka-Ciacek et al., 2021; Kilkey and Ryan, 2021). I add to that literature by engaging with the ways in which official definitions of membership overlap with and shape non-citizens' definitions and experiences of belonging.

The main focus of the chapter is the civic integration requirements of the British naturalisation process, which I interpret as exclusionary mechanisms that reduce citizenship to narrow understandings of belonging in the political community (Morrice, 2016a, 2016b). Furthermore, I explore how the mobilisation of notions of belonging to define membership in the political community shapes non-citizens' experiences of naturalisation and conceptions of citizenship. This mobilisation of belonging as criteria for inclusion or exclusion has been termed politics of belonging (Yuval-Davis, 2006) and is useful to expose the mismatch between official definitions of citizenship and individuals' expectations of membership, equality and protection.

I start the chapter with a brief discussion of the historical and political events that led Britain to decide to leave the European Union in 2016.

I then look at the relevant theoretical debates that inform my analysis of the implications of affective definitions of citizenship. The analysis is divided into three parts, the first examining the impact of Brexit on individuals' understandings of home. Here, I show how the destabilisation of their understandings of home preceded their naturalisation and was ignited by Brexit, leading them to seek security in naturalisation. Their accounts sit at the intersection between protective (Coutin, 2003) and defensive naturalisation (Ong, 2011; Aptekar, 2016) because they condense the anti-immigrant context in which the research was immersed and the historical construction of citizenship as security. In the second part of the analysis, I present participants' reflections on cultural elements of citizenship they encountered in naturalisation, which undermined their experiences of belonging in Britain. The result was an erosion of their sense of belonging and a series of reasons why they can never (again) claim to fully belong in Britain. In the final section I discuss how this cultural turn has, besides affective connotations, also moral undertones, which in turn emphasise a notion of citizenship as a virtue (Schinkel, 2010), further narrowing the gates to belonging.

The analysis I present focuses on the affective language participants used to discuss issues of belonging and citizenship. It concludes that the conceptual borders of the national community (Hampshire, 2011) encountered and produced in naturalisation created a sense of incomplete belonging, leaving participants feeling like less-than-equal citizens (Byrne, 2017).

The seeds of Brexit

The referendum to leave the European Union took place in June 2016; however, its seeds started to germinate many years before. The analysis I present here goes beyond the traditional understanding of naturalisation reforms being specifically aimed at non-European migrants (Muslims in particular) and Brexit being about restricting non-European migration. Instead, I pursue a conceptual distinction that hinges on the idea that the ethnonationalistic and anti-immigrant agenda behind both were a danger to EU citizens all along.

Undoubtedly, there has been a hierarchy of deservingness within the migrant population in Britain, where non-European migrants were constructed as 'less deserving' and more in need of assimilation. Consequently, British naturalisation reforms have historically followed a narrowing ethno-nationalistic trend (Mayblin, 2017; El-Enany, 2020; Donoghue and Kuisma, 2022) that revoked citizenship rights from colonial subjects and narrowed the access to citizenship for non-citizens. These narrow definitions of membership in the polity discursively constructed a gendered and racialised citizen (as well as sexualised, classed, etc.) that effectively could exclude anyone who was not born in Britain to (white) British parents. Brexit, I argue, is but the manifestation of this historical trend. Its clear focus on European migration could serve as a reminder of the fact that narrow definitions of membership create a hierarchy both within (citizens) and outside (immigrants) of membership. Although EU citizens were not at the bottom of that external hierarchy, the fact remains that they were constructed to be 'outside' of the political community. Such is the nature of ethno-nationalist understandings of citizenship.

Even when the focus was not EU citizens, the consequences of the reforms would one day impact them too. In 2002, the White Paper *Secure Borders, Safe Havens* (Home Office, 2002) was a response to increased anxiety around migration and multiculturalism in Britain (McGhee, 2009; Meer et al., 2009). It highlighted the need to redefine what it meant to be British and to strengthen the sense of community cohesion in Britain, which was interpreted to be in crisis after the social disturbances in the north of England (Yuval-Davis et al., 2005). That same year, the 2002 Nationality, Immigration and Asylum Act was introduced, establishing new knowledge of language and life in the UK requirements as well as citizenship ceremonies. These were the tools with which the British state was to create a new vision of citizenship, with stronger cultural requirements.

This new naturalisation model constituted a shift of responsibility onto immigrants for the perceived fragmentation of community along ethnic and cultural lines (Kostakopoulou, 2010). Furthermore, this continues the historical trend to defined 'the deserving and the undeserving, the familiar and the "other" in Britain' (Mayblin, 2017: 178), which was always linked to issues of migration and race (El-Enany, 2020). This resulted in shrinking definitions of what it meant to be British and an increasingly moralising and affective discourse around such definitions, calling for assimilation and learning to be British 'at a deeper level' (McGhee, 2009: 51).

Furthermore, within the context of the decline of empire, immigration was constructed as a threat and citizenship as privilege in all of Europe (Huysmans, 2005; Humphrey, 2013). The driving force of such conceptions was the legal differentiation of subjects, which resulted in a (racial, sexualised, gendered, etc.) hierarchy of entitlements and which hinged mainly on the citizen/migrant distinction (Mongia, 2018; Bassel and Khan, 2021). Thus, citizenship and the state are colonial legacies that have historically shaped migration and citizenship policies.

The particularism of the European context is centred around freedom of movement and the way in which it discursively turns *some* migrants into '*regional free movers*' (Favell, 2008: 703, italics mine). However, not all European citizens have had access to that label, with many individuals from new accession countries struggling to appropriate it (Rzepnikowska, 2019).

Since the beginning of the twenty-first century, the affective elements of the definition of citizenship have become clearer, in as far as they referred to belonging and privilege. The European freedom of movement right obscured the migrant/citizen distinction. The divide became increasingly more relevant in the UK through the moralising discourses of deservingness that widened the gap between migrants and citizens. As a result, the distinction between European and non-European migrants has been narrowing in public discourse (Guma, 2020), highlighting their differentiation from British citizens (Roos, 2019; Joppke, 2020).

This discursive construction of EU migration as producing 'European migrants' rather than the 'free regional movers' of the past influenced the experiences of those living in Britain and their attachment to their Europeanness (Favell, 2017). It is of utmost importance to avoid exceptionalising EU citizens' experiences in the British context because this 'distracts from the structural forces underlying it' (El-Enany, 2020: 212). The experiences presented in this chapter are to be considered in this context, which points to a longer history of relations and transformations of EU and British citizenship, considered to be the seed that germinated into Brexit. Thus, Brexit can be considered as the culmination of longer socio-political histories and development within British society (Outhwaite, 2017).

Affective citizenship and naturalisation

Traditional definitions of citizenship tend to focus on its three main dimensions: status, rights and identity (Joppke, 2019). In this chapter, I add the affective dimension, which is key to construct belonging to the nation state (Yuval-Davis, 2006). Furthermore, citizenship is a social and political construction steered by cultural interpretations of liberal democratic values that new citizens ought to conform to. These cultural interpretations produce concrete forms of belonging, which in turn are central to official definitions of citizenship, most visible in naturalisation regulations (Lähdesmäki et al., 2016: 239).

Thus, belonging is conceptualised as a device to draw and maintain boundaries between members and non-members of the polity (Blachnicka-Ciacek et al., 2021). It follows that I focus on the state politicisation of belonging and how it shapes membership, its regulation and management through policy.

To regulate belonging, the state mobilises emotions, which are validated, recognised and encouraged to define good citizenship and manage access to the national community. Scholarship on affective citizenship has helped our understanding of the emotional nature of different conceptions of citizenship (Berlant, 1997; Plummer, 2003; Fortier, 2010) by offering an explanation 'of contemporary conditions of personal life and subject formation, and how they relate to citizenship' (Fortier, 2016: 1042). Thus, the literature on affective citizenship is crucial to observe the way new citizens (ought to) feel and perform to be considered good citizens. Bringing emotions into the landscape of citizenship begs for a focus on simultaneous experiences of inclusion, or exclusion, mobility and otherness (Glaveanu and Womersley, 2021: 629) because they reveal the symbolic contours of the nation state.

Moral regulations are at the centre of affective governance as they determine who is the 'good citizen' by establishing which behaviours, values and skills are acceptable and necessary to access belonging and which are not. Moral citizenship can be most clearly associated with the assessment of 'good character' in naturalisation processes, in which the 'moral valence' of aspiring citizens is measured and assessed (Aptekar, 2016: 1147).

Civic integration requirements such as language tests, evidence of good character, citizenship tests and ceremonies are the most visible arm of the moralising policies that regulate access to citizenship for non-nationals. Aspiring citizens interpret such civic integration requirements in particular ways, which inform their behaviour and shape how they narrate their own lives in their naturalisation applications (Fortier, 2021). Linked to this, individuals perform certain behaviours, adhere to certain values, and contest others, to come up with their own definitions of citizenship, based on their experience of requesting access to it.

Participants of this research, whose identity and representations of home were disrupted by Brexit, sought naturalisation to get protection from Britain, the British state and its citizens (El-Enany, 2020; Fortier, 2021) given the sense of vulnerability this disruption provoked, which was linked to the status of migrants (Blachnicka-Ciacek et al., 2021).

Method

The above-mentioned theoretical approach has methodological implications, as it focuses on the intersectional character of 'the citizen' implied in this more 'personal membership' (Fortier, 2010: 25), which is nonetheless regulated and administered by the state. The most important implication is that an analysis of affective definitions of citizenship in the naturalisation process necessitates being complemented by the lived experiences of those who naturalised. Furthermore, given the complexity of the topic and its relevance in the context in which this research was embedded, it was necessary to focus discussions on issues of citizenship specifically. This is because political events and personal decisions about citizenship were so closely intertwined that a less focused approach would have drifted away from the specificity of the naturalisation context. Therefore, semi-structured interviews were conducted in 2017 in Brighton and Hove with European citizens who were in the process of naturalising or had recently naturalised as British citizens.

Participants were contacted through my social contacts, social media, official invitations shared on various mailing lists and through snowball methods. The various methods of recruitment ensured a varied sample, with participants from almost every European country, of various socio-economic statuses, a relatively even gender split, years of residence in the UK, etc. All participants had to be eligible for British citizenship and had to have either naturalised or made a decision about naturalisation. The interview topics were citizenship, naturalisation, European citizenship, emotions and Britishness. The sample consisted of 36 participants, with whom 38 interviews were conducted, as two were interviewed twice.

The interviews provided participants with a space to reflect about what it meant to be or become British. In such definitions, participants encountered and appropriated an affective language to discuss issues of belonging and being at home, both of which were often used interchangeably with citizenship.

Naturalisation: a shield against Brexit

Interviews revealed that in the context of Brexit, naturalisation became a homemaking strategy originating in the anxieties resulting from the political context. This attitude towards naturalisation has been termed 'defensive naturalisation' when it relates to mitigating a risk or 'protective naturalisation' when it constitutes a response to a clear threat (Godin and Sigona, 2022). Essentially, immigrants' pursuit of citizenship is a response to the political climate in an effort 'to protect themselves from criminalisation and anti-immigrant policies' (Aptekar, 2016: 1148). Citizenship is thus interpreted as security and naturalisation as 'temporally variable and linked to specific events' (Sredanovic, 2022: 3107)

This section examines the promise of security embedded in official definitions of citizenship and defensive naturalisation as a response. Brexit is deeply implicated in participants' practices of defensive naturalisation which associate migration with deportability and vulnerability, and citizenship with safety and protection, leading to a destabilisation of feeling at home in Britain.

Jens is a German citizen, who has lived in Britain for over 10 years working in the finance sector in London. Brexit had a deep impact on Jens' sense of being at home in Britain: '[Do you think the UK is your home?] I used to say yes, but after the Brexit vote and following the discussion at the political level I'm not so sure anymore. If you asked me in 2006 or 2011, it certainly felt like a different country.' This sense of estrangement led Jens to question whether he could feel at home in Britain. Such loss of certainty had an impact on his feelings of safety and belonging. Like Jens, Ina also felt that her sense of being at home had been undermined by the political context, saying 'and suddenly with the referendum, it just … it changed in terms of Britain, you know it just makes you think like "god, 52 per cent of the people have voted that they don't want EU migrants here"'. Ina is also a German dual citizen, who at the time of our interview had lived in Britain for more than 20 years and who had recently become a British citizen. For Ina, public opinion had an impact on how she feels and sees herself in Britain. She even borrows from public discourses when she suggests that she is a 'EU migrant'. Earlier in the interview, Ina told me that she never felt like a migrant.

For Ina and Jens, Brexit was a sudden change in how they felt about themselves and living in Britain. Their accounts are evidence that Brexit is a historical landmark, which provides a unique political context for examining the impact of political events on individuals' relationship with their country of settlement. For example, Lena (also originally from Germany) has lived in the UK for 26 years, and for her the referendum changed her perception of Britain entirely. Like Jens, she thinks that Britain 'is not the same place' anymore and that what she experienced as her home in the past years was a 'smokescreen', something to distract her from a reality that had always been there, saying 'I have learned that this isn't the country I thought it was. So that was the biggest disappointment, I think. … because I don't feel like home anymore. I felt very settled and then this happened and now I am not settled.'

Lena questions her own feelings of being at home and her own judgement all those years ago when she felt settled in Britain. These participants speak about how Brexit 'undermined their personal commitment to residing in the country' (Zontini and Genova, 2022: 645). Lena gives a good example of this when she tells me 'I just felt like I didn't really want to live here anymore.'

Some of those feelings of being unsettled were associated with a fear of not being allowed to stay. This speaks of an association of the status of migrants with deportability, a product of years of anti-immigrant discourses within the hostile environment in Britain. Pauline fears being sent back to her country of birth. She has lived and worked in the UK for 30 years; going back to France 'would be like moving to a foreign country' for her, which is why she is pursuing British citizenship: 'I do it for my own security in the future because I sense that things will get much worse before they get better. I think ... they will make it much more difficult, for EU citizens.'

Pauline has a general understanding of the everyday workings of the state and associates it with its anti-immigrant policies, which could affect her ability to remain settled in the UK. This sense of vulnerability was central to her decision to naturalise. Similarly, Aino felt that the government could do anything to her from the day after the referendum and confesses to have entered a state of panic and regret:

> I had this wave of panic; you know it's just that thing of 'what's going to happen' and you just think ... I am such a pessimist as well that I think the worst, and I thought wow they are going to kick me out, so I am going to get this done.

Aino is originally from Finland and has lived most of her life in Britain. She came to the UK to study when she was 18 years old, and never left. She was 40 at the time of our interview. Furthermore, Aino has kept the same job in higher education for more than 15 years. It would be fair to assume that she would feel safe in Britain, given her circumstances of relative privilege. However, Aino's fear of being kicked out, like Pauline's, was the main catalyst for her naturalisation application. Brexit and its destabilisation of their sense of belonging resulted in the undermining of their 'confidence in the stability of institutional structures, and influenced their relationship with and trust in British society' (Hall et al., 2022: 175; see also Godin and Sigona, 2022; Sredanovic, 2022). It is with, and as a result of, this distrust and uncertainty that participants embark on a defensive and protective naturalisation that uncovers an internalisation of the affective definitions of citizenship as safety. Furthermore, the belief in citizenship's promise of security is eroded (I argue) by the impenetrable hierarchy of belonging contained in the affective language with which naturalisation defines membership.

The erosion of belonging

This section focuses on experiences of naturalisation, specifically in relation to its cultural requirements. Many participants expressed a disenchantment with the newly acquired citizenship, which came with an internal hierarchy of belonging that seemed impenetrable to them. Certain cultural elements were key to blocking any sense of identification with Britishness. For example, language skills were repeatedly mentioned as a marker of true membership or lack thereof, as in the case of Kaiden, who said 'I am not British, you know ... everyone knows as soon as I open my mouth!'. For Kaiden, originally from Malta, his accent gives away that he is not British, suggesting that he cannot become British unless he gets rid of his foreign accent. Kaiden has lived in the UK for 10 years and works on a farm in the southeast of England. Similarly, Anne comments on how acquiring citizenship would not make any difference for her because she will never truly cross the line between citizen and migrant. Anne is a German-born French citizen who has lived in Britain for almost 20 years. She moved to France in the 1980s and became a French citizen, losing her German citizenship. Language was at the centre of her decision to naturalise in France and not to do so in Britain:

> I just don't feel ... I have not reached that level of language ... that I reached in France, even after 19 years. First time I say something, people ask me where are you from? So even if I have the passport, people will always consider me a foreigner, because they can hear me.

Anne identifies as French, and her language skills were key to that because 'people didn't think [I] wasn't from there'. However, her foreign accent in English closes the gate to belonging in Britain. In these examples, the collective construction of a hierarchy of belonging is visible because Kaiden and Anne both mention what others perceive when they speak. Thus, this emphasises the limited power of citizenship to override certain ethnocultural categories (Bloemraad and Sheares, 2017).

Thinking about the cultural impenetrability of belonging, I asked participants to define what it meant to be a citizen for them. Elías' response is revealing of the importance of belonging. He first defines the citizen in abstract as somebody who belongs, arguably conforming to official definitions of citizenship in terms of belonging (Home Office, 2002): 'somebody ... who has a sense of belonging with the rest of people who share that citizenship and ... is familiar with the laws, rules, customs of that country'. Elías is a dual citizen of Spain and Portugal, and in the process of becoming a British citizen. He has lived in Britain for more than 15 years, although intermittently; however, he might not fit his own definition of the citizen:

> probably the right thing to do when I get it is to say I am British and I am as British as everybody else, because under the law you are. But it's not ... it's not how I feel. I probably feel British enough ... I certainly feel more British than a lot of people who are British, but yeah, it's difficult.

It is interesting to see the centrality of feelings in his definitions of the citizen and his definition of his own acquired citizenship. While Elías is aware of the conflict between the legal and affective dimensions of citizenship, he asserts that naturalisation does not (and cannot) give access to the *right* feelings: 'for me nationality … naturalisation is not necessarily like I feel British as I feel my own place, because that is going to be a lie. I don't think anybody would…'.

The dilemma Elías presents is entirely affectively constructed, even when he discusses the legal aspect of his membership. His affective definition of the citizen led him to exclude himself from the category of British citizen. There are other instances in which the affective definitions got in the way of participants feeling that they could belong. Ina, who I presented in the previous section, spoke of her ceremony as an alienating experience:

> With the national anthem you know, obviously I've been in the UK, and you know in football matches and stuff they'll play it and I've sort of started singing along to it and it almost felt like … it's not quite my country, but almost, it's always sort of felt like quite a nice thing and you know, I sort of felt mostly part of it. And at the ceremony, I think the whole thing … I just felt so annoyed with it and then the national anthem played, and I just thought I'm really not feeling this at all! And now that I am actually a citizen and yet with all that had happened, with the referendum, I don't feel like 'tada! I'm British and this is all great!' And so, I was just in tears because this wasn't really quite the Britain that I wanted to feel part of.

It is impossible to separate her naturalisation experience from the impact Brexit had on her sense of belonging. However, the sense of loss is clear. A key element to her emotional response to the ceremony was the language used by the representative of the Queen, who emphasised the distinction between native citizens and new citizens, welcoming and inviting the latter to become full members of the community:

> [W]hat really, really got to me was that she was then talking about how now that we were British citizens, we were encouraged to become a part of our community and maybe consider volunteering for a charity. And I thought: I have been here 20 years! I've been volunteering for charities for many, many years and many different charities and I just found it so offensive that suggestion that 'well you've been a migrant so clearly so far you've not made a contribution but now that you are British you can be part of the community' … And the thing is that everyone would have been in the UK for many, many years … then sort of not acknowledging you know that we've clearly become a part of our community already.

The frustration that Ina felt when being welcomed into the community reflects her understanding of the citizenship ceremony as an event that constructs her as a newcomer, erasing her previous life in the UK (Byrne, 2014) and revealing a new hierarchy of belonging that forced her to reassess her own place in it. Other similar experiences revealed that participants often spoke of a 'scale of belonging' between native British citizens and naturalised British citizens. Francisco, a Paraguayan-Spanish dual citizen, who has lived equal amounts of time in Paraguay, Spain and the UK, clearly expresses this difference:

> An acquired nationality is not as heavy as a … like a birth given one, in my opinion. There might be terms … like right now wherever I go, I am going to be Spanish forever, there might be terms … like you have to stay here if you live abroad for more than three years you lose your nationality or something like that that I don't know.

For Francisco, the conditional nature of an 'acquired citizenship' affects its value. Inês, originally from Portugal and who recently became a British citizen, worries about the conditional nature of her new citizenship. Hoping she will not lose it in the future, she tells me how she will take the time to read about the conditions of deprivation to make sure that she can keep it: 'I heard somewhere that if you want to leave the UK for longer than two years or so you have to let the Home Office know. I'm not sure if this is right information, I'm just hoping they wouldn't be like "we're going to revoke your nationality." '

Although Francisco and Inês' concerns about the conditionality of citizenship are not in line with UK law, they are telling of their understanding of citizenship by naturalisation as being something provisional. This is related to the naturalisation process and ethno-nationalistic definitions of membership, which 'embed the conditionality of citizenship in popular consciousness' (Fortier, 2021: 39). Moreover, this understanding of the new citizenship as something that can be lost contrasts with earlier associations of safety and security. This inherent contradiction points to the idea that naturalisation does not give access to 'true' membership, the one that Elías and Francisco refer to when they speak of their birthright citizenship. The latter is defined in emotional terms, both in participants' experiences and in the naturalisation process, suggesting that they perceive their newly acquired citizenship as a less-than-equal citizenship, always 'at risk of being discursively (if less often legally) revoked' (Byrne, 2017: 323; see also Yeo, this volume).

In line with this perception, Elías thinks that he simply cannot fully become a true British citizen because he 'merely' naturalised as one later in life:

> I mean I don't know a lot of people naturalising as adults that really go and identify … it's a bit ain't it … I mean I'm not going to say I identify as British with a view of not offending all the British who are born here, you know they'd be like 'what the fuck' you know, 'he's not as …'?

The line dividing the native and the alien does not seem to allow any crossings, not even through naturalisation. These new citizens, regardless of their new legal status, regard native citizens as the original and legitimate category based on how they feel, giving birth to reflections on the illusion of belonging and revealing the danger of defining citizenship as belonging. Anne, Kaiden and Francisco decided not to naturalise because they felt they could never overcome or fulfil the cultural and affective requirements of the naturalisation process and truly become British citizens.

Virtualisation of citizenship

As seen above, Brexit and the naturalisation process had a significant impact on participants' definition of citizenship. A sense of disenchantment settled over our discussions of home, belonging and citizenship. However, and perhaps as a result of such disenchantment, participants started to develop their own discourses of belonging, turning their focus to the ways in which they can prove that they are (and were all this time) good citizens and 'feel British enough' (Elías). I interpret this as being the result of an integrationist and moralising agenda in citizenship policies.

An idea of integration was at the centre of participants' legitimising claims of belonging. They did not contest *that* they had to earn citizenship, but *how* to earn it. Their claims were anchored in moralising discourses that revealed their desirability through their willingness to integrate/assimilate. These narratives look suspiciously like official discourses of who is a good citizen and what good citizenship entails. Scholars have studied this mixing of integration with citizenship and referred to it as the virtualisation of citizenship (Schinkel, 2010) or deserving citizenship (Monforte et al., 2019). Here I take a deeper look at claims to deserving citizenship and the notions of good citizenship they rest upon.

In 2002, the Green Paper *The New and The Old* stated that integration is 'the basis of good citizenship' (Crick et al., 2002: 12). This is similar to the way Aleksander narrated his own decision to naturalise. He understands citizenship as a measure of integration and says that from the moment they decided to move from Poland to the UK six years ago, they (himself and his husband) knew they were going to apply for citizenship as soon as they could: 'When we moved here, we wanted to have citizenship as a proof that we are actually involved in this community.'

For Aleksander, their citizenship will reflect their involvement in the community and act as proof of integration. Integration here is symbolised also in the desire to integrate and precedes citizenship. Relatedly, Mikolaj says that his desire to acquire British citizenship is tied to his original desire to assimilate into British culture: 'And our goal was to try to assimilate as well, we heard about some Polish districts in London as well, but we tried to avoid it, we wanted to see the culture … So, in this sense we found that we could apply for citizenship.'

Avoiding Polish neighbourhoods and their curiosity to *see British culture* underly their claim to (good) citizenship. Elías also considers citizenship as a sign of integration. For him, naturalising was the logical thing to do because he feels 'very integrated' into his community. Acquiring citizenship for him was a way of consolidating that feeling: 'Once you are in a place on a long term [basis] it is easier to … you know, go all the way and try to integrate fully.'

This idea of integration and citizenship as overlapping mirrors the current conception of integration and good citizenship being connected in Britain. Learning about the country signals a desire to integrate, and the connection between learning and integration is considered 'common sense' and taken for granted (Fortier, 2021). Moreover, according to Schinkel (2010) this turns citizenship into something more than the acquisition or possession of rights; it is rather the performance of a virtue, symbolised in the desire to integrate or even 'feeling integrated'.

In line with this, Lazar, who is originally from Bulgaria and considering applying for British citizenship, thinks that only people who are *integrated* in the country should be granted citizenship. In his opinion, integration should be a requirement for citizenship and the problem of measuring integration could be resolved simply by testing language skills: '[granting citizenship to those who do not speak English] is not acceptable because you can't integrate in the society properly if you don't speak the language'.

He considers that non-nationals with little knowledge of the English language do not deserve to be granted citizenship. Furthermore, citizenship is turned into a cognitive competence (Delanty, 2003) when knowledge of the language and facts about history and society are assessed, something widely accepted by participants of this research.

This results in an assessment of migrants' 'linguistic, ideological, and religious allegiances being increasingly scrutinised as indicators of integration' (Duyvendak et al., 2010 in Chauvin and Garcés-Mascareñas, 2014: 427) and justified with liberal democratic values that transcend legal rights and obligations to include moral values and cultural traits, as well as feelings of attachment to the nation. Consequently, notions of integration and citizenship are closely related both in policy and in the experiences of participants.

Conclusion

In this chapter I have examined the ways in which Brexit and the naturalisation process influenced participants' expectations and definitions of citizenship, revealing a hierarchy of belonging that hindered their access to full membership. Such a hierarchy was intersectionally constructed with complex ethnocultural and affective definitions of membership in the state.

The accounts presented here associated citizenship with a sense of security, as a promise of equality and full membership, which was central to their aspirations in the context of Brexit. However, essentialist discourses on belonging and integration reveal the uncertain nature of citizenship (Fortier, 2021), with narrow perceptions of culture and linguistic skills.

The naturalisation process became a highlighter of the erosion of the participants' sense of belonging that started with Brexit. This is perhaps because the learning required by the naturalisation process highlighted a pre-existing British community, of which they had not been members yet, made up of 'native' British citizens. I interpret this phenomenon to be the consequence of the culturalist shift in naturalisation processes, which essentialises culture and belonging through narrow definitions of the nation and leaves aspiring or new citizens feeling as less-than-equal citizens (Byrne, 2017).

For many participants, becoming British responded to a need to acquire rights and feel safe. However, their experiences of the naturalisation process raised bigger questions about their feelings of identification and belonging. This dissonance between initial expectations and experiences within the process created a sense of disenchantment because new citizens felt othered. The process told the story of a reality that was unachievable and, therefore, relegated them to a group of quasi-citizens even after acquiring British citizenship.

Thus, it emerged that participants' defensive naturalisation had guided their expectations towards legal membership in the community. However, after naturalising, a new hierarchy of belonging became visible, which led to reflections on the moral elements of citizenship and highlighted the impenetrability of belonging. Furthermore, for some participants (Francisco, Anne, Kaiden), reflections about defensive naturalisation and a hierarchy of belonging occurred simultaneously and led them away from naturalisation. That is, while they identified a lack of British citizenship with vulnerability, they also considered that naturalisation would have no impact on their place in the hierarchy of belonging. This reveals how the British naturalisation process leads to an oversimplification of the experiences of migrants in their host communities, seeing integration, belonging and membership as stages in a linear journey – a linearity that participants' narratives presented here contests and interrupts (Fortier, 2021).

Participants' perceptions that they can never be British because they don't have the right feelings, accent, and so on, suggests that they internalised affective definitions of citizenship, which were exacerbated by the political climate. Before Brexit, some of the participants introduced here felt a sense of belonging that was disrupted by the political atmosphere. Therefore, further research could take Brexit as an opportunity to consider how political events change non-citizens' perceptions of themselves and their place in their communities. Moreover, Brexit taught us an important lesson about not dismissing the affective dimension of citizenship and the power of its instrumentalisation. A renewed focus on affective citizenship can help to take more seriously the inequalities within the political community and to demystify the value of citizenship as certainty and security.

References

Aptekar, Sofya (2016) 'Making sense of naturalization: What citizenship means to naturalizing immigrants in Canada and the USA'. *Journal of International Migration and Integration* 17(4): 1143–1161. https://doi.org/10.1007/s12134-015-0458-5

Bassel, Leah and Khan, Kamran (2021) 'Migrant women becoming British citizens: Care and coloniality'. *Citizenship Studies* 25(4): 583–601. https://doi.org/10.1080/13621025.2021.1926075

Berlant, Lauren (1997) *The Queen ofAmerica Goes to Washington City*. Durham, NC: Duke University Press.

Blachnicka-Ciacek, Dominika, Trąbka, Agnieszka, Budginaite-Mackine, Irma, Parutis, Violetta and Pustulka, Paula (2021) 'Do I deserve to belong? Migrants' perspectives on the debate of deservingness and belonging'. *Journal of Ethnic and Migration Studies* 47(17): 3805–3821. https://doi.org/10.1080/1369183x.2021.1932444

Bloemraad, Irene and Sheares, Alicia (2017) 'Understanding membership in a world of global migration: (How) does citizenship matter?'. *International Migration Review* 51(4): 823–867. https://doi.org/10.1111/imre.12354

Byrne, Bridget (2014) *Making Citizens: Public Rituals and Personal Journeys to Citizenship*. London: Palgrave Macmillan.

Byrne, Bridget (2017) 'Testing times: The place of the citizenship test in the UK immigration regime and new citizens' responses to it'. *Sociology* 51(2): 323–338. https://doi.org/10.1177/0038038515622908

Chauvin, Sébastien and Garcés-Mascareñas, Blanca (2014) 'Becoming less illegal: Deservingness frames and undocumented migrant incorporation'. *Sociology Compass* 8(4): 422–432. https://doi.org/10.1111/soc4.12145

Coutin, Susan Bibler (2003) 'Cultural logics of belonging and movement: Transnationalism, naturalization, and U.S. immigration politics'. *American Ethnologist* 30(4): 508–526. https://doi.org/10.4324/9781315252599-9

Crick, Bernard et al. (2002) *The New and the Old: The Report of the 'Life in the United Kingdom' Advisory Group*. London: Home Office.

Delanty, Gerard (2003) 'Citizenship as a learning process: Disciplinary citizenship versus cultural citizenship'. *International Journal of Lifelong Education* 22(6): 597–605. https://doi.org/10.1080/0260137032000138158

Donoghue, Matthew and Kuisma, Mikko (2022) 'Taking back control of the welfare state: Brexit, rational-imaginaries and welfare chauvinism'. *West European Politics* 45(1): 177–199. https://doi.org/10.1080/01402382.2021.1917167

Duyvendak, Jan Willem, Hurenkamp, Menno and Tonkens, Evelien (2010) 'Culturalization of citizenship in the Netherlands'. In Ariane Chebel D'Appollonia and Simon Reich (eds) *Managing Ethnic Diversity after 9/11: Integration, Security, and Civil Liberties in Transantlantic Perspective*. New Brunswick, NJ: Rutgers University Press, pp. 221–243.

El-Enany, Nadine (2020) *(B)ordering Britain: Law, Race and Empire*. Manchester: Manchester University Press.

Favell, Adrian (2008) 'The new face of East–West migration in Europe'. *Journal of Ethnic and Migration Studies* 34(5): 701–716. https://doi.org/10.1080/13691830802105947

Favell, Adrian (2017) 'European Union versus European society: Sociologists on "Brexit" and the "failure" of Europeanization'. In William Outhwaite (ed.) *Brexit: Sociological Responses*. London: Anthem Press, pp. 193–200.

Fortier, Anne-Marie (2010) 'Proximity by design? Affective citizenship and the management of unease'. *Citizenship Studies* 14(1): 17–30.

Fortier, Anne-Marie (2016) 'Afterword: Acts of affective citizenship? Possibilities and limitations'. *Citizenship Studies* 20(8): 1038–1044. https://doi.org/10.1080/13621025.2016.1229190

Fortier, Anne-Marie (2021) *Uncertain Citizenship: Life in the Waiting Room*. Manchester: Manchester University Press.

Glaveanu, Vlad P. and Womersley, Gail (2021) 'Affective mobilities: Migration, emotion and (im)possibility'. *Mobilities* 16(4): 628–642. https://doi.org/10.1080/17450101.2021.1920337

Godin, Marie and Sigona, Nando (2022) 'Intergenerational narratives of citizenship among EU citizens in the UK after the Brexit referendum'. *Ethnic and Racial Studies* 45(6): 1135–1154. https://doi.org/10.1080/01419870.2021.1981964

Guma, Taulant (2020) 'Turning citizens into immigrants: State practices of welfare "cancellations" and document retention among EU nationals living in Glasgow'. *Journal of Ethnic and Migration Studies* 46(13): 2647–2663. https://doi.org/10.1080/1369183X.2018.1535313

Hall, Kelly, Phillimore, Jenny, Grzymala-Kazlowska, Aleksandra, Vershinina, Natalia, Ögtem-Young, Özlem and Harris, Catherine (2022) 'Migration uncertainty in the context of Brexit: Resource conservation tactics'. *Journal of Ethnic and Migration Studies* 48(1): 173–191. https://doi.org/10.1080/1369183X.2020.1839398

Hampshire, James (2011) 'Liberalism and citizenship acquisition: How easy should naturalisation be?'. *Journal of Ethnic and Migration Studies* 37(6): 953–971. https://doi.org/10.1080/1369183X.2011.576197

Home Office (2002) *Secure Borders, Safe Haven: Integration with Diversity in Modern Britain*.

Humphrey, Michael (2013) 'Migration security and insecurity'. *Journal of Intercultural Studies* 34(2): 178–195.

Huysmans, Jef (2005) *The Politics of Insecurity: Fear, Migration and Asylum in the EU*. London and New York: Routledge.

Joppke, Christian (2019) 'The instrumental turn of citizenship'. *Journal of Ethnic and Migration Studies* 45(6): 858–878. https://doi.org/10.1080/1369183X.2018.1440484

Joppke, Christian (2020) 'Immigration in the populist crucible: Comparing Brexit and Trump'. *Comparative Migration Studies* 8(1): 49. https://doi.org/10.1186/s40878-020-00208-y

Kilkey, Majella and Ryan, Louis (2021) 'Unsettling events: Understanding migrants' responses to geopolitical transformative episodes through a life-course lens'.

International Migration Review 55(1): 227–253. https://doi.org/10.1177/0197918320905507

Kostakopoulou, Dora (2010) 'Matters of control: Integration tests, naturalisation reform and probationary citizenship in the United Kingdom'. *Journal of Ethnic and Migration Studies* 36(5): 829–846. https://doi.org/10.1080/13691831003764367

Lähdesmäki, Tuuli, Saresma, Tuija, Hiltunen, Kaisa, Jäntti, Saara, Sääskilahti, Nina, Vallius, Antti and Ahvenjärvi, Kaisa (2016) 'Fluidity and flexibility of "belonging": Uses of the concept in contemporary research'. *Acta Sociologica* 59(3): 233–247. https://doi.org/10.1177/0001699316633099

Mayblin, Lucy (2017) 'Asylum after empire'. In Lucy Mayblin, *Asylum after Empire: Colonial Legacies in the Politics of Asylum Seeking*. London: Rowman & Littlefield, pp. 175–180.

McGhee, Derek (2009) 'The paths to citizenship: A critical examination of immigration policy in Britain since 2001'. *Patterns of Prejudice* 43(1): 41–64. https://doi.org/10.1080/00313220802636064

Meer, Nasar, Dwyer, Claire and Modood, Tariq (2009) 'Embodying nationhood? Conceptions of British national identity, citizenship, and gender in the "veil affair"'. *Sociological Review* 58(1): 84–111. https://doi.org/10.1111/j.1467-954X.2009.01877.x

Monforte, Pierre, Bassel, Leah and Khan, Kamran (2019) 'Deserving citizenship? Exploring migrants' experiences of the "citizenship test" process in the United Kingdom'. *British Journal of Sociology* 70(1): 24–43. https://doi.org/10.1111/1468-4446.12351

Mongia, Radhika (2018) *Indian Migration and Empire: A Colonial Genealogy of the Modern State*. Durham, NC: Duke University Press.

Morrice, Linda (2016a) 'British citizenship, gender and migration: The containment of cultural differences and the stratification of belonging'. *British Journal of Sociology of Education* 38(5): 597–609. https://doi.org/10.1080/01425692.2015.1131606

Morrice, Linda (2016b) 'Cultural values, moral sentiments and the fashioning of gendered migrant identities'. *Journal of Ethnic and Migration Studies* 43(3): 1–18. https://doi.org/10.1080/1369183X.2016.1211005

Moss, Jonathan, Robinson, Emily and Watts, Jake (2020) 'Brexit and the everyday politics of emotion: Methodological lessons from history'. *Political Studies* 68(4): 837–856. https://doi.org/10.1177/0032321720911915

Ong, Paul M. (2010–11) 'Defensive naturalization and anti-immigrant sentiment: Chinese immigrants in three primate metropolises'. *Asian American Policy Review* 21: 39–55.

Outhwaite, William (ed.) (2017) *Brexit: Sociological Responses*. London: Anthem Press.

Plummer, Ken (2003) 'The new theories of citizenship'. In Ken Plummer, *Intimate Citizenship: Private Decision and Public Dialogues*. Seattle, WA: University of Washington Press, pp. 49–66.

Roos, Christof (2019) 'The (de-) politicization of EU freedom of movement: Political parties, opportunities, and policy framing in Germany and the UK'. *Comparative European Politics* 17(5): 631–650. https://doi.org/10.1057/s41295-018-0118-1

Rzepnikowska, Alina (2019) 'Racism and xenophobia experienced by Polish migrants in the UK before and after Brexit vote'. *Journal of Ethnic and Migration Studies* 45(1): 61–77. https://doi.org/10.1080/1369183X.2018.1451308

Schinkel, Willem (2010) 'The virtualization of citizenship'. *Critical Sociology* 36(2): 265–283. https://doi.org/10.1177/0896920509357506

Sredanovic, Djordje (2022) 'The tactics and strategies of naturalisation: UK and EU27 citizens in the context of Brexit'. *Journal of Ethnic and Migration Studies* 48(13): 3095–3112. https://doi.org/10.1080/1369183X.2020.1844003

Yuval-Davis, Nira (2006) 'Belonging and the politics of belonging'. *Patterns of Prejudice* 40(3): 197–214.

Yuval-Davis, Nira, Anthias, Floya and Kofman, Eleonore (2005) 'Secure borders and safe haven and the gendered politics of belonging: Beyond social cohesion'. *Ethnic and Racial Studies* 28(3): 513–535. https://doi.org/10.1080/0141987042000337867

Zontini, Elisabetta and Genova, Elena (2022) 'Studying the emotional costs of integration at times of change: The case of EU migrants in Brexit Britain'. *Sociology* 56(4): 638–654. https://doi.org/10.1177/00380385211063355

6

Brexit fears: anticipating and dealing with the loss of citizenship rights

Djordje Sredanovic

In this chapter I explore how members of different groups impacted by the Brexit process anticipate (but also, to a certain degree, dismiss) potential risks linked to the process, and how they deal with such risks.[1] The encounter between Brexit and the sociology of risk allows me to pursue two aims. The first is to understand the uncertainties linked to Brexit as something that those impacted by Brexit live with, and try to deal with, mobilising different unequally distributed resources (see also Sredanovic and Della Puppa, 2021). The second is to distance further the study of migration (and naturalisation) from the assumptions of maximising rational choice under stable conditions and with relatively complete information (see also Sredanovic, 2022). I use the results of a five-year qualitative research with EU27 citizens in the UK and Britons in Belgium, as well as with Britons living in the UK who have applied or have considered applying for the citizenship of another member state.

I argue that the risks deriving from the Brexit process have been rendered particularly complex by the combination of the reversal of well-established rights and by the long, uncertain and still not entirely completed process of negotiation between the UK and the EU itself.[2] From this point of view, examining retrospectively the responses to Brexit and how they have changed during the Brexit process itself is a way to understand the Brexit experience and how it might continue to shape the future of a significant proportion of the UK and EU populations, as well as a way to push forward the analysis of uncertainty in migration in general.

As in the rest of this book, the focus of the fears explored is on the loss of EU citizenship for British citizens (a development that endangers especially UK citizens living in another EU member state) and the loss of a substantial part of the protection linked to EU citizenship for EU27 citizens living in the UK. It should be noted, however, that third-country nationals have also been impacted by the developments of Brexit, especially if they had explored the possibility of obtaining the citizenship or permanent residence of an EU27 member state also in order to have the opportunity to move to the UK (cf. Della Puppa and Sredanovic, 2017; Della Puppa et al., 2021; Turcatto and Vargas-Silva, 2022).

Social research on Brexit has produced a body of knowledge on the perspectives of EU27 citizens in the UK and, even though to a lesser degree, on those of British citizens in the EU (the third group here considered, British citizens in the UK, have been less explored). Some of the issues here explored, such as the rise of xenophobia, worries about the loss of rights and those linked to the settled status procedure, have been the object of a number of publications, as I discuss below. However, there have been relatively limited attempts to theorise Brexit experiences from a point of view of the sociology of risk.

For the interviewees of my research, the risks associated with the loss of citizenship rights are further entangled with those linked to the future of British society post Brexit. For some of the interviewees, formal rights and the procedures to defend them were further seen as scarcely relevant in the face of their predictions of what the UK will be like after Brexit, especially in economic terms but also in political and social ones.

The loss of citizenship rights linked to Brexit has been the first serious loss of rights for many intra-EU migrants, including for many of the interviewees of this research. The experience of intra-EU migration before Brexit has been far from universally rosy. Migrants from later accession states have been the object of significant xenophobia, other than having seen their rights limited for several years (see e.g. Ciupijus, 2011). More generally, intra-EU migration has never been free of barriers, particularly against migrants with limited income (see e.g. Maas, 2013; Lafleur and Stanek, 2017). However, for at least some intra-EU migrants, EU citizenship has offered extensive protection and allowed highly successful migratory experiences (see e.g. Favell, 2008).

At the same time, certain aspects of the experiences of Brexit are hard to match to the existing theories of migrant uncertainty linked to the lack or the loss of rights. Deportability (De Genova, 2002) – the condition of undocumented migrants that makes them potentially always deportable and therefore exposed to particularly severe exploitation – seems applicable to the consequences of Brexit only in the most extreme of hypotheses. The condition of being 'in limbo', used prevalently to describe the uncertainty of those awaiting the results of an asylum application (Cabot, 2012; Haas, 2017), also does not seem to apply entirely.[3] The waiting that asylum seekers experience is characterised by severe limitations (typically strong limits to mobility and a prohibition to work) and open to extremely different outcomes (from full protection to the denial of rights and potential deportation), but the potential outcomes are still limited in number and predetermined (e.g. full asylum, subsidiary protection, humanitarian protection or refusal).[4]

What sets apart the case of Brexit is not so much the severity of the situation of those impacted by the process, or the degree of loss of rights, but the way in which the long negotiation in particular has made the process of Brexit open-ended and complex. As mentioned, EU27 citizens in the UK and Britons in the EU enjoyed extensive rights before Brexit, although for some EU27 citizens such rights kicked in only after their country of citizenship acceded to the EU. The populations impacted by Brexit are more diverse in terms of class, race and ethnicity than is commonly recognised in public discourse (Antonucci and Varriale, 2020). However, EU27 citizens, or at least West Europeans, in the UK have found more space in better-paid jobs (Johnston et al., 2015) compared to other migrant groups, and Britons in Belgium (another focus of this study) tend to have a more middle-class profile. British migration to Belgium differs from that to other EU member states because of the lesser relevance of lifestyle migration, more important in France and Spain (e.g. Ferbrache and MacClancy, 2020; MacClancy, this volume), and because of the role played by EU institutions in Brussels and the network of public and private organisations surrounding them, which attracts more professionals and to a degree seems to promote more EU-friendly attitudes among the local British population.

The dynamic, complex and difficult-to-calculate nature of the risks linked to Brexit makes it a good candidate for some insights into the sociology of risk that have been introduced only in a few cases in migration studies. The classic works in the field of the sociology of risk (starting from Beck, 1992) have insisted on the presumed 'democratic' – that is, indifferent to class or to other socially structuring dimensions – nature of contemporary risks, so it is not surprising that the classic sociology of risk has struggled to find an application to migration studies. However, later formulations (e.g. Tulloch and Lupton, 2003; Curran, 2013) have redefined risk as mediated by class, gender, age, ethnicity, migratory experience, and so on. Still, the general applications of the sociology of risk in migration studies, leaving aside the studies of how migrants are constructed as a risk by sectors of the more or less sedentary populations (e.g. Hier and Greenberg, 2002), are mostly focused on migratory projects as risky endeavours and on the ways in which migrants and migrants-to-be manage such risks (Williams and Baláž, 2012; Bradatan, 2016). Limited attention is given to the risk linked to lack or loss of rights, with a few exceptions, such as Le Courant's (2015) analysis of how undocumented migrants manage risks when interacting with migration authorities.

One extremely useful concept for understanding the *responses* of those impacted by Brexit to maintain their rights is that of protective citizenship, or defensive naturalisation. The concept has been mostly used in the US to indicate the naturalisations triggered by legislative measures that reduce the rights to which non-citizens are entitled, in particular the 1996 welfare reform that excluded migrants from most welfare measures (Coutin, 2003; Gilbertson and Singer 2003). However, the concept has further been used to describe naturalisations linked to a hostile political climate or to proposed legislation, rather than to already approved legislation (e.g. Félix et al., 2008). From this point of view, the naturalisations of members of the different groups impacted by Brexit can be considered defensive naturalisations linked to a hostile climate, and, especially for the measures taken before the introduction of the Withdrawal Agreement, anticipating a still indefinite but almost certainly negative evolution of the legal context.

Among the literature that has explored risk in connection to Brexit specifically, Antonucci and colleagues (2017) have linked the sociology of risk to the Brexit referendum, arguing that the Leave position is not linked to 'left behind' working-class voters but rather to a middle class that perceives globalisation as an existential risk. Two contributions, focusing on Central and Eastern European interviewees in the years before the Brexit referendum, have argued that the Brexit moment can be compared with the uncertainty created by the Yugoslav Wars (Drnovšek Zorko, 2020) and more generally with the post-socialist transition (Kay, 2020). Most contributions that address theoretically the risks of Brexit focus on EU27 citizens in the UK. These include Trąbka and Pustulka (2020), who show how the risks are contained by more consolidated migratory careers that allow access to naturalisation and other resources, as well as by less anchored careers that leave space to exit strategies; Teodorowski et al. (2021), who use a mental health reading to show issues of being 'on hold' as a result of the uncertainties of the negotiation and of rejection, linked both to individual hostility and the general political climate; and Hall and colleagues (2022), who discuss transnational resources that can be mobilised against uncertainty, including familiarity with, resources in and the possibility to live in different national contexts, family networks and the possibility to rely on collective organisation, mainly nationality-based ones. The only previous contribution that focuses on Britons in the EU is the study of British migration to Germany by Auer and Tetlow (2023), who suggest that the uncertainty of Brexit has not only accelerated such migration but also pushed migrants to engage in more risk-taking in enacting more rapidly the migration decision, as well as accepting worse salary conditions in the new country of residence.

The data presented here are based on in-depth interviews conducted between 2018 and 2022 as part of a research project on the impact of Brexit on the values and meanings of EU and national citizenships. The interviews were with EU27 citizens in the UK, British citizens in Belgium, and British citizens living in the UK who explored obtaining another citizenship as a result of Brexit. The interview guide included questions about the (expected and actual) consequences of the Brexit process for the lives of the interviewees; their responses in terms of application for nationality or other legal statuses; their own and their relatives' plans about potential further migration; and their attitudes towards the institutions involved in the negotiations and the negotiations themselves. The interviewees were mostly contacted through social media, including open calls on Twitter and announcements in Facebook groups for specific groups of nationals in the UK and Belgium, with further contacts made through the snowball procedure.

The group of interviewees included 34 EU27 citizens from 11 member states (7 Italian, 6 Spanish, 4 Polish, 4 Croatian, 3 French, 3 German, 2 Greek, 2 Dutch, 1 Austrian, 1 Belgian and 1 Hungarian), 16 British citizens living in Belgium, and 13 British citizens who had explored obtaining another citizenship on the basis of descendance, marriage to an EU27 citizen or a mobile lifestyle between the UK and the EU. The interviewees lived across the whole of Belgium and Great Britain (but with no interviewees in Northern Ireland), with some clustering in the larger Brussels, Manchester and London areas. The overall group of interviewees included 39 women and 24 men, ages ranging from the mid-twenties to seventies (with a slightly younger group on average among EU27 citizens in the UK and a slightly older group among Britons in Belgium). The interviewees were somehow skewed towards the middle class (especially among the Britons in Belgium, likely due to the attraction of EU institutions for middle-class professionals). They were largely white, and some had additional ancestry beyond British ancestry and those of the EU member states listed above, including Serbia, Chile and Northern Cyprus. All the names used are pseudonyms.

A diachronic point of view on Brexit and its risks

Examining the interviews conducted at different moments between 2018 and 2022, as well as the retrospective description of each interviewee's experience since the 2016 referendum (and for many the experiences beforehand), allows a timeline to be identified of how the Brexit risks were perceived. While there are significant internal variations, at least three main moments can be identified in the data collected (see also Sredanovic, 2022): a post-referendum moment of generalised uncertainty, without insight into the possible forms taken by Brexit (roughly up to early 2017); the period of negotiations between 2017 and 2019, with uncertainty driven by the wide range of possible outcomes; and the overlap of Brexit, the transition period and the COVID-19 pandemic, starting from 2020.

The referendum moment itself and the following months were those characterised by the most radical fears, including, for some of the interviewees, losing outright the right to reside and to work. This was discussed by Kate, one of the British interviewees in Belgium:

> For me personally I, I was concerned that at some point I might have to leave Belgium. And that I would, I would no longer be able to live and to work in Belgium as I do now, so that was, yeah, that was a fear that I had. That I have to go back to the UK.
>
> [Kate]

With the emergence of the details of the negotiations between the UK and the EU, between 2017 and 2019 some of the more radical fears retreated. However, the protracted negotiations between the EU and the UK, followed by the extended stalemate on whether to approve the Withdrawal Agreement in the UK Parliament between late 2018 and most of 2019, created further uncertainties. The possibility of deadlines being reached without an agreement opened the risk of a 'no-deal' Brexit, and at the same time the equilibrium in Parliament suggested in some moments the possibility of cancelling Brexit, with the overall result of leaving the situation open-ended.

Many interviewees described these years as being on hold, unable to plan any major life choices without knowing what Brexit would have entailed (see also Teodorowski et al., 2021). While several interviewees dealt with the uncertainty through a protective naturalisation, seen as the only sufficient guarantee to maintain most of their rights, others took a wait-and-see approach (Sredanovic, 2022). In the face of the possibility of a no-deal result, which entailed not only uncertainty about the status of British and EU citizens, but also possible sudden disruptions to the circulation of basic goods, a few interviewees prepared contingency plans, including the idea of leaving the UK before the end of the negotiations and staying abroad (see Sredanovic, 2021).

With the Conservative victory at the 2019 general election, which made Brexit a certainty, the fears shifted to knowledge of the loss of rights, as well as fears of future complications, and in particular the possibility of the UK government and, to a lesser degree, the Belgian one, reneging on the rights confirmed through the Withdrawal Agreement. The diffusion of the COVID-19 pandemic in 2020 on the one hand masked some of the impact of Brexit, both by emerging as a more salient risk and by introducing limits to mobility which superseded those related to Brexit. On the other hand, the pandemic compounded the uncertainties, with closures of services needed to comply with new regulations, situations of being stranded outside the UK, and the loss of employment without guarantees to access benefits for the most recently arrived (Turcatti and Vargas-Silva, 2022). The settled status process was made more complicated for many by the closure of public services and limits to local mobility linked to the COVID-19 lockdowns. Moreover, in 2021 the start of Brexit limitations to entry in the UK, combined with the pandemic-related limitations, increased the number of EU citizens who were refused entry, along with, for some months, the use of immigration detention for EU citizens not authorised for entry into the country. While one of my EU27 interviewees in the UK, Matea, discussed the difficulties of applying for pre-settled status when it was only possible to do so with Android phones and local authorities had closed their services because of the lockdown, the interviewees I met starting in 2020 had limited experience of international mobility during the pandemic.

Loss of rights

The loss of formal rights was the most obvious consequence of Brexit, and was also the component most exposed to the long negotiation between the UK and the EU. For my interviewees, the fears of categorically losing the right to reside in the country of residence was mostly confined to the first phase of Brexit (as in the quote from Kate above) and to some moments in which a no-deal Brexit seemed probable. The introduction of settled status in the UK (and of the 'M card' in Belgium for British residents who arrived before the end of the transition period) on the one hand presented routes to confirm one's right to stay. On the other hand, the new statuses entailed having to reapply for less rights than those held before Brexit, and the settled status in particular was the object of worries about the dematerialised procedure and the lack of physical proof of status (cf. Botterill et al., 2020; Elfving and Marcinkowska, 2021; Sredanovic, 2023).

Trąbka and Pustulka (2020), in discussing Polish migrants who were determined to stay in the UK, distinguish between well-anchored 'bumblebees', relying on resources and on a clear way to citizenship to dismiss the impact of Brexit, and newcomer 'honeybees', in the course of accumulating resources to be able to remain. In my interviews those most recently arrived, especially among the EU27 citizens in the UK, were paradoxically also the ones most ready to minimise the possible impact of Brexit, relying on their commitment to the new country of residence.

The right to work was a more significant concern for a number of interviewees. For some Britons interviewed in Belgium this was directly linked to the EU-related nature of their jobs, as the loss of EU citizenship could have meant the loss of the right to appear before the European Court of Justice or to work for EU institutions (the possibility that the British personnel were going to be asked to leave their jobs was avoided in the spring of 2018, at least for those holding permanent jobs within the European Commission and the European Parliament). More generally, however, a number of interviewees were aware that their right to work could be at risk. Valérie asked for reassurance from her employer, a local authority, that they would be able to sponsor her for a work visa if necessary, while Krisztina noted how a number of research job announcements that she might have been interested in applying for specified that the employer was unable to provide visa sponsorship. In some cases, Brexit was a trigger to try to change employment profile, as in the case of Claudia:

> Unfortunately Brexit put a lot of fear on me also for what concerns work, because I was working as a teacher and therefore I didn't have a permanent contract, I have always worked as a free-lance, also in Italy, and so I liaised with schools, language schools; I worked on-call on Italy, and as a free-lance here. I can say that Brexit scared me a lot, so I looked for a full-time job, my aim was to look for somebody to hire me with a permanent job.
>
> [Claudia]

British citizens residing the UK were those more clearly foreseeing the loss of opportunities in the EU, resulting from not being able to rely on the residence routes available for those present before the cut-off date. For some interviewees with significant cross-border activity this had significant implications. Economic interests linked to UK/EU travel often intersected with specific lifestyles and different forms of European and cosmopolitan identities. Other interviewees relied on UK/EU travel to maintain family and friendship relations, and in some cases anticipated care responsibilities, for example for ageing parents. UK/EU mobility was therefore a major issue in most of the interviews, both in terms of short-term mobility and in terms of the right to settle and/or return to a country different from that of residence (cf. Sredanovic, 2021).

Claudia, mentioned above, was unwilling to continue her migration project in the UK if travel to Italy was to become complicated, as she was not willing to live in a place from which she would not be able to visit her family frequently. More generally, a number of interviewees feared that border crossings might become lengthier. A specific problem for British citizens in the UK who obtained an M card emerged from border controls: normally entering the Schengen Area involves a stamp on the passport, which starts the 90-day visa-free period. Britons on the M card in some cases had their passports stamped, which opened up the fear of being considered an overstayer at the following border crossing despite their residence in Belgium.

Several interviewees also wanted to keep the option open of moving to a different EU member state, which for some of the Britons interviewed involved clear plans, while others simply wanted to safeguard a potential future lifestyle. For the EU27 citizens, the issue was rather that all statuses except citizenship allow only a limited number of years outside the UK before losing residence rights (Sredanovic, 2021).

Further, some interviewees, such as Stéphanie, expected EU27 citizens to be legally discriminated against in access to the real estate market and excluded from welfare at the beginning of their migratory experience. Katrin, who had a degenerative disease, was working at the time of the interview but knew that she would need to rely on welfare in the future. She similarly expected non-citizens to be excluded from welfare in the near future, partly because she expected the general economic situation of the UK to worsen significantly. Katrin's worries echo those of the disabled EU27 citizens in the UK discussed by Duda-Mikulin and Głowacka (2024), who saw the social pressure for all EU27 migrants to be workers benefitting the UK as an obstacle for disclosing their status and applying for benefits.

The variety and differences in the risks that interviewees linked to Brexit confirm that risks are experienced differently according to one's social position, even among groups with similar legal entitlements to rights, such as EU27 citizens in the UK and British citizens in Belgium. In particular, this emerges in terms of different expectations about citizenship rights, as well as in terms of what alternative resources interviewees drew upon as guarantees to limit the impact of Brexit, according to their class, migratory history, age and transnational networks (Sredanovic and Della Puppa, 2020).

Changes in society

For many of the interviewees, their expectations about the future of British society were equally if not more important than the loss of formal rights in understanding the long-term impact of Brexit. In some cases, such expectations about the future of the UK intersected with their fears about the loss of rights; in other cases, the discourse of rights was trumped by that about the future of the UK.

Firstly, across most of the interviews there was a lack of trust in the British government; such lack of trust was mentioned by Walter as a reason to apply for Belgian citizenship and by Krisztina as a reason to apply for British citizenship:

> I was too scared not to go for it [the citizenship application], if that makes sense. And I really fear for all my friends who for whatever reason, whether they are Slovakian, and they can't actually, and they don't want to renounce their citizenship back there ... I did not know what ... we still don't know what will happen to people. And I don't trust the British government to any degree.
>
> [Krisztina]

Along with the lack of trust in the UK government there was for many of the interviewees an expectation that the UK economy was set to be hit by a significant economic crisis. This was the expectation of some Britons in Belgium like Mira, but also that of a number of EU27 citizens, including Katrin and Claudia, with the latter seeing the weakness of the sterling as the main problem linked to Brexit:

> What scares me most is the mere economic side. From the point of view of what is lost generally on my salary, for what concerns the fact that the Sterling ... a salary in a [good] Sterling Pound [exchange rate] could have been a fairly good salary, and on the contrary it could even become the opposite.
>
> [Claudia]

For Claudia, who had arrived a few years before in the UK, and was due to marry a Briton but did not have such strong links with the country of residence, the economic situation was a reason to apply for settled status but avoid pursuing permanent residence.

A third social change that many EU27 citizens and some of the Britons saw in the UK was the emergence of an unwelcoming society, of which the referendum result was both a sign and an accelerator. Some interviewees were aware of news items about the rise of hate crimes after the 2016 referendum (research has confirmed the increase, although it seems that after the end of 2016 the level of hate crimes reported returned to previous levels – Devine, 2021). Other research studies confirmed the rise in experiences of hostility among EU27 citizens, which, in the case of Central and Eastern Europeans, was a continuation of previous experiences (e.g. Guma and Jones, 2019; Rzepnikowska, 2019; Sime et al., 2022), as well as how the referendum result offered legitimation to xeno-racism more generally (Patel and Connolly, 2019).

Many of the people I met felt rejected by the political context and, to different degrees, by the majority who had voted for Brexit; Stéphanie, for example, felt unwilling to explore permanent residence and citizenship exactly for that reason. Two interviewees, Daniel and Ignacio, related overt episodes of overt hostility with Daniel's Indian wife being harassed on a bus the day after the referendum and Ignacio being spat upon during the height of the COVID-19 pandemic. While Ignacio was quick to dismiss the event as a single occurrence in the interview, the episode related by David accelerated the family's decision to leave the UK for Norway. Other interviewees who did not mention overt hostility still perceived minor comments as othering, as in Piet's case or, as in Krisztina's case, avoided opening themselves to harassment in public:

> My biggest fear is nationalism, and there was a real wave of anti-European feeling ... anti-foreigner feeling ... What happened afterwards [the referendum] was really bad ... a foreign name in itself became ... you became a

> suspect … You went to a doctor and a young assistant would ask you how long have you been in the country.
>
> [Piet]

> For a couple of months I was quite paranoid. I genuinely, I was worried about speaking on the phone, and I was … I didn't wanna speak in Hungarian in front of other people. And I think by now that kinda turned into … I'm still wary in some situations, so I'm not gonna pick up the phone in certain situations, if there are people who I assume wouldn't like that.
>
> [Krisztina]

Trąbka and Pustulka in their analysis distinguish between 'economic', 'psychological' and 'institutional/legal' vulnerability (2020: 2666). Setting psychological risks apart might not capture the continuity between 'symbolic' issues such as feeling rejected and the possibility of overt discrimination. Moreover, there is a strong continuity between access to formal rights and social recognition, as even rights that are never used can be appreciated as proof of being treated as an equal (Sredanovic, 2014). However, a few of the interviewees I met distinguished rather clearly between their worries about Brexit and issues that had a material impact on them. In particular, interviewees with activist experience in the Remainer field (and, to some degree, some older and/or middle-class interviewees) presented Brexit mostly as an issue for what they saw as a deterioration of the political situation in the UK and more generally as a worsening of the British society. Variations of this discourse are relatively common in many of the interviews I conducted with Britons, as well as with some of the EU27 citizens, especially those who had spent a longer time in the UK. While some linked the discourse to some individual interests at risk because of Brexit, it is notable that others underlined how they did not have personal worries in play.

Similar to these cases are those of two EU27 interviewees who were otherwise not worried by Brexit, Ilaria and Fabien, who mentioned respectively the hostile political discourse about EU27 citizens and the risk of political crises in the UK, especially in Northern Ireland. In this sense the political context of the UK seems to a degree a residual worry linked to Brexit – something that was of variable importance for the different interviewees, but that tended to emerge only in subordination to other issues.

Containing the fears

As shown across the chapter, the interviewees I met had a range of worries about Brexit, but they also contained such worries to different degrees, mobilising different arguments and resources.

As mentioned, a recurring narrative across several of the interviews I conducted consists of minimising fears about the personal impact of Brexit, focusing rather on problems that involve collectives, and often the whole British society. To a certain degree, this shift from the individual to the collective or general appears a political discourse linked to Remainer positions many interviewees were familiar with. The interview with a British couple living in the UK, Lindsay and Colin, is interesting in this sense:

> **Lindsay:** We both work in travel and tourism, so …
> **Colin:** For me it wasn't that, it was the fact that we were detaching ourselves from a larger community, because Lindsay and I both lived and worked in Italy, and we both work in travel, so therefore we were in contact with people in all sorts of countries.

As they detailed later in the interview, both had good reasons to worry about Brexit: not only did they work in tourism, and therefore were exposed to a potential decrease in EU tourists, but they were also involved in organising tourism from the UK to Italy, which relied on EU freedom of movement. In this sense, Colin's shift from the potential personal economic damage of Brexit to describing Brexit in terms of British isolationism appears a deliberate change of register to address 'higher' concerns. In other cases, the narrative intersected with individual resources, including EU citizenship:

> This is very strange, what I am going to say, I never treated it [Brexit] personally, I am more worried about Britain. I am not worried about myself, because I feel I don't have nothing to fear … I am European, if I feel like if I don't want to live here anymore, I can move to Italy or to France, you know, I have all Europe. I never felt restricted in my movement or decisions about where I want to be … I live in the UK for reasons, for all these years, I like living here, and I just feel sorry for this country, when it will go bad, and everything is showing it will.
>
> [Elżbieta]

In Elżbieta's case the reliance on EU citizenship and the possibility of moving elsewhere in the EU intersects with pessimism about the future of British society, but the risk is reframed in terms of emotional and identity links with the country, excluding worries about a potential individual impact.

In other cases, while not shifting the narrative to a collective level, the risks of Brexit were delimited through references to resources to mobilise against it. This was the case with Ignacio who, as mentioned above, was one of the few interviewees to discuss a case of open aggression but was generally confident about his situation in the UK:

> It's a very privileged thing to say: I was sure that I was going to be able to stay anyway. Because I had a very good job, and … well, good qualifications, so

> I was sure that if I wanted to stay I'll be able to stay ... So I was not worried about me personally, also because I lived in London and the people I interacted with, my friends here, almost all come from a very international background ... there's British people too, but they are used to international backgrounds ... That's not the experience that many other Europeans were getting, friends of mine who lived in the North, and other people that I knew, in London, but in less protected environments.
>
> [Ignacio]

Ignacio was not the only one to discuss how more cosmopolitan and/or Remain-voting areas of the UK could offer more protection than Leave-voting areas – other interviewees in the UK, both EU27 and British, presented similar arguments, in a couple of cases expressing discomfort about continuing to live in a Leave area. Ignacio's main argument, however, is the reliance on his qualifications and line of work to allow him to stay in the UK, and it is worth noting that he immediately described the discourse as privileged. As described elsewhere (Sredanovic and Della Puppa, 2020), the resources available to contain the effects of Brexit are stratified according to class and legal status, as well as other dimensions including migratory background, age and family networks. As mentioned above, other interviewees who could not rely on a job role such as that of Ignacio relied, for example, on their commitment to the country of immigration or on their history of fiscal contributions. The above-mentioned French couple, Valérie and Fabien, who I interviewed in two distinct moments in 2018 and 2019, also referred to the numbers of British citizens living in France as a guarantee against hard forms of Brexit (see Sredanovic and Della Puppa, 2020 for a similar argument advanced by Italo-Bangladeshis interviewed by Della Puppa).

Discussion and conclusions

In this chapter I have shown how the risks and fears linked to Brexit have been characterised by a particularly dynamic nature. At the moment of writing, not only has Brexit been enacted and the transition period ended, but some of the residual issues, particularly around the status of Northern Ireland, seem to have reached at least a temporary solution. Still, most of the legal statuses available to EU27 citizens in the UK and Britons in the EU27 (with the exception of citizenship) and acquired as a safeguard against Brexit can expire, for example through a prolonged absence from the national territory. Even without this, worries remain about governments reneging on the guarantees given or, worse, about statuses being misunderstood or ignored in the many encounters, including those with private actors, that incorporate elements of migration control. The conditions currently available to the groups impacted by Brexit are less favourable than those promised by the Leave campaign before the referendum, and are likely less favourable than the conditions that seemed probable during the negotiations. Still, some of the uncertainties that I have found for the period leading up to the end of 2019 are not present in the later interviews, showing that a sub-optimal situation has some advantages over unpredictable risk. The co-presence, intersection and, at the same time, relative independence of the legal risks of Brexit and the risks linked to transformations of society are in line with the dynamics recognised by the sociology of risk, but have not been previously fully articulated in sociological analyses of Brexit. The ways in which different interviewees contained the risks of Brexit, not only relying on unequally distributed resources but also prioritising different responses (discursive and practical) depending on the resources available, brings into further doubt the democratic nature of contemporary risks. Brexit, as a 'national' phenomenon, opposing the UK to the EU, might be considered to have a similar legal impact at least within groups sharing the same citizenship and legal status (EU27 citizens, Britons in the UK, Britons in Europe). Despite this, it is clear how even within such groups both the impact of Brexit and the responses to contain it vary across different axes.

Two further points are worth making here. Firstly, in the interviews I conducted, there were some gender differences in the ways in which risks were discussed. Other aspects I have explored, including the uses of citizenship (Sredanovic and Della Puppa, 2023) and plans for mobility (Sredanovic and Della Puppa, 2020), showed very little difference along gender lines, with class, age and migratory history being more relevant in characterising different approaches to citizenship and mobility. On the other hand, in the corpus of interviews I have compiled there is a certain tendency for woman interviewees to characterise the risks of Brexit as being more extensive and far-reaching. This remains a tendency rather than a regular occurrence, as I met men with a very worried outlook and women who dismissed the possibility of Brexit becoming a serious problem for them, but I also met a few interviewees who conveyed a certain frustration with their male partners' relaxed attitude towards Brexit and its consequences:

> He [her partner] earns a lot more than I do … and so he's paid quite a lot of taxes, and … he thinks that they [the British government] are gonna be nice to him … And I am thinking 'well, you haven't read what's happening, they don't care' … That's a big worry for me, that I can see myself not staying here, because I have really got enough, I can see myself going somewhere else … He's more reluctant, to accept.
>
> [Marika]

Again, my data do not suggest generalised gender asymmetries in dealing with Brexit risks – I found more differences within couples composed of an EU27 and a British partner than between men and women in general. Further, it is worth noting that the Brexit fears that are stronger among some of the women I interviewed are not immediately apparent as 'gendered' fears – they are not linked, for example, with the possible retrenchment of gender-based rights linked to Brexit (cf. Dustin et al., 2019), but can be identified as a more wide-ranging worry about the future adverse decisions on the part of the British and, to a less degree, Belgian, governments. An economic dimension is present in the case of Marika and a couple of other interviewees, as the fact that male partners tend to consider Brexit less of a risk is also linked to their better job situations. While the sociology of risk has identified (with a critical approach) a stronger orientation to risk-taking in normative masculinities compared to normative femininities (cf. Hannah-Moffat and O'Malley, 2007), what seems to emerge from my interviews is not so much a gendered aversion to risk-taking, but rather a gendered tendency to risk envisaging.

Secondly, a major tactic mobilised by different interviewees to limit the impact of Brexit was a protective naturalisation.[5] Even in the first period of the Brexit process, in which the loss of rights was still difficult to anticipate, for many of the interviewees applying for citizenship was already seen as a way to be safe, despite the fact that most of them would have not explored naturalisation had Brexit not happened and felt safe enough with their EU citizenship (Sredanovic, 2022). However, the process of applying for permanent residence and then for citizenship was itself a source of uncertainty and, for some of the interviewees, fear (Sredanovic, 2022). More importantly, the Britons I met (both in Belgium and in the UK), and the EU27 citizens who were more worried about the loss of formal rights, tended to be more interested in naturalisation as a solution, but the EU27 citizens who were more worried about changes in British society were less willing to link themselves further to the UK by obtaining British citizenship. Defensive naturalisation cannot defend against risks that go beyond the domain of formal rights, such as economic downturns, but naturalising has a larger meaning that depends on the potential applicant's condition and resources (cf. Sredanovic and Della Puppa, 2020).

The interviews I conducted show a complex typology of fears, in part linked to the more uncertain period of the Brexit process and in part to the continued complexity of the Brexit case, showing the usefulness of the sociology of risk for the analysis of the case.

The limited role that the fear of expulsion has in the interviews testifies to the difference between the condition linked to the Brexit process and existing concepts developed within migration studies, including deportability and the asylum process related state of being in limbo. This is despite the fact that even before the Brexit referendum expulsions of EU citizens had reached significant levels both in the UK and in Belgium (see e.g. Lafleur and Mescoli, 2018), suggesting that the risk of expulsion is still perceived as limited to specific profiles of EU citizens (with rough sleepers being particularly targeted both before and after Brexit – Morgan, 2022).

The interviews also allow a further test of the theses on the loss of relevance of national citizenship: while the interviews with the Britons in Belgium testify to the relevance of EU citizenship, or rather of holding national citizenship of any of the EU member states, the claim that denizenship is an acceptable substitute for full national citizenship remains unconvincing. Finally, the analysis confirms how both risks and citizenship are experienced differently according not only to the legal status of the subjects, but also according to other aspects of their social position, including class, age, gender, migratory history and family network.

Notes

1 The chapter is based on research that has been made possible through a Newton International Fellowship of the British Academy (Grant NF171438) and a post-doctoral fellowship of the F.R.S-FNRS (Grant FC22951).
2 The EU freedom of movement rights were well established, but the degree to which individuals took the rights as granted depends on the moment of access to the EU of their country of citizenship (cf. Lulle et al., 2018, 2019) as well on whether they were citizens 'by birth' or through naturalisation (cf. Sredanovic and Della Puppa, 2020, 2023).
3 The expression 'in limbo' has been used in two volumes (Remigi et al., 2017, 2018) collecting the stories of EU27 citizens in the UK and British citizens in the EU, but the uncertainty that characterises these stories, while significant, is very different from the uncertainty described through the same expression in refugee studies.
4 One study that shows a more open-ended situation is that of Mountz et al. (2002) on people with temporary protection status (TPS) in the US, in which the uncertainty was compounded by political debates around whether to open roads to permanent residence and citizenship to TPS holders.
5 See also Godin and Sigona (2022), who in the context of Brexit distinguish between defensive naturalisations oriented towards safeguarding formal rights and protective naturalisations oriented towards limiting discrimination.

References

Antonucci, Lorenza and Varriale, Simone (2020) 'Unequal Europe, unequal Brexit: How intra-European inequalities shape the unfolding and framing of Brexit'. *Current Sociology* 68(1): 41–59.

Antonucci, Lorenza, Horvath, Laszlo, Kutiyski, Yordan and Krouwel, André (2017) 'The malaise of the squeezed middle: Challenging the narrative of the "left behind" Brexiter'. *Competition & Change* 21(3): 211–229.

Auer, Daniel and Tetlow, Daniel (2023) 'Brexit, uncertainty, and migration decisions'. *International Migration* 61(4): 88–103.

Beck, Ulrich (1992) *Risk Society: Towards a New Modernity*. London: Sage.

Botterill, Kate, Bogacki, Mariusz, Burrell, Kathy and Hörschelmann, Kathrin (2020) 'Applying for Settled Status: Ambivalent and reluctant compliance of EU citizens in post-Brexit Scotland'. *Scottish Affairs* 29(3): 370–385.

Bradatan, Cristina (2016) 'Highly skilled migrants: Risks and hedging mechanisms'. *Population, Space and Place* 22(5): 406–410.

Cabot, Heath (2012) 'The governance of things: Documenting limbo in the Greek asylum procedure'. *Political and Legal Anthropology* 35(1): 11–29.

Ciupijus, Zinovijus (2011) 'Mobile central eastern Europeans in Britain: Successful European Union citizens and disadvantaged labour migrants?' *Work, Employment and Society* 25(3): 540–550.

Coutin, Susan Bibler (2003) 'Cultural logics of belonging and movement: Transnationalism, naturalization, and U.S. immigration politics'. *American Ethnologist* 30(4): 508–526.

Curran, Dean (2013) 'Risk society and the distribution of bads: Theorising class in the risk society'. *British Journal of Sociology* 64(1): 44–62.

De Genova, Nicholas P. (2002) 'Migrant "illegality" and deportability in everyday life'. *Annual Review of Anthropology* 31: 419–447.

Della Puppa, Francesco and Sredanovic, Djordje (2017) 'Citizen to stay or citizen to go? Naturalization, security and mobility of migrants in Italy'. *Journal of Immigrant and Refugee Studies* 15(4): 366–383.

Della Puppa, Francesco, Montagna, Nicola and Kofman, Eleonore (2021) 'Onward migration and intra-European mobilities: A critical and theoretical overview'. *International Migration* 59(6): 16–28.

Devine, Daniel (2021) 'Discrete events and hate crimes: The causal role of the Brexit referendum'. *Social Science Quarterly* 102(1): 374–386.

Drnovšek Zorko, Špela (2020) 'Cultures of risk: On generative uncertainty and intergenerational memory in post-Yugoslav migrant narratives'. *The Sociological Review* 68(6): 1322–1337.

Duda-Mikulin, Eva A. and Głowacka, Marta (2024) '"I haven't met one": Disabled EU migrants in the UK. Intersections between migration and disability post-Brexit'. *Journal of Ethnic and Migration Studies* 50(6): 1530–1548.

Dustin, Moira, Ferreira, Nuno and Millns, Susan (eds) (2019) *Gender and Queer Perspectives on Brexit*. Cham: Palgrave Macmillan.

Elfving, Sanna and Marcinkowska, Aleksandra (2021) 'Imagining the impossible? Fears of deportation and the barriers to obtaining EU settled status in the UK'. *Central and Eastern European Migration Review* 10(1): 55–73.

Favell, Adrian (2008) *Eurostars and Eurocities: Free Movement and Mobility in an Integrating Europe*. Maiden, MA.: Blackwell.

Félix, Adrián, González, Carmen and Ramírez, Ricardo (2008) 'Political protest, ethnic media, and Latino naturalization'. *American Behavioral Scientist* 52(4): 618–634.

Ferbrache, Fiona and MacClancy, Jeremy (2020) *The Political Agency of British Migrants: Brexit and Belonging*. Abingdon: Routledge.

Gilbertson, Greta and Singer, Audrey (2003) 'The emergence of protective citizenship in the USA: Naturalization among Dominican immigrants in the post-1996 welfare reform era'. *Ethnic and Racial Studies* 26(1): 25–51.

Godin, Marie and Sigona, Nando (2022) 'Intergenerational narratives of citizenship among EU citizens in the UK after the Brexit referendum'. *Ethnic and Racial Studies* 45(6): 1135–1154.

Guma, Taulant and Jones, Rhys Dafydd (2019) '"Where are we going to go now?" European Union migrants' experiences of hostility, anxiety, and (non-)belonging during Brexit'. *Population, Space and Place* 25(1): e2200.

Haas, Bridget M. (2017) 'Citizens-in-waiting, deportees-in-waiting: Power, temporality, and suffering in the U.S. asylum system'. *Ethos* 45(1): 75–97.

Hall, Kelly, Phillimore, Jenny, Grzymala-Kazlowska, Aleksandra, Vershinina, Natalia, Ögtem-Young, Özlem and Harris, Catherine (2022) 'Migration uncertainty in the context of Brexit: Resource conservation tactics'. *Journal of Ethnic and Migration Studies* 48(1): 173–191.

Hannah-Moffat, Kelly and O'Malley, Pat (eds) (2007) *Gendered Risks*. Abingdon: Routledge-Cavendish.

Hier, Sean P. and Greenberg, Joshua L. (2002) 'Constructing a discursive crisis: Risk, problematization and illegal Chinese in Canada'. *Ethnic and Racial Studies* 25(3): 490–513.

Johnston, Ron, Khattab, Nabil and Manley, David (2015) 'East versus West? Overqualification and earnings among the UK's European migrants'. *Journal of Ethnic and Migration Studies* 41(2): 196–218.

Kay, Rebecca (2020) '"You get a better life here': Social in/security and migration in a time of geopolitical transformations'. *Scottish Affairs* 29(3): 305–320.

Lafleur, Jean-Michel and Mescoli, Elsa (2018) 'Creating undocumented EU migrants through welfare: A conceptualization of undeserving and precarious citizenship'. *Sociology* 52(3): 480–496.

Lafleur, Jean-Michel and Stanek, Mikolaj (eds) (2017) *South–North Migration of EU Citizens in Times of Crisis*. Dordrecht: Springer.

Le Courant, Stefan (2015) 'Le poids de la menace: L'évaluation quotidienne du risque d'expulsion par les étrangers en situation irréguliere'. *Ethnologie française* 45: 123–133.

Lulle, Aija, Moroşanu, Laura and King, Russell (2018) 'And then came Brexit: Experiences and future plans of young EU migrants in the London region'. *Population, Space and Place* 24(1): e2122.

Lulle, Aija, King, Russell, Dvorakova, Veronika and Szkudlarek, Aleksandra (2019) 'Between disruptions and connections: "New" European Union migrants in the United Kingdom before and after the Brexit'. *Population, Space and Place* 25(1): e2200.

Maas, Willem (2013) 'Free movement and discrimination: Evidence from Europe, the United States, and Canada'. *European Journal of Migration and Law* 15(1): 91–110.

Morgan, Benjamin (2022) 'What fresh hell? UK policies targeting homeless migrants for deportation after Brexit and Covid-19'. *Critical Social Policy* 42(1): 150–159.

Mountz, Alison, Wright, Richard, Miyares, Ines and Bailey, Adrian J. (2002) 'Lives in limbo: Temporary Protected Status and immigrant identities'. *Global Networks* 2(4): 335–356.

Patel, Tina G. and Connelly, Laura (2019) '"Post-race" racisms in the narratives of "Brexit" voters'. *Sociological Review* 67(5): 968–984.

Remigi, Elena, Martin, Véronique and Sykes, Tim (eds) (2017) *In Limbo: Brexit Testimonies from EU Citizens in the UK*. London: Byline Books.

Remigi, Elena, Williams, Debbie, De Cruz, Helen, Pybus, Sarah, Killwick, Clarissa and Blackburn, Paul (eds) (2018) *In Limbo Too: Brexit Testimonies from UK Citizens in the EU*. London: Byline Books.

Rzepnikowska, Alina (2019) 'Racism and xenophobia experienced by Polish migrants in the UK before and after the Brexit vote'. *Journal of Ethnic and Migration Studies* 45(1): 61–77.

Sime, Daniela, Tyrrell, Naomi, Käkelä, Emmaleena and Moskal, Marta (2022) 'Performing whiteness: Central and Eastern European young people's experiences of xenophobia and racialisation in the UK post-Brexit'. *Journal of Ethnic and Migration Studies* 48(1): 4527–4546.

Sredanovic, Djordje (2014) 'Quelle est la valeur de la nationalité/citoyenneté en Italie? Résultats d'une recherche auprès des migrants et des ouvriers italiens à Ferrare'. *Migrations Société* 153–154: 47–61.

Sredanovic, Djordje (2021) 'Brexit as a trigger and an obstacle to onwards and return migration'. *International Migration* 59(6): 93–108.

Sredanovic, Djordje (2022) 'The tactics and strategies of naturalisation: UK and EU27 citizens in the context of Brexit'. *Journal of Ethnic and Migration Studies* 48(13): 3095–3112.

Sredanovic, Djordje (2023) 'The vulnerability of in-between statuses: ID and migration controls in the cases of the "Windrush generation" scandal and Brexit'. *Identities* 30(5): 625–643.

Sredanovic, Djordje and Della Puppa, Francesco (2020) 'Aspettative, immaginari e progettualità di mobilità e stanzialità nel quadro della Brexit: Cittadini dalla nascita e «naturalizzati»'. *Polis* 34(1): 85–108.

Sredanovic, Djordje and Della Puppa, Francesco (2023) 'Brexit and the stratified uses of national and European Union citizenship'. *Current Sociology* 71(5): 725–742.

Teodorowski, Piotr, Woods, Ruth, Czarnecka, Magda and Kennedy, Catriona (2021) 'Brexit, acculturative stress and mental health among EU citizens in Scotland'. *Population, Space & Place* 27(6): e2436.

Trąbka, Agnieszka and Pustulka, Paula (2020) 'Bees & butterflies: Polish migrants' social anchoring, mobility and risks post-Brexit'. *Journal of Ethnic and Migration Studies* 46(13): 2264–2681

Tulloch, John and Lupton, Deborah (2003) *Risk and Everyday Life*. London: Sage.

Turcatti, Domiziana and Vargas-Silva, Carlos (2022) '"I returned to being an immigrant": Onward Latin American migrants and Brexit'. *Ethnic and Racial Studies* 45(16): 287–307.

Williams, Allan M. and Baláž, Vladimir (2012) 'Migration, risk and uncertainty: Theoretical perspectives'. *Population, Space and Place* 18(2): 167–180.

7

Brexit and Brits in Spain: lifestyle migration and political agency

Jeremy MacClancy

The academic literature on lifestyle migration is already large, and it continues to grow. While the range of topics covered within this sub-field of the social sciences becomes ever richer, one theme strangely ignored is lifestyle migrants acting as political agents. It is as though moving to cheaper, warmer climes in order to live a more pleasurable life should dovetail with lack of community engagement. It is supposed that the underlying logic to this style of migration is that such people move to luxuriate, not to agitate.

But does shifting to sunnier climes and cheaper goods preclude the possibility of marshalling and exercising power? The response of this ethnographic chapter is a resounding negative. Given the opportunity, some lifestyle migrants will spontaneously begin to act politically. And if some proposed measures are seen as a direct threat to general migrant interests, emergent leaders among their number can rally impressive cohorts to the cause in a surprisingly short period. That is the key theme and thrust of this chapter.

Given common misconceptions about Britons residing in Spain, I cannot emphasise strongly enough that those who go to live there as retirees are the minority of British migrants to the country. The majority of Britons living in Spain are employed, whether full- or part time, whether Spain is their main place of work or they commute between there and the UK. There are large estates on the coast where a very high percentage of the occupants are elderly migrants, but there are also very sizeable populations of Britons in all the urban centres of the country. And even on the coast, many British residents have jobs.

For convenience of exposition, this chapter is divided into the following sections: a brief chronology of post-war British settlement in the province of Alicante, southeastern Spain; migrants' millennial turn to town-hall business; reactions to the referendum; the post-referendum rise of anti-Brexit groups; migrants' predicament today. My ethnographic material is grounded in repeated annual field trips to Alicante province since 2006. In a gesture towards collaborative fieldwork, I provided all interviewees with my list of questions at least 48 hours before the interview; I emailed my draft text to all participants and then invited them to a collective seminar and lunch for their comments. I am grateful to them all for their contribution, and for being so open with me.

A key theme within this chapter is the broad range of effects the results of the Brexit referendum has had on Britons living on the Continent. My discussion relies on the interviews I carried out in Alicante province in 2019. Given the importance of the issue to Britons, there has been surprisingly little ethnographic work done on Leavers and Remainers, whether in the UK or abroad. The only exceptions I am aware of are the work by the ethnographic sociologist Micheala Benson, who has looked at the variable consequences of Brexit on British migrants of different means and ethnicities, and the paper by the anthropologists Katharine Tyler, Cathrine Degnen and Joshua Blamire (forthcoming) on stereotyping of Leavers and Remainers within the UK, while Collard and Webb's revealing work on British migrants' party affiliation was via an online questionnaire (Benson 2020; Collard and Webb 2020). Thus, my discussion of these interview findings and their analysis can be viewed as a rare contribution to the needed fieldwork-grounded ethnography of a central, contemporary but neglected topic within the discipline.

A brief history of Brits in Alicante

Spain has long been the most favoured destination for Britons moving to the Continent, and Alicante the most popular province within the country. In 2010, 34 per cent of Brits who migrated to Spain chose Alicante for their new abode. In total, about 7 per cent of the provincial registered population was British. Another 8 per cent were from a variety of other EU member states. In nine municipalities there were more foreigners than locals, and in several of those the majority of immigrants were British (Huete et al., 2013: 337–338; Ortiz, 2015; *La Vanguardia*, 2018). All these figures are underestimates, as until very recently many resident Britons chose not to register.

In the late 1950s the interests of an energetic mayor of a depressed fishing village chimed with those of national planners. With the support of central government he oversaw the massive, rapid development of his municipality. Benidorm now has the largest number of high-rise buildings per hectare in the world. However, because of the hoteliers' restrictive practice, construction companies in the area could not build equally dense conurbations nearby. Instead, they put up second homes: substantial houses on large plots for the well-to-do. They then shifted to southern Alicante, creating large estates (*urbanizaciones)* of smaller homes on smaller sites. By the advent of the millennium, there was so little coastline still available for development that they moved inland, putting up isolated *urbanizaciones* which, with populations of up to 16,000, might dwarf the head village of their municipality. These estates may have such a sufficient range of services that resident Britons do not need to leave the area or even to speak Spanish.

It is important to emphasise the diversity of these migrants. It is not just the elderly retired, but the middle-aged and parents bringing up young children as well. Many have jobs, whether full- or part time; some return to the UK to work for several weeks every month or so. They might have moved for a better life but that does not need to exclude continuing employment (Huete and Mantecón, 2012; O'Reilly, 2020: 5). Some take advantage of the shift to retrain in new skills, becoming yoga instructors or teachers of modern languages. Some reinvent themselves, creating a novel past to suit their new present. Some migrants were said to become expert builders or plumbers 'on the plane over'. A few reinventers indulged in more radical transformations, claiming military or sporting distinction. As one couple said to me, 'The main reason we're here in Spain: we're anonymous, and can be anybody we want to be.'

In 2019, I interviewed 29 Britons, most living in the Alicantine interior, about their reasons for migrating. A majority said they disliked contemporary development in Britain: too much red tape, street hostility, over-liberal laws, a failure of pedagogical vision. In contrast, Spain had a milder, usually warmer climate and had a lower cost of living. Several stressed their love of the country: its culture, sense of community, food, local friendliness, landscape, the light late in the day. Many could live in a bigger house than their previous one in the UK; some didn't have the money to buy a house at all in Britain. Many quotidian essentials were cheaper, municipal taxes not so high, and access to health services speedy and of good quality. Most interviewees led socially very active lives and were quietly proud they contributed to the maintenance or creation of local services. None voiced regret at making the move.

Lifestyle migrants learn to be political agents

In 1999 the Spanish government implemented an EU measure enabling residents who came from another EU member state to participate in municipal elections. For the first time, Britons could publicly accuse elected officials of incompetence or worse, and seek to replace them. They and other foreigners were so successful that by 2007 three dozen, the majority British, had become councillors, albeit in small or comparatively small municipalities (MacClancy, 2019: 373). It is difficult to generalise about these Britons, as they are so assorted. Most already had some experience of public activity and organisation, especially in their new, Alicantine place of residence.

Many felt marginalised in municipal meetings, as though they'd been included on a local party ticket for the sake of electoral support from the British population. Some were so disenchanted by the disinterest of local party representatives that they stood as independents: on election, some entered coalitions in order to gain municipal clout. In at least one municipality the foreigners plus some locals formed their own party. In one case the electoral results were so evenly divided that the new incomer councillors held the balance of power, giving them disproportionate leverage in town-hall matters.

In interviews, these British councillors also complained of corruption, nepotism, clientelism and ademocratic practices. In contrast, they would speak in moral terms of the need for 'fairness' and 'justice'. As one put it to me, 'I'm a mean Scotsman': he judged local service providers to be grossly greedy, 'just taking money from the expats. This is unfair. Lots of things are unfair in this world, and I'd like to rebalance it.' Despite the obstacles apparently put in their way, some did think they had achieved worthwhile goals during their term of office, and could reel off a list of initiatives they had thought up and had implemented: securing large EU grants; initiating and managing health campaigns; creating a charitable system to aid the needy; rebranding the municipality's tourist strategy; and so on.

Brexit: reactions

In spring 2019, I interviewed 28 migrants who had left Britain years before to reside in Alicante province. All were born British, bar two who were spouses from non-European countries. I interviewed roughly equal numbers of men and women. All were in their fifties or older, bar one adult son. Six had jobs, most of them part time, and one periodically commuted to the UK. To the extent one can assign them to socio-economic classes, all were members of a broad middle class. All lived inland except three, who lived on the coast. Of the 26, 20 said they were for Remain, six for Leave. The majority underlined that they firmly upheld their particular stance: they wished to make no further qualifications. However, while interviewees classified themselves in unambiguous terms as either Remain or Leave, four in fact held mixed positions which tended to gyre around a much more intermediate space.

I reviewed separately my interview transcripts of Remainers and Leavers, and tried to group their reasons for voting the ways they did. I found the majority of reasons given by all interviewees, no matter their voting preference, could be categorised into a small set of general factors, which I term familial; international trade; belief in larger units; belief in the benefits of the EU; identity.

Remainers: several voiced familial concerns about the future of their adult children, still in the UK, in particular ones who had their own businesses. Several mentioned the effect of Brexit on trade and on workers. An ex-accountant worried about the UK as a single player within the global market: 'If the EU was a company, England would be just a subsidiary, with nothing to gain by leaving; only by staying and trying to change it.' Several argued that the benefits of joining together with other nations surpassed economic considerations: the larger the group, the better the chance of defending group interests and representatives. 'The wider you go the more representative you can be,' said one couple. Some tied bigger units with conviviality, linking that with a shift towards a more harmonious, larger whole: 'We ought to work towards a world where we all work together, with more tolerance and understanding.' These concerns about conviviality and larger units dovetailed with support for general mobility within the EU. Thanks to this free and easy movement across borders, formerly sternly guarded, 'People were gelling.' This mobility both exemplified and reminded people that 'This world belongs to us all.' They regarded freedom of movement both as an opportunity for individuals to take advantage of, and as a valorised dimension of identity. They did recognise the EU did not work perfectly. However, that was a reason for internal reform, not for departure. Finally, all those interviewed said they were British; several added that was not their only social identity and nor was it necessarily the most important. They were not 'British and only British', but rather 'British and ...'

Leavers: Two interviewees emphasised the early effect of Brexit on trading relations. They thought these would be temporary, 'bumps along the road'; in the long term the UK economy would prove to be resilient. The City of London was too well established to stop being a European centre of finance. One acknowledged that being a member of the EU was beneficial for trade, 'But they'll be there anyway.' Some argued that belonging to smaller units led to a stronger identity. It was always better to run one's own show, at both household and national levels. One made the point by talking about the village where he lived: 'Pueblo del Moro wants to be Pueblo del Moro. Its people want to retain autonomy. They don't need anyone else. Without identity they're awash, they're nothing. The EU brings a conformity they don't embrace, attitudes they don't follow.'

The EU was not just out of kilter with the UK; it was corrupt as well: its bureaucrats were powerful but unelected; they wasted money but, it was claimed, did not get their accounts signed off. Leavers approved of the idea of free movement but not if they were refugees or 'terrorists and Islamic fundamentalists'. One interviewee summed up by stating that the European Union had become 'the longest exercise in collective stupidity'. Another, a well-to-do businessman, underlined the power of British identity as a core attribute of who he thought he was; he, his father, his grandfather and other kin had all fought in the British Army. Another pointed out that the British were not federalists, evidenced by the number of compatriots who had gone into combat and died. Both regarded these military efforts as individual contributions to the collective aim of maintaining the sovereignty of their country. Brexit would enable them to regain it.

Brexit: an eruption of emotions, a clash of views

Some Remainers stated to me that their reaction to the result of the referendum was one of profound 'disbelief'; they were 'stunned', 'absolutely dumbfounded', 'shocked', 'mesmerised'. Some said they had felt sick, wept or cried openly. One spotted a broader range of reactions: 'Almost everyone shocked. But many of them said, "Good!" '

I do not wish to over-dramatise, though it might make for a more striking picture. Some were not so moved by the result. In the words of one, who shifted into Spanglish, 'There was a lot of shock, but not much reaction. The pueblo was tranquilo.'

Some revealed they had been taken aback by the voting patterns of some friends and acquaintances. But, however great their surprise, they soon realised it was better not to broadcast one's opinions. Yet discussions would break out again whenever the press printed scare stories: they might be unsettled by questions about the future of their pensions or continued access to health care, and whether they needed to apply for a residence permit and a Spanish driving licence.

Several decades ago, the anthropologist James Boon generalised about meetings between people with very different understandings of the world: they usually exaggerated or lampooned the attitudes of their interlocutors (Boon, 1983). If this is so, we should expect Remainers and Leavers to caricature each other. That is nothing new. The interesting question is how they portray the other. I found, in the course of our interviews, that Remainers above all commented on Leavers' ideas of the past, their concept of their common homeland and the sources of their opinions; Leavers criticised Remainers in particular as ill-informed.

Some Remainers carped at Leavers as being so backward looking they still believed in 'gunboat' diplomacy. To them, Leavers' Brexit was 'a retrogressive step, going back to a time no longer existing'. Their view of history was also deeply partial: 'Leavers have forgotten the state of England at the time of entry to the EU': the three-day week, devaluation still a very recent memory, the UK then very much 'the poor man of Europe'. Some Remainers, well aware of Leavers' portrayal of the Second World War, thought hope lay with the younger generation, who had not been forced to live through the conflict nor live among the scarred ruins of once-bombed cities.

Several Remainers judged Leavers' view of the country as overly homogeneous, as skating over ethnic and geographic diversity. Among some Leavers, this silence about variety dovetailed with 'xenophobic nastiness'. Some Remainers were 'very upset by the racial hatred Brexit has excited'. One remarked that there had been no reference to Scots' view. Two, with much foresight, pointed out the similar omission of Northern Ireland as a possible source of contention: 'What really galls me is the total disregard for the border ... A hard border again: it doesn't bear thinking about.'

Remainers tended to see themselves as informed, and frequently slammed Leavers as ignorant. One spontaneously talked about her in-laws who voted Leave because of two programmes they had viewed on television: 'They'd not thought further than their nose. "Rule Britain shit!"' She suspected their views, at root, were racist. Others complained of Leavers' talk about sovereignty as light on evidence, and of Leavers themselves as not thinking the issues through, of undervaluing free movement within Europe, and failing to consider what life would be like for their grandchildren.

Some Remainers remarked that at the time of the vote people, whichever way they had leant, knew less about the consequences of Brexit. In their opinion, the government had failed to educate the electorate sufficiently. At the time of interview some thought, given the dire forecasts of many economists, that Leavers would vote differently if the referendum were to be reheld. I found no evidence of this.

Some Leavers were just as critical of 'Remoaners'. For them, the key reason for residents voting Remain was fear. They feared losing their pensions and cover for health care. One Leaver said to me this was 'arrogant nonsense' propagated by 'fear-mongers'. A minute's thought would expose their lack of logic, as the Spanish government would not wish to lose so many tens of thousands of residents who maintained such a high number of local jobs. 'Brexit bad for the economy? That was said by people who didn't understand economics.'

Several Remainers placed the blame at the feet of government, leading Leave agitators and the press. A generation of governments, whoever was in power at the time, exploited the EU as a scapegoat. If an unpopular political decision had to be made, politicians would claim, if possible, that their hands were tied by the EU. The benefits of membership were too rarely advertised. In Spain, for example, whenever a public project received some funds from the EU, its flag was boldly included on outsize billboards; in contrast, in the UK, a similar project would only make reduced reference to its EU contribution. These Remainers contended to me that this consistent marginalisation or downplaying of the EU held pro-Remain MPs back from lauding the organisation for the ways it had benefited the UK. Some emphasised the ignoble, mendacious style of too many Leave politicians: the sum consequence was 'the knee-jerk reaction of voters pushed by people with their own agendas, thinking of their own pockets'. The influence of the press, especially tabloids aligned with the right, also came under attack. Some Remainers were disappointed to see that even *The Guardian* could portray British residents on the coast as almost exclusively aged retirees relying on the sun to extend their last days.

I did interview two couples where partners had voted opposite ways. Given the general ambience of mutual recrimination between Remainers and Leavers, I asked how they coped. Both couples said they did not talk about it.

My interviewees had quickly learnt how to contain the worst excesses when meeting diehards of the opposite camp. The more offensive public statements tended to be made online. Some interviewees revealed that, early on, they had joined a chat room occupied by those of the opposite camp. The abuse they received was so great and so speedy, they said, that they left the group rapidly. On one inland estate dominated by Britons, the coordinator of the online discussion group found the number of posts about Brexit was so high, and the exchanges so charged, that she moved the debate into a separate subsection. I was granted access to this e-forum where I saw participants speaking much more openly than my interviewees had done. For instance, some Leavers publicly criticised the volume of immigrants – 'changing the genetic make up of the UK for ever' (in a UKIP Warwick poster stuck up by a Leaver) – and their purported ability to exploit the benefits system. Others queried how democratic a second referendum would be: 'You can't move the goalposts just cos you lost. Suck it up buttercup.'

These references to immigrants and 'genetic make up' are all too revelatory. Some Remainers lamented that Leavers failed to distinguish between migrants, legal or illegal, and asylum seekers. One said with sorrow that he had 'found out that a lot of people in the UK are racist, which is a shame.' Some Remainers questioned how representative Leavers were, since so many were of senior generations, 'foaming through their clenched dentures'. Remainers openly wondered what sort of UK Leavers wanted, as they spoke so very little about Northern Ireland or even Scotland. Leavers might talk about 'the United Kingdom', but wasn't attention more focused on the noun than the adjective? It was argued they were true 'Little Englanders', as that would be more or less what they would be left with: 'And they have the cheek to call us Remainers "traitors."'

There were commonalities, shared by those on either side of this apparent political polarity. Stalwarts at either end on the political spectrum accused those at the opposite pole of telling 'lies' to argue their cause. They might classify their political adversaries as 'ignorant', 'thick' and 'stupid', substituting 'derisory drivel' for factual evidence. Some saw those on their far horizon living in a state of unreality: 'beyond reason', guilty of 'mass delusion', comporting themselves like Flat Earthers, who had 'voted for a unicorn'. I do not wish to overstate this case. The geographer Ben Rogaly, who did research in a small British city, uncovered that many of its inhabitants strongly resisted everyday racism by working to create and uphold a boundary-crossing, non-elite cosmopolitanism (Rogaly, 2020). Something like this was occurring in my own field site in Alicante province, Spain, as several members of the estate I have already referred to posted their maintained wish that its residents retain a sense of balance and strive to achieve a convivial co-residence. They wanted to share their lived space in as non-aggressive and friendly a manner as possible.

Brexit: back to the future

None of my interviewees said the referendum had altered their opinions about returning to the UK.[1] They might have to go back, but those who were planning to do so gave increasing age or family as their reasons. The rest, the great majority, were clear-minded, resolute: 'This is my home.'; 'Nothing would make me go back to England. I feel comfortable and at home here. There are no instances under which I'd go back.'

In fact, Brexit had had a securing effect, only sharpening their commitment to staying put. Some Remainers said they would not return as 'Brexit has so polarised the population'; Britons were now less compassionate, more racist and bigoted. A few were open that if obliged to leave Spain, they would migrate to another sunny country with an advantageous cost of living, such as the Philippines or Thailand. What charms the UK had held for them was by then outweighed by its miserable climate and high prices. They preferred to turn into serial transnationals than become begrudging returnees.

Concern about income could, however, trump all other factors. Possible causes for moving home that interviewees spoke about included the freezing of their pensions; losing free access to healthcare services; and a major drop in the exchange rate between the euro and sterling. When I first met with Britons in Alicante in 2018 to discuss these issues, most said they would not take Spanish citizenship even if it guaranteed them permanent residence and unhindered access to various services provided by the state. However, the next year many interviewees said they were prepared to give up their British citizenship if it ensured they could stay in Spain. 'We'll do whatever it takes.' Only one interviewee was adamant they would remain British, no matter what.

Brexit: what chance of a dialogue?

If we try to characterise the views of either side in the most general, yet informative, terms possible, Remainers emerged as people who hold an open-ended vision of the world, with their face to the future. They stated their belief in larger rather than smaller groups. Members of these larger associations would work to practise a sustained conviviality and a functioning harmony. The EU, which exemplifies these broader groups, would be the home for a creative multiculturalism enabled by a pervasive, productive tolerance. Remainers acknowledged they were British but that was not their only or even their most important source of identity.

Leavers were notably different. They regarded themselves as stalwarts of a properly representative democracy upheld by a formerly homogeneous population enjoying a well-grounded economy in a relatively compact country. The millions of those who had died for the country justified its continued existence. Leavers' vision can be characterised, without oversimplification, as internally focused and usually backward looking. It is an ideal of a supposedly stable, pacific society where people could salute their fellows in an unproblematic manner, a society where all of its members had contributed fairly to the Commonwealth. For Leavers, being British in their terms was easily the most significant group identity they held dear. Only family could come before it.

It is hard to gauge the racist dimension to Brexit discourse, both Leaver and Remainer, as interviewees were circumspect, even when edging towards comments they were aware could be classed as such. 'You've to be really careful when talking about migrants, as people'll call you a racist.' Two Remainers did discuss the matter without apparent restraint. One attacked the government for preferring immigrants over natives: 'foreigners' in the UK were 'stealing *my* pension, because they're claiming child benefit'. I was not given permission by the other interviewee to print their comment about migrants to Britain. A third was even more cautious. They opened their comment by stating 'Not being racist', before adding, 'The UK has done too much for people coming into the country.' To them, Spain had an admirable system because an immigrant had to gain a NIE (*Numero de Identificación Extranjero*), issued by the National Police, 'in order to do anything'. Britain, they claimed, did not appear to have a similar system.

At least one British commentator has spoken of Leavers in the UK as an unusual mix of free-marketeers and those who want to see their vision realised: a return to a stable society on the lines of post-war UK (O'Toole, 2019). Leavers in Spain took a different tack, speaking more in socio-political terms than economic ones. They were not resolute neoliberals, but regarded the 'bumps' on the road a worthy price to pay to achieve their dream. After the referendum, some analysts put forward the contested argument that a significant number of Leavers were people trapped in 'left behind' places, neglected parts of post-industrial UK. They had voted to leave the EU out of a sense almost of despair, for the sake of an alternative which just might prove more promising than their present predicament (Edwards, n.d.) Alicantine Leavers do not fit this frame: the ones I interviewed were not indigent and all bar one of those few interviewees who did appear less comfortably off than the majority I spoke with propounded Remain without noteworthy qualification.

Though the positions maintained by Remainers and Leavers appear opposed, they are articulated by a common set of coupled concepts: expansiveness vs. centripetality, multiculturalism vs. cultural coherence, forward-looking vs. historically grounded, unrestricted mobility vs. relative stability, globally oriented vs. Anglocentricity. Not everyone fitted this binary scheme. One Remainer interviewee chastised the government for spending money on immigrants rather than boosting her pension. Another was anti-EU but cited financial 'self-interest' as sufficient reason for voting Remain. Yet another leant towards Remain because she wanted her adult children, resident in the UK, to enjoy the benefits of a healthy jobs market. A fourth said he was a Remainer but voiced opinions associated with Leavers throughout our encounter. I asked him why: 'In my heart I'm a Leaver. But my brain says Remain.'

Whether Remainer or Leaver, some interviewees backed their position by reference to geography. For one Leaver, 'We are an island, therefore difficult to take over, so it can't be more over-run by migrants.' In contrast, a Remainer saw insularity in negative terms: 'Britain is a stupid ... island out in the Channel: but it needs Europe to be something, desperately.' One self-flattering Remainer summarised the differences between camps in geographically bound terms: Leavers had an 'island mentality', Remainers a 'gypsy pirates' one. In other words, Leavers were nationally fixed, home-based types, Remainers transnational voyagers, open to new worlds, their face to new winds.

Here, opposed visions tend to go hand-in-hand with mutual incomprehension, as several interviewees confessed. One pair thought the argument for Remain so patent they 'couldn't imagine people wouldn't see the benefits of being in the EU'. Yet, as one astute Leaver noted, 'When you ask Remainers, "Why did you vote that way?", they can't really tell you. And it's the same for Leavers.' Though advocates of both sides upheld a utopia and disparaged that of their opponents, Remainers and Leavers utilised much the same vocabulary. But they interpreted the terms differently according to opposed values. The common result was that arguments from either camp were not engaging with each other, but rather sliding past one another.

Brexit: campaigning

Several interviewees said they felt numb on hearing the referendum result. That feeling soon turned into a sustained emotional state they regarded as akin to grieving. Their deeply unhappy state could last weeks, or for some even longer. This 'bereavement', as some of them styled it, was blended with worry, concern about the future and what they classed as severe depression. But some of the more energetic were not prepared to remain passive on the sidelines: they began to talk, and to organise.

The word first spread among neighbours; email extended the circle and then social media enabled explosive growth. For example, in the days immediately following the referendum Britons in Almeria, southeast Spain, had come together to form Europats. Within less than two months, its database held about 1,000 email addresses and, within a year, 6,000. Many of these freshly formed groups had one or several activists knowledgeable in IT within its governing circle, keeping their sophisticated websites up to date, and monitoring the lively discussions on their Facebook pages. The use of IT was central to these groups' organisation, spread, rate of growth and speed of response to new events: the velocity of interaction enabled by IT became a social factor of its own.

In early 2017, 11 groups agreed to form a broad EU-wide coalition, British in Europe (BIE), with c.30,000 members. Members of its Steering Committee teleconferenced weekly, or more frequently, to debate strategy and agree on actions. In turn, its members disseminated information and decisions to their respective groups and the public via its websites and social media. The coalition was so successful that some groups soon began to question their continued independent existence.

These activists' political experience before Brexit was mixed. Though some had none, several had engaged in campaigns in the UK, and many of them had previous careers in public service. But it is noteworthy how few had campaigned on other earlier issues in Spain. For British residents, participating in municipal politics and initiating anti-Brexit groups appeared to follow relatively separate trajectories.

Their actions had effect, preventing the British government from forgetting their concerns. Among other focused efforts, they intervened in legal actions in the Supreme Court, lobbied members of both chambers in Parliament as well as MEPs, participated in the launch of a European Citizens' Initiative to guarantee EU passports for Britons after Brexit, and co-organised anti-Brexit rallies in London, Madrid and other major cities. Together with other leaders of BIE, they met with national politicians in their respective countries of residence, as well as with the European Commission's chief Brexit negotiator, Michel Barnier.

They were also listened to. In October 2016, evidence about the triggering of Article 50, provided by Fair Deal for Expats, was referred to by High Court judges. Bremain saw information it supplied restated by MPs in the House and even the words of one of their lobbyists quoted in parliamentary debate. In 2018, one Bremain representative emailed me: 'We have considerably influenced the content of the EU proposals on citizens' rights—it is evident every time we submit new information, as the proposals have changed before our eyes, sometimes even using the exact same language' (Sue Wilson, 'Bremain's work goes on!', Bremain's January newsletter, January 2020, bremaininspain.com).

In April 2017 David Jones, Minister of State at DeExEU, met with anti-Brexit campaigners based in Spain, where he underlined the wish of the British government that these groups take their demands to the Spanish government as well. At the end of the meeting, Jones thanked them 'for telling us things and ideas we'd not thought of'. One of the activists understood this to mean that DExEU was partially reliant on the campaigners for information, and wished them to do its work for them: informing the Spanish government of the relevant issues and their concerns before the British government engaged in serious negotiation on key issues. One can view this as the empowerment of the campaigners by the British government, which recognised their privileged, intermediary position by asking them to soften up the Spanish government, in effect, on their behalf. To follow this logic, the British government was acknowledging its own relative ignorance, and augmenting the role of the activists.

Brexit: affective activism

Activism can bear both political and individual benefits. An outstanding example is Sue Wilson, Chair of Bremain in Spain. In 2019 she confessed she had been 'a political virgin' up until the referendum: 'I felt perfectly content in Spain and in ignorance, and felt that any decisions made in Westminster were of little consequence to me.' The referendum result made her 'a different person. It turned me into a campaigner'. Many members of Bremain said much the same, referring to the 'damage' the result had made 'to their sense of security, their health and well-being, and the anxiety it causes about the future'. Wilson had observed her vocabulary had become stronger, a 'common side-effect among Bremain campaigners'. Activism had led to her learning new skills, and had given her the confidence to speak at very large public events, something previously inconceivable to her: 'I value one thing about Brexit: that it has given me a passion and commitment to change my future and, I hope, the future of others' (Wilson, 2019).

Given the hours she spent campaigning since 2016, the example of Wilson is out of the ordinary. However, the general point stands: participating in the anti-Brexit movement could transform negative affect into a positive reformulation of self, enabling the construction of a novel social network, one held together by a newly coherent set of shared interests and fortified by common passions. Much of this was exemplified in an article in the January 2020 e-newsletter of Bremain in Spain:

> We have all been through so many emotions in the past four years, none of them easy to deal with. We have cried, we have shouted, we have pleaded ...
>
> ... we must focus on the positives as much as possible. We've made new friends, we've learnt new skills, we've discovered new passions. Most important of all, we have learnt to appreciate our European home more than ever before. We may hate Brexit with a passion, but we cherish our lives in Spain—Brexit cannot change that. (Sue Wilson, 'Bremain's work goes on!', Bremain's January newsletter, January 2020, bremaininspain.com)

The notion of identity being employed here is both highly individual and profoundly social. Activists strove to remould a central sense of self. The groups wished to stimulate members' consciousness of their personal agency to give them a sense of belonging within a newly constructed community. They recognised members might feel isolated from what they had regarded as their social group: 'Britons in Spain'. The common end was the creation of a novel 'Remainer' collectivity, of agents and activists committed to the cause and well aware they were not isolated but an integral part of a common body. This could allow energetic campaigners to turn private despair into public zeal, regrounding their sense of security in the process.

These days, most anthropologists conceive of identity as central to both individuals and social groups, yet at the same time dynamic and contested. If this is so, then it is unsurprising that some activists saw the referendum as an infrequent example of what they call identity 'theft'. One member of the Bremain Council wrote to me: 'I was raised in Britain, worked in Germany, have lived in Spain for twelve years, and am going to Italy soon to marry my Italian boyfriend, where we will live. I feel very, very European. How can people take that from me?'

Some saw their agency compromised by what they regarded as politicians' marginalisation of them, an attitude given voice in the slogan, 'We are not bargaining chips!' Acting in an activist manner was a means to oppose openly this classificatory dispossession, a way to hold fast to their threatened identity. A Greek anthropologist commenting on that country's financial crisis regarded nationals' identification with much broader indignation as a means to explicate, and so contain, the crisis (Theodossopoulos, 2013: 208). The situation in Spain was parallel: for both Greeks hamstrung by a harsh policy of austerity, and British residents arguing against Brexit, giving voice to their indignation reinforced agency. It was empowering.

Some opponents criticised them as 'keyboard warriors' (activists whose battlefields are confined to their computers) or 'snowflakes' (elegant figures who cannot survive beyond strictly delimited conditions). In response, some Remainers inverted the symbolism, appropriating these denigratory terms for themselves, revalorising them as they went. Their aim was to blunt their opponents' barbs, by turning their would-be slurs into badges of self-reference, worn with pride.

Let us compare the styles of councillors and activists, throwing into relief their differences and similarities. Britons in municipal elections strove to uphold what they regarded as a quotidian ethics. While both they and the activists had to follow administrative regulations, the latter had to operate in much more open-ended, intercultural spaces: here, persuasive arguments had to be based on rights-based language, not a claimed everyday morality. Further, 'Europe' was not a relevant term in the discussions I held with councillors in 2015; they were above all concerned with local issues, not ones beyond the national (MacClancy, 2019; Ferbrache and MacClancy, 2021). By definition, the EU and 'Europe' were central frames within which anti-Brexiteers operated. And, as members of the EU, campaigners acted on their right to claim rights. Councillors might have seen their efforts in ethical terms towards a just end, but the activists spoke within the terms of rights-based language: in other words, within political, social and legal coordinates. Moreover, in perhaps their most innovative move, they attempted to help create a new mode of citizenship, one not contained by national boundaries. Yet, exactly what EU citizenship might enable or entail remains a labile, disputed notion. Activists exploited this zone of disputation as a space in which they could develop their argument. The legal theorist Patricia Mindus has contended that a mass citizens' movement offers the greatest possibility of separating EU citizenship from national ties (Mindus, 2017: 92–94). This argument, if right, underlines the potential power the activists enjoyed to guide the rethinking of EU citizenship.

Accommodating to the post-Brexit life?

This chapter has been about lifestyle migrants and political agency in Spain. What comes across is that political activity among this distributed population is fragmented rather than pervasive. Those who became involved in municipal politics did not tend to join anti-Brexit campaigns. Those who did participate in these campaigns were surprisingly ignorant of a parallel political campaign by well-to-do foreign incomers 10 to 15 years previously, against the flagrant expropriations of the regional government in the same area (Janoschka, 2009). It is as though each domain was a separable sphere of historically grounded activity.

It is also important that the Brexit dispute is kept within its appropriate bounds. At its height, the anti-Brexit campaign was clearly very important to many British residents, in several different ways, as detailed above. That does not mean it necessarily dominated their lives. Not all residents were activists; indeed, the British consul in Alicante questioned to me how representative the campaigners were. In contrast to the style of activists, one interviewee emphasised to me how essential it was to park Brexit within broader contexts to retain a wider perspective. Whatever happened, their lives were more than Brexit: '*Jeremy!* There's wine to drink! Coffee to be had! Life to be lived!'

In a similar manner, those I reinterviewed two years or so after the referendum stressed that though some of their British neighbours had returned to the UK since, Brexit was not the sole or even major cause for their departure. Instead, they pointed out that numbers have been declining for many years. The major stimulus had been the economic fallout from the banking crisis of 2008. Many incomers who had had jobs, such as working in bars or restaurants, went home when their employment ended. That loss, and the worsening exchange rate of the pound to the euro, had made their way of life too precarious.

It remains indisputable that Brexit has altered migrant lives, to a degree. A significant percentage of residents used to shuttle between the two countries, whether as 'summer swallows' or periodic commuters. The implementation of Brexit forced them to choose where they wished to be officially resident, and therefore taxable. The present regulation is that an unregistered non-EU member can only stay for 90 days out of every six months. This did not suit those who did not wish to register or have their travel constrained. So they went back to the UK. Also, it is thought many of the unregistered but permanently resident did register, while the rest returned to Britain or chose to remain, moving even further into a netherworld of illegality. By definition, we do not know how many of the unregistered left Spain and how many have stayed.

The councillors remain in place, despite initial fears they would have to stand down on the day Brexit was implemented. Though their numbers have declined slightly, they continue to act as political agents within their municipalities. In a like manner, the anti-Brexit campaigners keep the struggle up though their demonstrations are neither so frequent nor so numerous. These days their main battle-site appears to be the web, where distinguished contributors – retired ex-ministers, a former Deputy PM – vent their spleen on successive issues. Between the councillors and the campaigners there seems to be even less contact than before. They travel on different trajectories.

My final point has to be that the anti-Brexit campaign will not go the way of its Valencian expropriation predecessor. The anti-expropriators won their case. It was closed, then forgotten. Brexit is too broad, too long-lasting an issue to be neglected in the same way. The cumulative consequence of the councillors remaining in office and the campaigners' example is that today's lifestyle migrants and their successors-to-come know that political agency, of different kinds, remains within their remit. Acting politically can dovetail, not clash, with developing their style of life.

Note

1 For contrasting examples of the effect of Brexit on British migrants' decisions on whether to remain or return to the UK, see Giner-Monfort and Huete (2021); Sredanovic (2021).

References

Benson, Michaela (2020) 'Brexit and the classed politics of bordering: The British in France and European belongings'. *Sociology* 54(3): 501–517.

Boon, James (1984) Other Tribes, *Other Scribes: Symbolic Anthropology in the Comparative Study of Cultures, Histories, Religions and Texts*. Cambridge: Cambridge University Press.

Collard, Sue and Webb, Paul (2020) 'UK parties abroad and expatriate voters: The Brexit backlash'. *Parliamentary Affairs* 73(4): 856–873.

Edwards, Jeanette (n.d.) *Fault Lines: Europe, Brexit and Anthropology*. Douglass Distinguished Lecture, Society for the Anthropology of Europe, given at Vancouver, November 2019.

Ferbrache, Fiona and MacClancy, Jeremy (2021) *The Political Agency of British Migrants: Brexit and Belonging*. London: Routledge.

Giner-Monfort, Jordi and Huete, Raquel (2021) 'Uncertain sunset lives: British migrants facing Brexit in Spain'. *European Urban and Regional Studies* 28(1): 74–79.

Huete, Raquel and Mantecón, Alejandro (2012). 'Residential tourism or lifestyle migration: Social problems linked to the non-definition of the situation'. In Omar Moufakkir and Peter M. Burns (eds) *Controversies in Tourism*. Wallingford: CAB International, pp. 160–173.

Huete, Raquel, Mantecón, Alejandro and Estévez, Jesús (2013) 'Challenges in lifestyle migration research: Reflections and findings about the Spanish crisis'. *Mobilities* 8(3): 331–347.
Janoschka, Michael (2009) *Konstruktion Europaischer Identitaten in Raumlich-Politischen Konflikten*. Weisbaden: Franz Steiner Verlag.
La Vanguardia (2018) 'Diecisiete municipios españoles tienen mayoría de población extranjera'. *La Vanguardia*, 25 April. www.lavanguardia.com/vida/20180425/442999739349/diecisiete-municipios-espanoles-tienen-mayoria-de-poblacion-extranjera.html (accessed 12 April 2020).
MacClancy, Jeremy (2019) 'Before and beyond Brexit: Political dimensions of UK lifestyle migration'. *Journal of the Royal Anthropological Institute* 25(2): 368–389.
Mindus, Patricia (2017) *European Citizenship after Brexit: Freedom of Movement and Rights of Residence*. London: Palgrave Macmillan.
O'Reilly, Karen (2020). *Brexit and the British in Spain*. Project Report. London: Goldsmiths. https://doi.org/10.25602/GOLD.00028223
O'Toole, Fintan (2019) 'Dreams of empire, blitz spirit, a country in decline... how competing visions of the past are driving Brexit'. *The Guardian*, Review supplement, 2 November: 12–13.
Ortiz, Alberto (2015). 'Los extranjeros, infrarrepresentados en los municipios donde son mayoría'. *La Vanguardia*, 3 May. www.lavanguardia.com/politica/20150503/54431002135/los-extranjeros-infrarrepresentados-en-los-municipios-donde-son-mayoria.html (accessed 12 April 2020).
Rogaly, Ben (2020) *Stories from a Migrant City: Living and Working Together in the Shadow of Brexit*. Manchester: Manchester University Press.
Sredanovic, Djordje (2021) 'Brexit as a trigger and as an obstacle to onwards and return migration'. *International Migration* 59(6): 93–108.
Theodossopoulous, Dimitrios (2013) 'Infuriated with the infuriated? Blaming tactics and discontent about the Greek financial crisis'. *Current Anthropology* 54(2): 200–221.
Tyler, Katharine, Degnen, Cathrine and Blamire, Joshua (forthcoming) 'Leavers and Remainers as "kinds of people": Accusations of racism amidst Brexit'. *Ethnos*. https://doi.org/10.1080/00141844.2022.2155208
Wilson, Sue (2019) 'Bremain in Spain's Sue Wilson: How Brexit changed our lives'. *Dispatches Europe*, 22 May. https://dispatcheseurope.com/bremain-in-spains-sue-wilson-how-brexit-changed-our-lives/ (accessed 17 April 2020).

8

'We are the European family': unsettling the role of family in belonging, race, nation and the European project

Hannah Jones

Introduction

In the years-long 'Brexit moment', evidence of turmoil about belonging, nationalism and dislocation has been all around. While some have reached out for solace and connection, gestures of connection can themselves alienate others, through claiming attention for one experience of the pain of nationalist rejection while seemingly ignoring histories of longer, more acute racialised border violence (Emejulu, 2016; Piacentini, 2016). This chapter reckons with one mode of seeking connection and belonging: the appeal to (metaphorical) (trans)national family. In doing so, I seek to understand the appeal of this call, its limitations and – tentatively – its possibilities for a more inclusive solidarity that can take into account histories of violence enacted through practices of nation and family.

The title of this chapter comes from an encounter with work by German photographer and 2000 Turner Prize winner Wolfgang Tillmans, which promotes a 'Remain' vote in the EU referendum (see Tillmans, 2016a). Frustrated by the official Remain campaign, Tillmans worked with artists and other collaborators in his Between Bridges project to produce his own publicity materials.[1] Using background images from his previous works in the series Vertical Landscapes (1995–), overlaid with short messages promoting voter registration and a Remain vote, the posters were distributed as open-source files which the public were encouraged to print and display, and use on social media. Hard copies were also distributed. Around 25 designs emphasised themes including having a democratic voice, youth mobility, and transnational familial and cultural links.

The poster which helped to trigger the thinking in this chapter states (Figure 8.1): 'It's a question of where you feel you belong. We are the European family.' Seeing this particular poster shared on social media in the aftermath of the referendum result, it became clear that it also acted as a source of comfort for some, a reassertion of connectedness and belonging across national borders within the European Union, no matter what the referendum said. The 'question of where you feel you belong' is not a simple one. It is cross-cut by questions of power, history and personal circumstances – including during the 'Brexit moment' of uncertainty, anxiety and anger. The feeling of where one belongs is not a personal feeling but a public feeling (Ahmed, 2007; Cvetkovich, 2012). While 'family' is often thought of as a source of comfort, connection and safety, it is also – much like nation – an exclusive institution, and one that involves power, hierarchy, submission and oppression within its empirical and figurative manifestations. It is much easier to imagine family, and belonging to one, as an undifferentiated comfort and good, for those who have not experienced domestic abuse, ostracisation or family breakdown. Similarly, it is much easier to imagine national belonging or homeland as an easy or unproblematic 'good feeling' for those who have not experienced racism, citizenship discrimination, transnational separation or diasporic melancholy. One does not simply 'choose' to belong to a nation, or family; it depends on a reciprocal relationship which might be denied in a way that goes to the very essence of who a person is seen to be (Ahmed et al., 2003).

In many ways, Brexit is not a unique moment. It is one within which echoes and hauntings of earlier and ongoing divisions of racialised nationhood and practices of family inclusion and exclusion resonate in powerful ways (Bhambra, 2017). This chapter considers the fractures visible in the Brexit debates as just one example of how borders and inclusion/exclusion across them, and one's belonging, can change without oneself changing or moving in any way. In doing so, the trope of (trans)national belonging evoked through a metaphor of family, as in Tillman's work, is re-examined. While both family and nation tend to be used rhetorically as if they are timeless and fixed, the next section of the chapter considers how they actually parallel one another in their blurrings, shiftings and contradictions. Some contradictory attempts to fix shared family forms and (trans)national ideals are highlighted, including both rejection of queer families and racialised religious groups from the nation, and the reincorporation of one of these groups in order to stigmatise the other.

To extend this recognition of shifting forms of family, and the implications of family in constructing race and nation, the next sections consider examples of family practices used to construct the position of racialised insiders and outsiders to The European Family. Firstly, drawing on Ann Laura Stoler's work on the codification of intimate relationships in Dutch colonies and Gloria Wekker's critical autobiographical reflections on being a 'postcolonial' Dutch subject, I point to (a) how intimate family practice is a fundamental part of constructing both race and nation, and (b) how the European project (of developing and maintaining European power)

Figure 8.1 Wolfgang Tillmans, pro-EU/anti-Brexit campaign, 2016. (Image credit: Digital, available online at https://tillmans.co.uk/campaign-eu)

always involved the labour and bodies of those deemed outside the racialised European Family and continent.

Coming back to the current moment, I consider how state-sanctioned marriage and patriarchal presumptions continue to be instrumental in maintaining racialised border controls in Europe. This is explored with particular reference to the case of Mohamed Bangoura, a six-year-old boy deprived of his British citizenship in 2018 on the basis of his mother's marital status while out of the UK without his parents.

As another example of how one's belonging can shift without one moving or changing, and to demonstrate the immediacy of how intimate family and history intervene in current bordering and racialising practices, I draw on my own experience of becoming a dual national in response to the Brexit result, which I pursued in response to being made to feel an outsider, but clearly from a position of citizenship privilege. Keeping in mind the historical contingency and the racialised, classed and gendered power relations at play in the status of citizenship/family, this experience is put into conversation with the contemporaneous ways in which holding dual nationality – or just the potential of it – has become a risk, particularly mobilised against those suspected of terrorist involvement, such as in the case of teenage mother Shamima Begum.

Having laid out these complexities of what the 'European family' and 'the question of where you feel you belong' might mean, but recognising the deep appeal of familial connection, I return to contemporary political art to look for other possibilities of reimagining family, race and nation. In this instance, I consider the work of Gillian Wearing in her projects *Family Monument, A Real Birmingham Family* and *A Real Danish Family*, which have attempted to expand the connection between real and imagined families and place identities in ways that rely less on fixed and exclusive ideal types.

The final section of the chapter draws these cases together to make sense of what an imaginary of national or European family might enable or foreclose. Here, I return to Tillmans' posters but bring them into conversation with Wearing's work, which begins with the intimate (and 'real') and reflects on the local, regional and national collective. Might this provide an alternative way of imagining connection and solidarity without closure and exclusion?

Shifting and reifying European family

> Christian democracy protects us from migration, defends the borders, supports the traditional family model of one man, one woman, considers the protection of our Christian culture as a natural thing. (Orbán quoted in Reuters, 2018)

Family is an inherently gendered and racialising category in the context of Western Europe. State sanctioning of intimate relationships has historically served to organise economic relationships, national inclusion and practices of racialisation. There have always been alternative formations of family and practices called family, which reject the normative model or enact it in alternative ways (longstanding examples include informal adoption or cross-generational care arrangements), alongside more recent changes in the cultural and legal acceptance of same-sex unions. Similarly, the 'EUropean' subject exists in multiple forms, often transgressing the normative vision of whiteness, Europeanness or legitimacy.[2] If this were not the case, there would be little need for the proclamations of those such as Hungary's prime minister Viktor Orbán, who fear these everyday 'alternative' ways of being might prove more attractive than his 'Christian, one man, one woman' dream. Family, however defined, tends to relate back to obligation, care and biological relatedness (whether real or fictive). The home and family are most often used metaphorically to mean comfort, but can also be places of repression, control and violence (e.g. Barrett and MacIntosh, 1982; Ahmed et al., 2003).

One parallel between the European Union and the project of the modernised normative family is their continual reinvention; their reimagining of restrictive structures (patriarchy, national borders) while still hanging onto the original form and therefore the problems of exclusive, hierarchical logics. The European Union project is at one level of course about breaking down national borders – in terms of trade certainly and, in an idealistic vision, in terms of a peace project between European nations previously divided by war and political conflict. However laudable this may seem, there are limits to this vision both in its idealistic form and in practice. The most obvious being that the transnational, borderless ideal itself has borders, ones that are increasingly fiercely guarded in part as a result of the freedom of movement within the territory: Fortress Europe. Like families, nations themselves have shifting internal allegiances and rivalries.

Even those who have lauded the post-national idealism of the EU project (e.g. Favell, 2019) recognise that EU freedom of movement and related easy connections beyond national legal and affective belonging is, in the simplest terms, only available to EU citizens. The Schengen Area of frictionless movement and the removal of internal borders has since its inception been dependent on enforcing ever more stringent external borders. Increasingly, this also involves enlisting neighbouring countries in the process of restraining entry to the EU for 'immigrants', in return for partial access to movement within the EU for those neighbouring countries' citizens (Grzymski, 2019). The boundaries of who 'belongs' to the European family is strictly policed – even to the extent of reinstating internal EU borders (Lendaro, 2016).

The European dream of liberalism, the free market and free movement is not just premised on exclusion, but also challenged from 'within' by far-right illiberal populism in countries such as Poland and Hungary (Graff et al., 2019: 551), and increasingly in more longstanding EU family member countries. Politicians' claims to defend 'Christian marriage' are mobilised as a reason for defending EU borders (from Muslims). Elsewhere, those apparently on the opposite end of a political spectrum use a defence of LGBT+ rights to likewise stigmatise and exclude Muslims from inclusion in the Euro/national family (Puar, 2007), while minority fundamentalist Muslim, Jewish and Christian groups form coalitions in opposition to queer families (Barnabas Fund, 2019; Haynes, 2019; Volpe, 2019).

The persistence of family in empire

'The European' can hardly be imagined without an understanding of Europe's embroilment with geographies and peoples of the world (Goldberg, 2006). Both national identity and race/racism as we currently understand and experience them have been produced through histories of colonial conquest, genocide, slavery and resource extraction by Europeans (Bhattacharyya, 2018). This developed through physical force, certainly, but also through technologies of family and reproduction. Anthropologist Ann Laura Stoler's (1989, 2002) landmark work on Dutch colonial practices is exemplary in demonstrating how this worked in practice, in this instance through the transforming practice of 'concubinage', or informal but institutionally accepted coupledom, in which norms of race and gender not only related but constituted one another. The 'European family' considered in Stoler's work is a projection and construction of 'European' identity and pretended superiority, as performed in parts of the world dominated and ransacked by European national powers, to sustain this power through the ongoing construction of racialised privilege. Within the relationships formed by early European settlers and local women, in both everyday relations and formal bureaucratic rulings, race as a category was constructed over time through the instigation of taboos and how they related to material changes in circumstance:

> Unions between Annamite women and French men, between Javanese women and Dutch men, between Spanish men and Inca women produced offspring with claims to privilege, whose rights and status had to be determined and prescribed. From the early 1600s through the 20th century the sexual sanctions and conjugal prohibitions of colonial agents were rigorously debated and carefully codified. (Stoler, 1989: 637)

'White' or 'European' superiority and separateness from locals had to be maintained in order to maintain colonial authority. White poverty, sickness and old age was shipped back to Europe (Stoler, 1989: 655). When white supremacy was thought to be 'in jeopardy, vulnerable, or less than convincing', colonial elites moved from endorsing concubinage to bringing European women to colonies as wives in 'full-blooded' European families (639). As such, the colonial project was intimately entwined with social and legal constructions of family. While intimate life involved personal feeling and connection, this was recognised as either a political tool or political threat in connecting or separating groups through defining entitlement (or not) to resources, rights and respect.

Stories of promise of membership of The European Family ultimately thwarted by race are visible too in the embers of European empires. In *White Innocence* (2016), gender theorist Gloria Wekker considers her own 'European family' story and how it fits into ongoing, multi-layered European racialising regimes. She writes:

> My own family migrated to the Netherlands in December 1951, when my father, who was a police inspector in the Surinamese force, qualified to go on leave for six months to the 'motherland,' where we eventually stayed permanently ... The regulation for leave in the motherland was of course meant for white Dutch civil servants only, who should not 'go native,' losing their sense and status of being Dutch, but my father had risen to a rank where he qualified for that perk ... It was only decades later that I realized that the reason why we found our first house in the old Jewish neighbourhood of Amsterdam was that 70 percent of Jews in the Netherlands were abducted during World War II. (Wekker, 2016: 8)

Wekker continues:

> My family became subject to the same postwar disciplining regime that was meant for 'weakly adjusted,' white lower-class people and orientalised Indonesians ... The postwar uplifting regime consisted of regular unexpected visits from social workers, who came to inspect whether we were duly assimilating, that is, whether my mother cooked potatoes instead of rice, that the laundry was done on Monday, that we ate minced meatballs on Wednesday, and that the house was cleaned properly. (Wekker, 2016: 9)

In her account, Wekker highlights the nature of European racialising logic. Firstly, there were the same regulations as described by Stoler, intended to keep Dutch colonial officers connected to the *motherland*. Then, when the Wekkers exceptionally took up this offer, they found themselves reclassified from Dutch (colonial) citizens to 'undesirables', ostracised from national belonging through the surveillance of their family life – and the inseparability of racialising processes of class and classed processes of racialisation (see also Virdee, 2014) – while noting that the home they found was itself cleared by the internal European racial 'regulation' of the Holocaust.

The Wekkers are one way to reconceive a quintessentially 'European Family' as exceeding the bounds of European continental territory, or as a family that exists in relation to Europe, its history and present. They grew and lived in a European-controlled territory and took advantage of the myth-making of that territory which, to maintain loyalty and order, relied in part on the idea that the wealth of and belonging to Europe was available to its imperial subjects. In moving to the 'motherland' within Europe, the racial differentiation at the heart of European identity and 'civilisation' was demonstrated again, with the policing of behaviours within the continent of Europe – even, ironically, where the cleanliness and fastidiousness, which apparently needed to be inculcated within families, such as the Wekkers, were made more difficult by the less 'civilised' housing conditions in Amsterdam than in Suriname ('having come to the motherland, we did not have an indoor shower and had to bathe in a tub in the kitchen, as was usual [in the Netherlands] at the time' – Wekker, 2016: 8). Thus, 'The European Family' was policed, codified and reimagined outside the territory of continental Europe, as part of the wider project of defining and defending white supremacy. This expectation of welcome and inclusion in a European empire that was taught to imperial subjects, only to find the opposite on arrival in the 'motherland', is something mirrored elsewhere, including more recent reverberations in the case of the 'Windrush Scandal' in the UK (Wardle and Obermuller, 2018; de Noronha, 2019; see also the Introduction by Sredanovic and Byrne, and the chapters by Yeo and Rzepnikowska, this volume).

Taken together, we can see through these examples, crossing time and continents, a way of imagining The European Family differently. It is both a national and an intimate project, one that assigns legal rights through governmental regulation of personal relationships, and one that reasserts that only some are truly recognised as family members.

The persistence of marriage as bordering technology

I have so far discussed the ways in which ideas of an inclusive transnational family of the EU are challenged by the barriers around the EU, tensions within it and the ongoing familial connections and denials associated with colonial adventures of individual EU member states. However, in an era of superdiversity, we can see that both reconfigured transnational relations and reconfigured familial relations can still end up in a bitter reminder of the restrictions of inclusion in both national and intimate families.

Consider the case of six-year-old British-born Mohamed Bangoura. In 2018, he was refused re-entry to the UK and thereby separated from his mother for two weeks until the matter was resolved following campaigning, media outcry and support from his MP and MEP. Mohamed had been visiting his uncle in Belgium over the summer. His mother, Hawa Keita, had come to the UK from Guinea and the Home Office claimed it had sent her a letter revoking Mohamed's passport in March 2018, on the basis that 'Mohamed was only entitled to British citizenship through his mother or her husband, but neither was settled in the UK when he was born' (BBC News, 2018). That is to say, Mohamed was registered as having British citizenship for the first six years of his life, but at that point, the Home Office apparently identified new information about his parents' visa status and revoked his citizenship – leaving him effectively, in the words of media reports, 'stranded and stateless' (BBC News, 2018). Keita stated that she never received the letter and consequently did not anticipate problems when Mohamed went to visit family and friends for the summer holidays. It was only on the return to the UK that border guards reported a problem.

In the mainstream news coverage, the case was resolved when Mohamed was issued with a temporary travel document enabling him to be reunited with his mother – following pressure from both MPs and journalists. The final outcome for Mohamed and his mother was not made public.

What did emerge more quietly in legal analysis was that this is not an isolated case (Hickman, 2018). The problem with Mohamed's status derived from the marital status of his mother. Both of Mohamed's parents were legally resident in Britain at the time of his birth, and his biological father's name was entered on his birth certificate. His parents assumed that he qualified for British citizenship because of having one parent who was 'a British citizen or has settled status (i.e. the right to remain in the UK permanently) at the time of [his] birth' (Hickman, 2018). Mohamed would qualify through his father, who was a British citizen, and it was on this basis that his passport was issued. The problem arose because in British citizenship law, it is the husband of the mother who counts as the 'father' for citizenship purposes – and not the biological father. Keita was still married to another man, who was not a British citizen; they were separated, and he was living in Guinea (Crisp and McCann, 2018). This was what the Home Office had discovered, and on this basis had revoked Mohamed's citizenship lawfully, though perhaps not fairly. Other cases where citizenship has been denied on the same principle exist; one case heard around the same time in court prompted a judge to make a 'Declaration of Incompatibility' stating that the legal situation is incompatible with human rights law and should be changed by government (Hickman, 2018). While the British Nationality Act 1981 made it possible to receive British nationality through one's mother as well as one's father, it retained this patriarchal attachment to marriage, which expects a mother to be in a married relationship with the father of her children.

It is not clear how Mohamed's parents' marital status 'came to light' at the Home Office. It is worth noting, however, that it is not only in this situation that the apparently anachronistic importance of marital status determines residence and citizenship rights. Civil partnership and established non-marital (but evidentially cohabiting, coupled and romantic) relationships are now considered valid family connections in immigration applications to the UK. However, the marriage route still remains the 'safest' in terms of convincing authorities of a valid and legitimate connection – hence the Home Office's fascination with the idea of 'sham marriages' (Wemyss et al., 2018). While marriage and family continue to be considered valid reasons for transgressing national borders, the policing of the 'truth' of the romantic relationships underpinning marriage contracts becomes a concern of the migration-minimising state. In the UK, the Home Office has demonstrated this through its high-profile and militarised raids on wedding ceremonies, often in the company of local journalists who will publicise further the government interest in identifying the absence of true love (Jones et al., 2017: 69; see also Yeo, this volume).

There are countless examples of the way in which gendered and racialised familial relations are policed as a way of enforcing (trans)national borders, often reinforcing potentially repressive relations within the intimate family: the privileging of family reunification as a means of attaining residence in a territory; discriminatory income thresholds for being allowed to bring a foreign spouse into a territory; the strange logic of the 'Surinder Singh' route to family reunification in the UK through which British citizens could avoid the income threshold otherwise required to bring their non-EU spouse to join them by moving to another EU country and becoming qualifying European nationals; the 'primary purpose rule' in the UK which, between 1983 and 1997, required applicants for family reunification visas to demonstrate 'that the marriage was not entered into primarily to obtain admission to the United Kingdom' (Immigration Rules as cited in Young Justice, 1993: 3); the barbaric 'virginity testing' of South Asian women seeking UK visas, to ascertain whether they were 'really' new brides; the recognition (or not) of same-sex marriage within immigration regimes; the rejection of asylum claims grounded on homophobic persecution on the basis of a judge's assessment of a claimant's sexuality and relationships; and the mobilisation of claims to respectability and stability of family relationships by those who would otherwise question the institution's conservatism, in order to attain geographical security (Lutz, 1997; Chávez, 2013; Sirriyeh, 2015; Wemyss et al., 2018; Griffiths, 2021).

Until now, I have discussed the crossing of borders largely through a lens of entering (or being rejected from) belonging to a particular/new trans/national family. However, another way in which family practices and lived experiences of bordering are parallel is that one can be a member of more than one family (intimate or national) at once – and that this multiple membership itself, while mundane, can also fundamentally bring into question some of the claims about absolute loyalty or belonging that lie at the base of both institutions.

Dual nationalities: citizens of the world/nowhere

Talking about family is personal. So let me give a personal example. My maternal grandfather came to the UK from Germany in 1938, when he was 12, travelling with his parents from Nuremberg where, had they stayed, they would not have survived. Once in England, they were all made stateless by the removal of German citizenship from all Jews by the Nazi government. Later they were naturalised as British citizens. As I discovered after the Brexit vote, this fortunate escape from unspeakable consequences had become my own opportunity to acquire ongoing EU citizenship, whatever happened to UK membership.

It was only after the referendum that I found out that descendants of those Jews, trade unionists and others who had been deprived of German citizenship between 1933 and 1945 were entitled to 'restoration of citizenship', as a form of cross-generational reparation from post-war German governments. I learnt some German at school but had always felt uneasy visiting Germany because of this family history, and doubt that I would have pursued this citizenship at all if it had not been for the threat of Brexit.

The number of British people seeking restitution of German citizenship as I have increased dramatically since the Brexit vote – from around 20 per year before 2015 to 3,380 in the two years following the referendum (Harpin, 2018). There has been some news coverage of this, in which people affected tend to emphasise either their wish to travel freely and maintain EU rights after Brexit, or rediscovering their family history and roots as German Jews (BBC One, 2017). The central motivation for me was less the ability to skip passport queues than a feeling of threat – perhaps irrational, but viscerally felt. The feeling of the walls closing in; the feeling of the necessity of collecting as many passports as possible in case of the need to flee.

While many non-UK citizens from other EU countries are feeling uncertain about their ability to stay in the UK, many UK citizens are considering whether they will be forced to stay, whether they want to or not, in a place that may continue to change in unanticipated ways. That latter group of people may say 'lucky you!' in response to my explaining that I am a dual British-German citizen now. Indeed, it is a privilege to now hold not one but two of the world's most 'powerful passports' in terms of mobility through visa-free travel (Passport Index, 2019). But I am not sure if luck is the right word. What is? The instinct to apply for 'restitution' of my German citizenship was born of fear, possibility and a cheeky desire to play the insane citizenship system at its own game. The absurdity of having both passports when I have no desire to live in Germany with all its hauntings, or away from the UK with its more familiar ghosts. The question about what my Grandpa would have thought of it. The absurdity of applying for restitution of a citizenship I have never had, when without the removal of it from my grandparent neither my mother nor I could exist. The idea of being grateful my great-grandparents had to leave behind their home, friends and belongings to survive; the idea of not being grateful that they were able to when so many others could not escape.

This is all part of a complicated, entangled family legacy, a European legacy and a European family legacy. But, at present, my citizenship and residency are not in question. For me, dual nationality is an option, an opportunity. But I gained it at the same time that others are finding that dual nationality – or even just eligibility for it – puts them at risk of having one citizenship removed, or even of being rendered stateless. The legal processes that have enabled this denial of one membership of national family, casting out by reinstating another, has been documented by Nisha Kapoor (2018) in her work on understanding the counter-terror matrix, and it has been brought to public attention by the case of Shamima Begum (see also chapters by Prabhat and by Yeo, this volume).

Begum, a British teenager, travelled to Syria in 2015 at the age of 15 with two friends of the same age, planning to join the Islamic State (IS) militant group. Four years later, she was found in a Syrian refugee camp by a *Times* journalist and her presence highly publicised – as was the imminent birth of her third child. At 19, two of her children had already died in refugee camps, and her Dutch husband – an IS fighter – was being held in Kurdish detention in Syria.

Begum told journalists she wished to return to the UK with her child, but, following successive frontpage headlines such as 'No Regrets, No Remorse, No Entry' (*The Sun*, 15 February) and 'Jihadi Bride Wants Baby on NHS' (*Metro*, 15 February), British Home Secretary Sajid Javid revoked her UK citizenship; she was no longer considered part of the British/European family ('You're Up Brit Creek', *The Star*, 20 February). Nor was her baby son, who died at a few days old. This was a populist move, linked to the outrage at Begum's apparent involvement in IS. However, it was controversial in less populist milieus for two main reasons: firstly, the removal of her British citizenship made her stateless – an action forbidden in both UK law and the Universal Declaration of Human Rights; secondly, as a child her involvement in IS was the result of abuse, meriting her protection (Yusuf and Swann, 2019). The statelessness question was argued on a technicality – that because Begum's mother was 'believed to be' a Bangladeshi national, Begum was entitled to apply for Bangladeshi citizenship until her 21st birthday (BBC News, 2019). Since she had made no such application, she was made stateless by Javid's actions; the Bangladeshi government made it known they would reject any application from her. What we see here is that fundamental tenets of human rights law, established as principles of European (and global) life after the Nazi Holocaust, are not maintained for those who are deemed not European *enough*. National citizenship – like family – is not a 'question of where you feel you belong', but a question of power. It is a racialised and gendered power to exclude individuals and groups from not only (trans)national family belonging on the basis of tracing intimate family genealogies that trump individual lives but, through this, to exclude them from humanity.

It is important to put this case in conversation with German attempts at reparation through restitution of citizenship to descendants. Both illustrate how membership of a (trans)national family is both dependent on and analogous to membership of the intimate family, and that how a person 'feels' may not allow then to be part of either kind of family if (parts of) that family rejects them. This is reinforced by the revelation that following the post-referendum rise in applications for restitution of German citizenship, the High Commission began refusing applications, often on the basis that citizenship could only be passed through the paternal line in German law until 1953 (Connolly, 2019).

Real families

> We … asked people what they thought the 'family' was, and they said the usual things – 2.4 children and a mum and dad, and so on. And then we asked them about their own families, and it was very different: 'Oh, it's just me and my mum.' (Wearing quoted in Aspden, 2014)

The metaphor of The European Family' is very real, both as a post-national form of belonging and an intimate relation governed by post-national EU regulations and enforcement. Calls like that reproduced by Tillmans, to a particular and bounded solidarity which leaves the idea of 'family' unquestioned, form part of that regulation and exclusion, even when the intention is something like the opposite – and even when the author is someone who has elsewhere explored more boundary-blurring forms of intimacy or family (e.g. Tillmans, 1992, 1993). The 'question of where you feel you belong' is not the simple personal choice or affiliation implied by Tillmans' poster, but something regulated by power and privilege that is shaped through forces of class, race, gender, sexuality, history and nationality.

Membership and full recognition within this family is at the expense of others who are not part of the family. Attempts to join are rebuffed as an intrinsic part of maintaining a feeling of belonging – and power – for existing members. But are there other ways of constituting family as a form of non-exclusive connection?

Gillian Wearing won the Turner Prize in 1997, three years before Tillmans. In the years since then, family and relationships have become a major theme of her work. This extends to a number of her pieces, but here it is particularly relevant to focus on three of them: *Family Monument/A Typical Trentino Family* (2007), *A Real Birmingham Family* (2014) and *A Real Danish Family* (2017) (Figures 8.2, 8.3 and 8.4). Through each of these interventions, Wearing has engaged in studies of the contested nature of belonging, place and connection through a seemingly simple device of constructing a bronze sculpture as a monument to local family. My suggestion is

Figure 8.2 Gillian Wearing, *A Typical Trentino Family*, 2009. Bronze on marble base. © Gillian Wearing, courtesy Galleria Civica di Arte Contemporanea, Trento, Italy and Maureen Paley, London

Figure 8.3 Gillian Wearing, *A Real Birmingham Family*, 2014. Bronze. © Gillian Wearing, courtesy Ikon Gallery, Birmingham and Maureen Paley, London

that these engagements provide a more capacious understanding of connections across, within and regardless of borders, while also drawing attention to the wider wounds from which the Brexit debate can distract. While my attention to Tillmans' work begins with a metaphor of family which I have tethered back to empirical families, Wearing's work starts with empirical families but ties them to bigger questions of place, connection and belonging. In her first piece in this series, she worked with a gallery in Trento, Italy, to engage with local concerns about the demise of the nuclear family and falling birth rates. To explore these questions, a statistical profile of the 'typical' family in the city was put together (a heterosexual married couple with two children), and families fitting that profile were invited to audition to be cast as a bronze statue for public display.

After the Trento piece, Wearing wanted to explore less the 'typical' family, but 'real families'. It was in the Birmingham and Danish pieces that the project developed in more expansive ways. Foremost, candidates to become the 'real family' cast in bronze simply had to identify themselves as a family; they could be a group of people constructed in any way (or a single person), as long as they self-identified as family. This in itself invited a contemplation of the various meanings of 'family', as we can see from the statement from Wearing quoted above. Further, the tying of each project to a place identity

Figure 8.4 Gillian Wearing, *A Real Danish Family*, 2017. Bronze and oil paint. SMK – National Gallery of Denmark, Copenhagen. © Gillian Wearing, courtesy SMK, Copenhagen and Maureen Paley, London

(whether city or nation) invited an examination of what such belonging might mean. Where this element might easily have created precisely the kind of exclusions I have critiqued around the idea of The EUropean Family above, in practice a more historically and sociologically minded recognition of shifting belongings was able to prevail, in dialogue between the artists, curators, the 'judges' invited to help choose the final families, and the accompanying TV shows, events and their audiences (Fabricius et al., 2017). Though the statue often appears as the focus of each of these projects, the process of engaging 'real families' and a debate about belonging and representation, through the selection of the family, is really at the heart of each work.

For *A Real Birmingham Family*, Wearing encouraged a broad and open idea of family and also an emphasis on belonging to a place (the city of Birmingham). The family chosen were two sisters, Roma and Emma Jones, and their two sons (and Emma's pregnancy bump). Ikon Gallery, through which the project ran, stated that 'No limits were placed on how the twenty-first[-]century family might define itself' (Ikon, 2014) and the sisters said:

> Our family is made up of two sisters who are single parents that support each other and play a major part in each other's lives. We have lived in Birmingham all our lives, in many different areas across the city. Being mixed race we feel at home here as it's so diverse and multicultural.
>
> ... We feel it highlights the fact 'family' is an indestructible bond between people that is universal. It doesn't matter how it is made up. (Jones family quoted in Authi, 2013)

This challenge to the idea of the nuclear family differed from the statue built in the original *Family Monument* project in Trento, which had focused on statistical norms and finding a final 'perfect family', as one newspaper described it (Drake, 2007). Even in the statue of the nuclear family of the Giulianis, there was challenge to the fixity of local belonging, with the group including a Greek wife, an Italian husband, their daughter, son and dog. Wearing made clear that one motivation for developing a similar project in her hometown of Birmingham was to move from the perfect family to a real family and highlighting a variety of forms families can take (Brown, 2014).

The beyond-the-nuclear-family approach appeared to be in retreat in the following work, the 2017 *A Real Danish Family*, which resulted in a statue of Yenny and Michael Lysholm Thorsen and their child. However, the apparent nuclear family ideal was subverted, in that the decision-makers emphasised the Lysholm Thorsens' story: Yenny became pregnant within weeks of them meeting, and they decided to marry quickly to become parents while recognising their relationship may not last forever. This seemed to please both marriage enthusiasts and 'modernisers' identifying the contingency of family units. Further, this Real Family also emphasised quietly the transnational making of Danish families: Yenny was born in Colombia and grew up in Denmark, adopted by white Danish parents; Michael was born to Danish parents living in Italy.

What these Real Families offer is not only an engagement with the variety of family structures and their change over time (which is also evident in the statues themselves, with both Emma Jones and Yenny Thorsen pregnant when they posed). They also gesture, perhaps less visibly, to the ways in which families and belonging are made up across place and time, even when a particular family is embedded in a particular place (Jones and Jackson, 2014). As the curators' publication from *A Real Danish Family* notes, not only are people in families made up of connections across places and times, but creating the *Real Danish Family* involved global connections including a British artist, Danish families and judges, a sculptor in London and a bronze casting workshop in China (Fabricius et al., 2017: 45).

More than Brexit wounds

Perhaps Tillmans and Wearing would see themselves as having similar conceptions of the family: Tillmans, I am sure, would argue that his call to the 'European family' we are all in was intended as an inclusive one. It was, after all, part of an explicitly political intervention with an impulse to maintaining transnational relationships. But as outlined above, the weight of the signification of 'The European Family' is too heavily racialised, both in symbolism and in continuing legal, institutional and everyday practices, for this message to be an inclusive or liberatory one. What Wearing's work discussed here offers and Tillmans' anti-Brexit work does not is an opening to question the (located) family – without necessarily jettisoning anything of worth it may contain. This is not simply a result of the end process of the families chosen and cast in static bronze, but in the conversation about making and remaking families, transnational families, queer families, race, marriage and time.

Tillmans' comments on the nature of belonging and connection he and others find in the European Union project were underlined by comments he made on his 'Anti-Brexit' blog, such as: 'We have in the last decades become a European family, with much less dividing us than connecting us' (Tillmans, 2016b). This statement presaged the 'we have more in common than what divides us' sentiment which became associated with British Member of Parliament Jo Cox after her assassination at the hands of an anti-EU white supremacist misogynist in June 2016. Like the More in Common project to memorialise Cox, Tillmans' politics are moderate rather than radical or revolutionary (Jones, 2019). Tillmans told *The Guardian* newspaper in 2016: 'I'm an activist for moderation … I have lived here for 26 years and contributed to British taxes … I have been the recipient of the Britain's biggest art prize … So, I think I'm allowed to speak on something I believe passionately in' (Tillmans quoted in O'Hagan, 2016). This appeal to the narrative of the good and worthwhile migrant, rather than a claim to universal rights, matches his calls for solidarity with 'refugees from terror and war' (Tillmans, 2016b), which similarly remain mired in tropes of undeserving vs. deserving travellers (signalled by refugees), with less attention to the complications of the journeys of those whose movement is neither EU sanctioned nor within the narrow scope of the recognised refugee (Jones et al., 2017: 120–140).

The problem with such a position is the same as the problem with the call to The European Family – most specifically to the definite article in this phrase, which reinforces an idea of an exclusive and identifiably bordered European ideal, which necessarily cuts out other possibilities. This contrasts with a reading of Tillmans' background images to his EU posters, 'photographic images of horizon lines between sea, cloud and sky', as about 'the non-solidity of borders speak[ing] to the predicament of the political situation we are in' (Demircan, 2016: 35). Perhaps there was possibility there for a more encompassing response of solidarity rather than solidity; but the nature of engaging with a political moment and its hegemonic insider/outsider logics lends itself to reproducing the enclosure of The European Family rather than the possibilities of a less bordered connection.

My suggestion is that the idea of belonging to a/the European family can only begin to be an inclusive vision if, as in these works by Wearing, we take as our starting point the lived experience of actual families in/across/between Europe. That is, if we recognise that families are partial, shifting, separated, traumatic, as well as connected, whole, comforting – and that the same goes for nationhood. The Brexit moment's shifts in dual nationality and hence dual allegiance within/across/outside 'The European Family' are a direct response to The European Family's own closures and containments, but also rely on a re-awakening or re-evaluating of transnational and trans-historical familial connection. The 'question of where you feel you belong' can contradict – yet still co-exist with – power structures that allocate belonging.

In examining some non-normative examples of European families, I do not intend to reclaim a celebratory notion of this concept. Rather, the cases I outline are about trauma, fear and disruption as much as attachment, comfort and support. The point is, these experiences of family are as much a part of the fabric of 'EUropean' experience as any other; indeed, they haunt the imagined ideal of a cosy, safe, home which EUropean family conjures and allows for only some.

Naturalisation and denaturalisation

As many contributions to this volume also discuss (see, for example, chapters by Prabhat, Yeo, and Sredanovic, this volume), Brexit has not just changed the citizenship rights available to UK and EU citizens, but has also led to many citizens seeking to change their citizenship to maintain or extend rights in ways they would not otherwise have considered. This draws attention to the ways in which the taken-for-granted nature of national belonging and rights to belong are always contingent and uneven. Read in this way, the recurrence of the term 'naturalisation' throughout the volume in its meaning of obtaining full citizenship of a place in which one resides is particularly striking. The 'natural' in naturalisation takes us to ideas that there is something inherently natural, taken for granted, of essence in having full citizenship rights in the place where one lives. And yet the process itself belies that this is not the case by the very existence of the possibility, or necessity in many cases, of changing this status, and doing so only with the permission of the state, to which one must prove one meets particular (sometimes opaque, often arbitrary) requirements. As I and other authors in this volume have discussed, the naturalisation process involves either detaching oneself from another nationality (or having been detached in the case of being stateless) or adding an additional legalistic allegiance/belonging which may be seen as competitive and in itself draw attention to the mythical nature of the ways in which national citizenship is treated as if exclusive, fundamental and timeless. And that fundamental unchangeability of nationality/citizenship is further undermined in practice by the ways in which naturalised citizens (or specifically, at present, Muslim dual nationals in the UK) have a less powerful British citizenship than others, in that their government may be able to sever their connection at will.

Much like Wearing's distinction between idealised family and 'Real Family' (i.e. family as lived connection rather than fixed ideal type), empirical, lived citizenship is not natural nor fixed or dependable, though in many cases it may feel so. And Brexit has brought both of these existing fragilities and myths to light in various ways.

Since the referendum and increasingly since withdrawal, applications to revise citizenships, to add British citizenship to existing EU status, to add another EU citizenship to British status, or to relocate in order to avoid such realignment, have increased in ways that both highlight how integrated Tillmans' 'European family' is in terms of cross-border living, but also how fragile that integration is in the face of material and political shifts. The effects of this on 'real families' can be seen, for example, in research by Zambelli et al. (2023) with multi-status families (i.e.

self-defined family units in which the members hold different citizenship or migration status) living in the UK and/or the EU in the wake of Brexit, for whom changes to residence rights have changed for some but not all family members, creating 'an externally imposed but deeply intimate division' (5) and situations in which new dependencies are created through reliance on attachment to one family members' status for other family members to be able to remain together. Even for those families who might all be able to attain settled status, the uncertainty around what this might mean and how long it might last (see Sredanovic, this volume) meant that life plans and expectations might be fundamentally shifted. Here, the idea of a family as somehow internally the same, and permanent, like the idea of a nation or group of nations as fundamentally the same and permanent, was starkly revealed as fantasy by the tectonic shifts of Brexit. This is certainly not to say that these fragilities, inconsistencies or ironies were new – but that they became more visible to a greater number of people, harder to look away from, and also perhaps affected a greater number of people in a sudden shock rather than in the usual, slow contradiction of everyday life.

What Brexit has perhaps naturalised is the dislocation of taken-for-granted ideas of family/familial-like affinities within and beyond the nation/family of nations. That these ruptures coincide with the visibility of the Windrush Scandal and political citizenship deprivation makes it clear, for those willing to see, that this condition is not novel or specific to Brexit shifts, but part of an ongoing low rumble of differential inclusions and exclusions. I am not suggesting that this violently shifting dis/inclusion of rights and belonging is somehow 'natural', but rather that it is an underlying condition of the current order of nation statehoods, which the EU project did not diminish. Attention to the ways in which citizenship (or its lack, or duplication) is lived and unequal is as important to understanding and reimagining connection as is greater attention to the lived (rather than the imagined) family and all its contradictions.

Notes

1 'Between Bridges is a foundation (est. 2017) for the advancement of democracy, international understanding, the arts and LGBT rights by Wolfgang Tillmans.' See: www.betweenbridges.net/anti-brexit-campaign.php (accessed 11 June 2020).

2 The capitalisation EUrope/EUropean is used to acknowledge that the European Union does not include all of Europe, but in fact erects borders within the continent around its members (see, for example, Grzymski, 2019).

References

Ahmed, Sara (2007) *The Cultural Politics of Emotion*. Durham, NC: Duke University Press.

Ahmed, Sara, Castada, Claudia, Fortier, Anne-Marie and Sheller, Mimi (eds) (2003) *Uprootings/Regroundings: Questions of Home and Migration*. London: Berg.

Aspden, Peter (2014) 'Statue of a family: By Gillian Wearing'. *FT Magazine*, 18 July. www.ft.com/content/171e7030-0d3c-11e4-bcb2-00144feabdc0 (accessed 11 June 2020).

Authi, Jasbir (2013) 'Meet the Joneses – the real Birmingham family of two single mums and sons chosen for library statue'. *Birmingham Mail*, 28 August. www.birminghammail.co.uk/news/local-news/meet-joneses---real-birmingham-5794999 (accessed 11 June 2020).

Barnabas Fund (2019) 'Answer to prayer as House of Lords committee calls on House to debate Relationships and Sex Education law after receiving hundreds of letters of concern'. *Christians in Crisis International Ministry*, 3 April. https://christiansincrisis.net/persecution-news/archives/259-2019-april/9836-answer-to-prayer-as-house-of-lords-committee-callson-house-to-debate-relationships-and-sex-educationlaw-after-receiving-hundreds-of-letters-of-concern.html (accessed 11 June 2020).

Barrett, Michèle and McIntosh, Mary (1982) *The Anti-Social Family*. London: NLB.

BBC News (2018) 'British boy "stateless" in Belgium after passport rejected'. *BBC News*, 6 September. www.bbc.co.uk/news/uk-englandsouth-yorkshire-45433403 (accessed 11 June 2020).

BBC News (2019) 'Shamima Begum will not be allowed here, Bangladesh says'. *BBC News*, 21 February. www.bbc.co.uk/news/uk-47312207 (accessed 11 June 2020).

BBC One (2017) 'British Jews, German passports' (prod. by Richard Pearson and Mike Smith). *BBC One*, 2 May. www.bbc.co.uk/programmes/b08mfgsj (accessed 11 June 2020).

Bhambra, Gurminder K. (2017) 'Locating Brexit in the pragmatics of race, citizenship and empire'. In William Outhwaite (ed.) *Brexit: Sociological Responses*. London: Anthem Press, pp. 91–100.

Bhattacharyya, Gargi (2018) *Rethinking Racial Capitalism: Questions of Reproduction and Survival*. London: Rowman and Littlefield.

Brown, Mark (2014) 'Ordinary Birmingham family to be immortalised in city centre statue'. *The Guardian*, 29 October. www.theguardian.com/artanddesign/2014/oct/29/ordinary-birmingham-family-immortalised-statue-gillian-wearing (accessed 11 June 2020).

Chávez, Karma R. (2013) *Queer Migration Politics: Activist Rhetoric and Coalitional Possibilities*. Chicago, IL: University of Illinois Press.

Connolly, Kate (2019) 'Descendants of Jews who fled Nazis unite to fight for German citizenship'. *The Guardian*, 10 July. www.theguardian.com/world/2019/jul/10/jews-fled-nazis-descendents-german-citizenship (accessed 11 June 2020).

Crisp, James and McCann, Kate (2018) 'Six-year-old British-born boy left stranded and "stateless" after Home Office revokes his passport'. *The Telegraph*, 5 September. www.telegraph.co.uk/news/2018/09/05/six-year-old-british-born-boy-left-stranded-stateless-home-office (accessed 11 June 2020).

Cvetkovich, Ann (2012) *Depression: A Public Feeling*. Durham, NC: Duke University Press.

de Noronha, Luke (2019) 'Deportation, racism and multi-status Britain: Immigration control and the production of race in the present'. *Ethnic and Racial Studies* 42(14): 2413–2430.

Demircan, Saim (2016) 'Wolfgang Tillmans and the EU'. *Art Monthly*, June, 397: 35.

Drake, Cathryn (2007) 'Gillian Wearing, 24 March–10 June 2007, Galleria Civica di Arte Contemporanea, Trento'. *Map Magazine*, 11 September. https://mapmagazine.co.uk/gillian-wearing (accessed 11 June 2020).

Emejulu, Akwugo (2016) 'On the hideous whiteness of Brexit: "Let us be honest about our past and our present if we truly seek to dismantle white supremacy" '. *Verso Blog*, 28 June. www.versobooks.com/blogs/news/2733-on-the-hideous-whiteness-of-brexit-let-us-be-honest-about-our-past-and-our-present-if-we-truly-seek-to-dismantle-white-supremacy (accessed 11 June 2020).

Fabricius, Jacob, Torp, Mariane and Bogh, Mikkel (2017) *Gillian Wearing: Family Stories*. Berlin: Hatje Cantz.

Favell, Adrian (2019) 'Brexit: A requiem for the postnational society?' *Global Discourse* 9(1): 157–68.

Goldberg, David Theo (2006) 'Racial Europeanization'. *Ethnic and Racial Studies* 29(2): 331–364.

Graff, Agnieszka, Kapur, Ratna and Walters, Suzanna Danuta (2019) 'Introduction: Gender and the rise of the global right'. *Signs: Journal of Women in Culture and Society* 44(3): 541–560.

Griffiths, Melanie (2021) '"My passport is just my way out of here". Mixed-immigration status families, immigration enforcement and the citizenship implications'. *Identities: Global Studies in Culture and Power* 28(1): 18–36.

Grzymski, Jan (2019) 'Seeing like a EUropean border: Limits of the EUropean borders and space'. *Global Discourse* 9(1): 135–151.

Harpin, Lee (2018) 'Surge in British Jews applying for German citizenship since Brexit'. *The Jewish Chronicle*, 21 October. www.thejc.com/news/uk-news/surge-in-british-jews-applying-for-german-citizenship-since-brexit-1.471269 (accessed 11 June 2020).

Haynes, Jayne (2019) 'Protests, smears and a headteacher's tears: How LGBT equality at Anderton Park school divided a community'. *Birmingham Mail*, 25 June. www.birminghammail.co.uk/news/midlands-news/protests-smears-headteachers-tears-how-16333108 (accessed 11 June 2020).

Hickman, Karma (2018) 'Plight of stranded British-born boy highlights citizenship discrimination'. *Bishop & Sewell*, 6 September. www.bishopandsewell.co.uk/2018/09/06/plight-of-stranded-british-born-boy-mohamed-bangour/ (accessed 11 June 2020).

Ikon (2014) 'A Real Birmingham Family'. *Ikon*. www.ikon-gallery.org/event/a-real-birmingham-family (accessed 11 June 2020).

Jones, Hannah (2019) 'More in common: The domestication of misogynist white supremacy and the assassination of Jo Cox'. *Ethnic and Racial Studies* 42(14): 2431–2449.

Jones, Hannah and Jackson, Emma (eds) (2014) *Stories of Cosmopolitan Belonging: Emotion and Location*. London: Routledge.

Jones, Hannah, Gunaratnam, Yasmin, Bhattacharyya, Gargi, Davies, William, Dhaliwal, Sukhwant, Forkert, Kirsten, Jackson, Emma and Saltus, Roiyah (2017) *Go Home? The Politics of Immigration Controversies*. Manchester: Manchester University Press.

Kapoor, Nisha (2018) *Deport, Deprive, Extradite: 21st Century State Extremism*. London: Verso.
Lendaro, Annalisa (2016) 'A "European Migrant Crisis"? Some thoughts on Mediterranean borders'. *Studies in Ethnicity and Nationalism* 16(1): 148–157.
Lutz, Helma (1997) 'The limits of European-ness: Immigrant women in Fortress Europe'. *Feminist Review* 57: 93–111.
O'Hagan, Sean (2016) 'Wolfgang Tillmans: "I see myself as a product of European cultural exchange" '. *The Guardian*, 8 May. www.theguardian.com/artanddesign/2016/may/08/wolfgang-tillmans-eu-referendum-remain-campaign-posters (accessed 11 June 2020).
Passport Index (2019) 'Global passport power rank 2019'. *Passport Index*. www.passportindex.org/byRank.php (accessed 11 June 2020).
Piacentini, Teresa (2016) 'Refugee solidarity in the everyday'. *Soundings* 64: 57–61.
Puar, Jasbir K. (2007) *Terrorist Assemblages: Homonationalism in Queer Times*. Durham, NC: Duke University Press.
Reuters (2018) 'Hungary will defend traditional families, stop demographic decline, Orban says'. *Reuters*, 25 May. www.reuters.com/article/us-hungary-orban-idUSKCN1IQ0V8 (accessed 11 June 2020).
Sirriyeh, Ala (2015) '"All you need is love and £18,600": Class and the new UK family migration rules'. *Critical Social Policy* 35(2): 228–247.
Stoler, Ann L. (1989) 'Making empire respectable: The politics of race and sexual morality in 20th-century colonial cultures'. *American Ethnologist* 16(4): 634–660.
Stoler, Ann L. (2002) *Carnal Knowledge and Imperial Power*. Oakland, CA: University of California Press.
Tillmans, Wolfgang (1992) 'Like brother like sister: A fashion story'. *i-D Magazine* 110, November: 80–87.
Tillmans, Wolfgang (1993) *Lutz, Alex, Suzanne and Christoph on the Beach*. London: Maureen Paley Gallery.
Tillmans, Wolfgang (2016a) 'EU campaign: Vote remain 23 June'. *Wolfgang Tillmans*. http://tillmans.co.uk/images/stories/misc/EU%20Campaign%20Wolfgang%20Tillmans%20-%20Updated_16.06.pdf (accessed 11 June 2020).
Tillmans, Wolfgang (2016b) 'Statement from 26 May 2016'. *Wolfgang Tillmans*. https://tillmans.co.uk/campaign-eu#mayx26 (accessed 11 June 2020).
Virdee, Satnam (2014) *Racism, Class and the Racialized Outsider*. Basingstoke: Palgrave.
Volpe, Sam (2019) 'Hackney faith leaders "shouldn't have signed harmful LGBT+ letter" '. *Hackney Gazette*, 25 April. www.hackneygazette.co.uk/news/22933963.hackney-faith-leaders-shouldnt-signed-harmful-lgbt-letter/ (accessed 18 July 2020).
Wardle, Huon and Obermuller, Laura (2018) 'The Windrush Generation'. *Anthropology Today* 34(4): 3–4.
Wekker, Gloria (2016) *White Innocence: Paradoxes of Colonialism and Race*. Durham, NC: Duke University Press.
Wemyss, Georgie, Yuval-Davis, Nira and Cassidy, Kathryn (2018) '"Beauty and the beast": Everyday bordering and "sham marriage" discourse'. *Political Geography* 66: 151–160.
Young Justice (1993) *The Primary Purpose Rule: A Rule with No Purpose. London: Justice*. https://files.justice.org.uk/wp-content/uploads/2015/01/06171917/PrimaryPurposeRuleRuleWithNoPurpose.pdf (accessed 10 June 2024).

Yusuf, Hanna and Swann, Steve (2019) 'Shamima Begum: Lawyer says teen was "groomed"'. *BBC News*, 31 May. www.bbc.co.uk/news/uk-48444604 (accessed 18 July 2020).

Zambelli, Elena, Benson, Michaela and Sigona, Nando (2023) 'Brexit rebordering, sticky relationships and the production of mixed-status families'. *Sociology*, OnlineFirst. https://doi.org/10.1177/00380385231194966

Conclusion: the long Brexit

Djordje Sredanovic and Bridget Byrne

There is a risk that Brexit can be viewed as a novel break point in the history of citizenship and migration. Yet, across this book we have shown how the Brexit process should be understood within longer histories of changes in migration and citizenship policies both in the UK and in the EU. Prabhat's chapter shows the parallels between the withdrawal of legal status from both British and EU citizens and the earlier withdrawal of status from Commonwealth citizens. Yeo further links the Brexit process with the reinforcement of denaturalisation powers in the UK. Barrios Aquino highlights the continuity between the Brexit process and the restrictive turn towards the acquisition of British citizenship in the early 2000s (a process that had parallels in much of Europe – see Rea et al., 2018), while Jones discusses how the ideas of membership intertwined with Brexit find a place in a longer history of defining families through gender and race.

At the same time, Brexit has undoubtably touched the complex system of EUropean (cf. Isin and Saward, 2013) political memberships: it has changed the relationship between the UK and the EU, but it has also had consequences for a wider range of supranational institutions, from the European Economic Area to Schengen, to the Common Travel Area between the UK and the Republic of Ireland, with further implications for the Good Friday Agreement. Nas and Baykal's chapter shows one such consequence of Brexit – the disapplication in the UK of the Ankara Agreement and the other agreements that have established a range of rights for Turkish workers and their families across the EU. The changing nature of EU/UK relations has wide-ranging consequences, as shown across different chapters focusing on the UK (Rzepnikowska, Barrios Aquino), the EU (MacClancy) and both (Prabhat, Nas and Baykal, Sredanovic, Jones). Sredanovic and MacClancy in particular highlight how both EU27 citizens in the UK and Britons in the rest of the EU had often relied on EU freedom of movement to manage their transnational lives, and that Brexit has disrupted such practices.

Given the wide-ranging consequences of Brexit for different groups, fears and countermeasures are a further theme crossing the whole book. Political mobilisation, of Remainers, but to a certain degree also of Leavers, has been one of the answers, as MacClancy's chapter shows for the British in Spain. Naturalisation, both in the UK and in the EU27, is the safest legal way to safeguard part of the rights endangered by Brexit, as both Barrios Aquino and Sredanovic in particular show. However, even citizenship does not give full protection: firstly, Yeo's chapter shows how denaturalisation powers and denaturalisations are on the rise. In addition to this, Barrios Aquino's interviewees did not expect their formal citizenship to make them accepted as British or help them avoid discrimination, while Sredanovic distinguishes between fears linked to formal rights and fears, such as xenophobia or economic crises, that citizenship cannot really protect them from. Similarly, Rzepnikowska' chapter shows the tensions between the loss of rights and growing hostility on the one hand, and the capacity of convivial relations in a neighbourhood to contain the negative impact on the other.

In the following sections of this final chapter, we consider the ways in which inequality and difference have shaped experiences of Brexit. At the same time, we argue that, while we are several years beyond the 2016 referendum, the process of Brexit remains ongoing and far from concluded. We conclude by considering the challenges that this offers to researchers who wish to understand the ongoing and future implications of this complex legal and political process for the legal rights of citizens and migrants.

The internal differences of Brexit

One recurring theme both in the chapters of this book and in the previous literature about Brexit is the attention to the internal differences and inequalities in the impact and experiences of Brexit. Legal status is a first obvious axis of inequality in the experiences of Brexit: being a British, EU27 (or dual) citizen, being a third-country national, having family links with status holders, having naturalised (or having the opportunities for naturalisation – see Sredanovic, 2022, 2023a) or holding permanent or temporary Brexit-specific legal status correspond to different experiences of Brexit. Among EU27 citizens in the UK, nationality is a further factor of differentiation, not only because of the continued freedom of movement for the Irish and the Commonwealth citizenship rights of the Maltese and Cypriots. We discussed in the Introduction how the seniority of accession of one's country changes the perspectives on Brexit (Lulle et al., 2018; Moreh et al., 2020). In addition, in the Introduction, we discussed how the experiences of Brexit are stratified according to race (Benson and Lewis, 2019; Benson, 2020), gender (Dustin et al., 2019), class, migratory history, age and family networks (Lulle et al., 2018; Sredanovic and Della Puppa, 2020,

2023 – see further Antonucci and Varriale, 2020 for a wider theoretical perspective). O'Brien (2021) is among the juridical studies focusing on different vulnerabilities in the context of Brexit. Other, ethnographic, studies have further focused on the specific racialisation of Central and East Europeans (Rzepnikowska, 2019, and in this volume; Sime et al., 2022) and of Roma (Patel et al., 2023), as well as of how Brexit impacts young (Lulle et al., 2018, 2022; Sime et al., 2020, 2022; Moskal and Sime, 2022) and older people (Giner-Monfort and Huete, 2021).

In this section we want to focus further on one dimension that has been less covered by the chapters in this book: the different impact and meaning of Brexit among the countries and territories of the UK. Indeed, the ethnographic work on the UK presented in this book focuses mostly on England (although Sredanovic also conducted interviews in Scotland and, to a lesser degree, Wales), even if we have been mindful of the internal diversity of the UK in building our theoretical frame. Brexit has an impact also beyond what are usually assumed to be the borders of 'Europe', including the introduction of harder borders between British, French and Dutch territories in the Caribbean (Boatcă, 2021). The impact of Brexit on the Crown Dependencies and British Overseas Territories has received limited attention in the literature (but see Mut Bosque, 2020); on the other hand, there has been more attention to the specific impact on Scotland, Wales and Northern Ireland. The greater reliance on EU structural funds, a history of bilateral engagements within the EU framework, and the fact that Scotland and Northern Ireland (differently from England and Wales) have seen majorities for Remain, have brought into focus differences in the impact of Brexit (see e.g. Birrell and Gray, 2017). From a legal point of view, most of the impacts of Brexit are in the field of policies reserved to the national government. The major exception is Northern Ireland: not only, as mentioned in the Introduction, because most people born in Northern Ireland have a claim on the citizenship of the Republic of Ireland, but also because the Good Friday Agreement, on which a large part of the institutional and political architecture of Northern Ireland depends, was created with reference to EU norms (Cochrane, 2020). From a social and political point of view, the devolved nations have even more specificities. In the case of Northern Ireland, the vote has seen the Nationalist/Unionist divide overlap with the Remain/Leave one, with the peace in the area further endangered by issues around the management of the UK/Republic of Ireland border (Cochrane, 2020). While the Northern Ireland Assembly has been deeply divided on Brexit issues and suspended between 2017 and 2020 and again between 2022 and 2024 also due to the fallout from Brexit, the governments of Scotland and, to a certain degree, Wales have been more active in advocating for safeguarding EU norms and the rights of EU27 citizens

(Birrell and Gray, 2017; Pietka-Nykaza et al., 2020). Ethnographic work on the experiences of EU27 citizens in Wales (e.g. Guma and Jones, 2019) has not shown particular differences from the larger number of studies conducted in England, but some of the work conducted in Scotland has shown how the Scottish context, while not free of problematic situations (e.g. Sime et al., 2020), has to a degree contained some of the negative consequences of Brexit (e.g. Kay, 2020; Gawlewicz, 2020). Ethnographic work in border areas of Northern Ireland (Wilson, 2020) has further shown how the importance of EU funding, cross-border economic activity and the fears for peace in Northern Ireland have spurred a Europeanist identity among the population of the areas, as well as some scepticism towards Brexit even among Unionists.

The political perspectives of Brexit

One of the major impacts of the 2016 referendum beyond the citizens' rights perspectives explored in this book has been the consolidation of Eurosceptic and Europhile political orientations in the UK, and the emergence of Leave and Remain identities. We have seen in MacClancy's chapter in this book how these have been important for many British in Spain (and cf. Ferbrache and MacClancy, 2021 for a France/Spain comparison). Beyond that, Brexit has been recognised as central for the 2017 and, even more, the 2019 UK general election (Sobolewska and Ford, 2020). How relevant this division will be in the near future is more difficult to anticipate. At the moment of writing, the Labour Party under Keir Starmer seems to be mostly avoiding the topic of Brexit, given the difficulty for the party in building majorities on the topic in target constituencies. Furthermore, the Brexit process has had a significant impact on UK migration policies beyond those specifically linked to UK/EU migration. Already during the referendum campaign, the Leave side targeted not only the free movement of EU citizens but also the migration of third-country nationals, including the 'Breaking point' poster which attacked the flows of refugees and advocated an exit from the EU in order to close the borders to such flows (see e.g. Abbas, 2019). The outcome of the 2016 referendum did not only bring legitimacy to anti-EU27 (and in particular anti-Eastern European) xenophobia, as discussed in particular by Rzepnikowska in her chapter in this book. It further reinforced a wider range of xenophobic and racist positions, as shown for example by Patel and Connelly (2019) and Hall (2023).

In addition, the Brexit process has seen, as mentioned in the Introduction, a harshening of the wider UK migration policies. While it is difficult to establish exactly how much Brexit has influenced such change in policies, there was a significant acceleration in restrictive policies with the election of Boris Johnson as leader of the Conservative Party in 2019, with restrictive positions continuing with the brief premiership of Liz Truss and then with the premiership of Rishi Sunak. Since 2019, the rhetoric against EU27 citizens has become more hostile. Not only was the end of free movement celebrated with a public campaign in the final months of 2020, but a number of new administrative measures have been taken to the effect of hindering EU27 citizens' access to British citizenship.[1]

However, the recent Conservative governments particularly targeted asylum policies. Such focus is also linked to Brexit: among the other EUropean institutions, the UK has abandoned the Dublin Regulation, which defines the movement of asylum seekers across most of the European Economic Area, and the procedures for the return of asylum seekers to the 'first safe country' (Ibrahim, 2022). One of the consequences has been the increase in arrivals of asylum seekers from France to the UK (including the shift of some arrivals from the Channel Tunnel to arrivals by sea), as well as the interruption of agreements to return the asylum seekers to France. Stopping such arrivals became a priority of recent Conservative governments, expressed by the slogan 'stop the boats' (Morgan and Willmington, 2023). Brexit is far from being the only cause of this development: movements of refugees from France to the UK were significant well before Brexit (and indeed are proof that the Dublin Regulation limits refugees' access to family links and opportunities for settlement – cf. Schuster, 2002), and UK governments have shown hostility towards asylum seekers since at least the 1990s (Stevens, 1992). However, the recent measures taken, from attempts to remove asylum seekers to Rwanda for the duration of the asylum application (Drakeley, 2023), to the use of barges to house asylum seekers, to the Illegal Migration Act 2023 which aims to close access to asylum for most arrivals to the UK (Morgan and Willmington, 2023), all show an acceleration of draconian anti-immigration policies since the Brexit process.

The legacies of Brexit

As discussed in the Introduction and across the chapters of this book, the rights of EU27 citizens in the UK and British citizens in the EU (or at least of those who have not naturalised) have been often managed through ad-hoc solutions. As mentioned in the Introduction, the UK introduced (permanent) settled status for EU27 citizens able to prove a five-year residence and (temporary) pre-settled status for those with less than five years of residence. While pre-settled status has been conceived as due to expire after five years without a settled status application, on 21 December 2022 the High Court decision declared it unlawful to withdraw the status due to the mere absence of a further application (Laffan and Telle, 2023). As a result, the UK government was forced to extend by two years pre-settled statuses that come to expiration (making the status automatically permanent has been considered by the government, but this option has not been clarified at the moment of writing). Regardless of the recent developments regarding pre-settled status, there are limits to the time that can be spent outside the UK before losing the right to return: six months in a year for pre-settled status, five continuous years for settled status. In this sense, if the loss of residence rights has been (for the moment) averted for expiring pre-settled statuses, there are certainly EU27 citizens who have lost their right to reside in the UK by spending prolonged periods abroad. British citizens in the EU have seen different procedures to safeguard their right to stay in the country of residence (cf. More, 2020). In some cases non-compliance (even if unintentional) has led to expulsions, with Sweden being particularly active in this field (O'Carroll and Duncan, 2023). In this case too, British citizens who have moved to another EU state (or to the UK or a third country) have often lost the linked status. In this sense, Brexit has left in its wake both significant populations with legacy statuses linked to Brexit and a more difficult to quantify group of people who have already lost such statuses.

Further, the statuses have extended to third-country nationals who are relatives of EU27 or British citizens.[2] In these cases, the issue is not only holding a legacy status subject to expiration or loss, but also depending on family links to hold this status and being open to miscategorisation (during border controls, but also in accessing rights). Finally, along with the established legacy status holders, new populations of British citizens in the EU and EU27 citizens in the UK are developing within the framework of visa-based immigration. Both in the UK and in the EU, short-term entries are visa-free (but will be subject to electronic travel authorisations by the end of 2024 in the UK and by mid-2025 in the EU), while work and settlement require visas. Along with the potential for creating overstayers on both sides of the Channel, this means that there increasingly will be populations who share a nationality but have significantly different rights depending on the date of arrival (and on whether they have lost the Brexit legacy status in the meantime). As mentioned in the Introduction and Prabhat's chapter, the UK in particular has already seen a major scandal with another legacy status population, with pre-1973 migrants from the Colonies and the Commonwealth (and their children) treated as undocumented in the 'Windrush generation' scandal (Bawdon, 2019; Gentleman, 2019; Shankley and Byrne, 2020). It is in this sense that there is a potential of future miscategorisation and unlawful denial of rights for the holders of Brexit legacy statuses, particularly if, as in the UK, there are no physical IDs to prove one's status (Sredanovic, 2023b).

Future lines of research

The above-mentioned issue of the legacy status holders and of inequal rights among nationals who arrived before and after the end of the transition period is a major question for the long-term consequences of Brexit, and one of the main topics that would need research in the future, both for its policy implications and for the changes brought to migration and mobility between the UK and the EU. More generally speaking, there is still limited research on how Brexit has changed and will change the migratory flows between the UK and the EU. While there have been studies about return and onward migration of those already on the territory before Brexit (e.g. Sredanovic, 2021; Godin and Sigona, forthcoming), we still know little about the new migratory forms and experiences linked to post-Brexit arrivals. Within this general question, while we now have a significant body of work on onward migration to the UK of third-country nationals who had naturalised elsewhere in the EU (cf. Montagna et al., 2021), and some exploration of the answers to Brexit of those already in the UK (Sredanovic and Della Puppa, 2020; Morad et al., 2021; Turcatti and Vargas-Silva, 2022; Formenti, 2023), we know little about how Brexit has disrupted the plans of potential onward migrants with this profile. We further have limited information about the experiences of EEA, non-EU migrants in the UK.

In the case of Britons in the EU, ethnographic studies in particular have focused on a small number of countries – to our knowledge, France, Spain, Belgium and Germany (in addition to MacClancy and Sredanovic in this volume, see MacClancy, 2019; Benson, 2020; Ferbrache and MacClancy, 2020; Kulz, 2022). While Britons were present in smaller numbers in other EU member states, this still means that we have a limited understanding of the differences in such experiences (e.g. those of the British in Sweden, considering also the higher number of expulsions). Finally, the impact of Brexit on third-country nationals, descendants of migrants from other countries and people of colour has been underexplored. Some of the few ethnographic studies of Leavers (Patel and Connelly, 2019; Hall, 2023) have highlighted a general xenophobia and racism rather than a specific hostility against EU migrants. We have one study on the British in the EU looking specifically at the experiences of Britons of colour (Benson and Lewis, 2019), along with some of the above-mentioned studies that have looked at EU27 and British citizens of colour (and/or naturalised before migration) as part of a wider study. Along with this, we also have some studies of the political answers to the referendum and Brexit among the people of colour who had voting rights in the referendum because of their British or Commonwealth citizenship (see Begum, 2023). Beyond these cases, however, the links between race and Brexit have been explored more in theory than empirically.

If we have shown across this book that Brexit is part of longer transformations and histories both on the UK and the EU side, we want to conclude by emphasising that Brexit is far from finished. In these final pages we have highlighted both how the major transformation in UK/EU mobility will have long-term consequences for a variety of groups of people and how Brexit had ripple effects on migration policies and flows beyond the groups directly impacted by Brexit in their formal rights. While the impact of Brexit on citizens' rights has been often sidelined in public discourse, even during the negotiations between the UK and the EU, we invite scholars and the larger public to continue to consider the impact of Brexit on citizens' rights well beyond the already long transition period.

Notes

1 Changes to the guidance documents of the Home Office include not admitting EU settled status as a basis to apply for British citizenship without fulfilling further integration requirements and the need to check the candidate's compliance with EU treaty rights for the ten years before the application.

2 The Brexit experiences of mixed-status families in the UK have been explored by Zambelli et al. (2024), but we still know little of the developments after the end of the transition period.

References

Abbas, Madeline-Sophie (2019) 'Conflating the Muslim refugee and the terror suspect: Responses to the Syrian refugee "crisis" in Brexit Britain'. *Ethnic and Racial Studies* 42(14): 2450–2469.

Antonucci, Lorenza and Varriale, Simone (2020) 'Unequal Europe, unequal Brexit: How intra-European inequalities shape the unfolding and framing of Brexit'. *Current Sociology* 68(1): 41–59.

Bawdon, Fiona (2019) 'Remember when '*Windrush*' was still just the name of a ship?' In Devyani Prabhat (ed.) *Citizenship in Times of Turmoil? Theory, Practice and Policy*. Cheltenham: Edward Elgar Publishing, pp. 173–197.

Begum, Neema (2023) '"The European family? Wouldn't that be the white people?": Brexit and British ethnic minority attitudes towards Europe'. *Ethnic and Racial Studies* 46(15): 3293–3315.

Benson, Michaela (2020) 'Brexit and the classed politics of bordering: The British in France and European belongings'. *Sociology* 54(3): 501–517.

Benson, Michaela and Lewis, Chantelle (2019) 'Brexit, British People of Colour in the EU-27 and everyday racism in Britain and Europe'. *Ethnic and Racial Studies* 42(13): 2211–2228.

Birrell, Derek and Gray, Ann Marie (2017) 'Devolution: The social, political and policy implications of Brexit for Scotland, Wales and Northern Ireland'. *Journal of Social Policy* 46(4): 765–782.

Boatcă, Manuela (2021) 'Thinking Europe otherwise: Lessons from the Caribbean'. *Current Sociology* 69(3): 389–414.

Cochrane, Feargal (2020) *Breaking Peace: Brexit and Northern Ireland.* Manchester: Manchester University Press.

Drakeley, Rhys (2023) Loophole or law-breaking? Rwanda plan's inconsistency with international refugee law. *York Law Review* 4: 141–181.

Dustin, Moira, Ferreira, Nuno and Millns, Susan (eds) (2019) *Gender and Queer Perspectives on Brexit.* Cham: Palgrave Macmillan.

Ferbrache, Fiona and MacClancy, Jeremy (2021) *The Political Agency of British Migrants: Brexit and Belonging.* Abingdon: Routledge.

Formenti, Ambra (2023) 'On the road again: Onward migration and transnational subjectivity among Portuguese-Guinean migrants in Peterborough (UK)'. In Jill Ahrens and Russell King (eds) *Onward Migration and Multi-Sited Transnationalism: Complex Trajectories, Practices and Ties.* Cham: Springer, pp. 219–239.

Gawlewicz, Anna (2020) '"Scotland's different": Narratives of Scotland's distinctiveness in the post-Brexit-vote era'. *Scottish Affairs* 29(3): 321–335.

Gentleman, Amelia (2019) *The Windrush Betrayal: Exposing the Hostile Environment.* London: The Guardian.

Giner-Monfort, Jordi and Huete, Raquel (2021) 'Uncertain sunset lives: British migrants facing Brexit in Spain'. *European Urban and Regional Studies* 28(1): 74–79.

Godin, Marie and Sigona, Nando (forthcoming) 'Infrastructuring exit migration: Social hope and migration decision-making in EU families who left the UK after the 2016 EU referendum'. *The Sociological Review.* https://doi.org/10.1177/00380261231194506

Guma, Taulant and Jones, Rhys (2019) '"Where are we going to go now?" European Union migrants' experiences of hostility, anxiety, and (non-)belonging during Brexit'. *Population, Space and Place* 25(1): e2198.

Hall, Natalie-Anne (2023) 'Trajectories towards political engagement on Facebook around Brexit: Beyond affordances for understanding racist and right-wing populist mobilisations online'. *Sociology* 57(3): 569–585.

Ibrahim, Yasmin (2022) *Migrants and Refugees at UK Borders: Hostility and 'Unmaking' the Human.* Abingdon: Routledge.

Isin, Engin F. and Saward, Michael (eds) (2013) *Enacting European Citizenship.* Cambridge: Cambridge University Press.

Kay, Rebecca (2020) '"You get a better life here": Social in/security and migration in a time of geopolitical transformations'. *Scottish Affairs* 29(3): 305–320.

Kulz, Christy (2022) 'British migrants in Berlin: Negotiating postcolonial melancholia and racialised nationalism in the wake of Brexit'. *Ethnic and Racial Studies* 45(7): 1326–1346.

Laffan, Brigid and Telle, Stefan (2023) *The EU's Response to Brexit: United and Effective.* Cham: Palgrave Macmillan.

Lulle, Aija, Moroşanu, Laura and King, Russell (2018) 'And then came Brexit: Experiences and future plans of young EU migrants in the London region'. *Population, Space and Place* 24(1): e2122.

Lulle, Aija, Moroşanu, Laura and King, Russell (2022) *Young EU Migrants in London in the Transition to Brexit.* Abingdon: Routledge.

MacClancy, Jeremy (2019) 'Before and beyond Brexit: Political dimensions of UK lifestyle migration'. *Journal of the Royal Anthropological Institute* 25(2): 368–389.

Montagna, Nicola, Della Puppa, Francesco and Kofman, Eleonore (2021) 'Onward migration: An introduction'. *International Migration* 59(6): 8–15.

Morad, Mohammad, Della Puppa, Francesco and Sacchetto, Devi (2021) 'The dark side of onward migration: Experiences and strategies of Italian-Bangladeshis in the UK at the time of the post-Brexit referendum'. *British Journal of Sociology* 72(5): 1311–1324.

More, Gillian (2020) 'From Union citizen to third-country national: Brexit, the UK Withdrawal Agreement, no-deal preparations and Britons living in the European Union'. In Nathan Cambien, Dimitry Kochenov and Elisa Muir (eds) *European Citizenship under Stress: Social Justice, Brexit, and Other Challenges*. Leiden: Brill Nijhoff, pp. 457–481.

Moreh, Chris, McGhee, Derek and Vlachantoni, Athina (2020) 'The return of citizenship? An empirical assessment of legal integration in times of radical socio-legal transformation'. *International Migration Review* 54(1): 147–176.

Morgan, Jennifer and Willmington, Lizzy (2023) 'The duty to remove asylum seekers under the Illegal Migration Act 2023: Is the government's plan to 'Stop the Boats' now doomed to failure?'. *Common Law World Review* 52(4): 103–109.

Moskal, Marta and Sime, Daniela (2022) 'Young Europeans in Brexit Britain: Unsettling identities'. *Global Networks* 22(2): 183–196.

Mut Bosque, Maria (2020) 'The sovereignty of the Crown Dependencies and the British Overseas Territories in the Brexit era'. *Island Studies Journal* 15(1): 151–168.

O'Brien, Charlotte (2021) 'Between the devil and the deep blue sea: Vulnerable EU citizens cast adrift in the UK post-Brexit'. *Common Market Law Review* 58(2): 431–470.

O'Carroll, Lisa and Duncan, Pamela (2023) 'Sweden has expelled 1,100 British nationals since Brexit'. *The Guardian*, 4 April.

Patel, Tina G. and Connelly, Laura (2019) '"Post-race" racisms in the narratives of "Brexit" voters'. *The Sociological Review* 67(5): 968–984.

Patel, Tina G., Martin, Phil, Brown, Philip and Tyler, Pip (2023) 'Racialisation, the EU Referendum result and sentiments of belonging in the UK: A consideration of Roma populations'. *Journal of Contemporary European Studies* 31(4): 1178–1191.

Pietka-Nykaza, Emilia, Leith, Murray Stewart and Clark, Colin (2020) 'Scotland and Brexit: Citizenship, identity and belonging'. *Scottish Affairs* 29(3): 293–304.

Rea, Andrea, Bribosia, Emmanuelle, Rorive, Isabelle and Sredanovic, Djordje (eds) (2018) *Governing Diversity: Migrant Integration and Multiculturalism in North America and Europe*. Brussels: Éditions de l'Université de Bruxelles.

Rzepnikowska, Alina (2019) 'Racism and xenophobia experienced by Polish migrants in the UK before and after the Brexit vote'. *Journal of Ethnic and Migration Studies* 45(1): 61–77.

Schuster, Liza (2002) 'Sangatte: A false crisis'. *Global Dialogue* 4(4): 57–68.

Shankley, William and Byrne, Bridget (2020) 'Citizen rights and immigration'. In Bridget Byrne, Claire Alexander, Omar Khan, James Nazroo and William Shankley (eds) *Ethnicity, Race and Inequality in the UK: State of the Nation*. Bristol: Policy Press, pp. 35–50.

Sime, Daniela, Moskal, Marta and Tyrrell, Naomi (2020). 'Going back, staying put, moving on: Brexit and the future imaginaries of Central and Eastern European young people in Britain'. *Central and Eastern European Migration Review* 9(1): 85–100.

Sime, Daniela, Tyrrell, Naomi, Käkelä, Emmaleena and Moskal, Marta (2022) 'Performing whiteness: Central and Eastern European young people's experiences of xenophobia and racialisation in the UK post-Brexit'. *Journal of Ethnic and Migration Studies* 48(19): 4527–4546.

Sobolewska, Maria and Ford, Robert (2020) *Brexitland: Identity, Diversity and the Reshaping of British Politics*. Cambridge: Cambridge University Press.

Sredanovic, Djordje (2021) 'Brexit as a trigger and an obstacle to onwards and return migration'. *International Migration* 59(6): 93–108.

Sredanovic, Djordje (2022) 'The tactics and strategies of naturalisation: UK and EU27 citizens in the context of Brexit'. *Journal of Ethnic and Migration Studies* 48(13): 3095–3112.

Sredanovic, Djordje (2023a) 'Brexit and citizenship by descent: A relational understanding of defensive pragmatism and of the rediscovery of belonging'. *Revue Européenne des Migrations Internationales* 39(2–3): 109–129.

Sredanovic, Djordje (2023b) 'The vulnerability of in-between statuses: ID and migration controls in the cases of the "Windrush generation" scandal and Brexit'. *Identities* 30(5): 625–643.

Sredanovic, Djordje and Della Puppa, Francesco (2020) 'Aspettative, immaginari e progettualità di mobilità e stanzialità nel quadro della Brexit: cittadini dalla nascita e «naturalizzati»'. *Polis* 35(1): 85–108.

Sredanovic, Djordje and Della Puppa, Francesco (2023) 'Brexit and the stratified uses of national and European Union citizenship'. *Current Sociology* 71(5): 725–742.

Stevens, Dallal (1992) 'Race relations and the changing face of United Kingdom asylum policy'. *Patterns of Prejudice* 26(1–2): 96–102.

Turcatti, Domiziana and Vargas-Silva, Carlos (2022) '"I returned to being an immigrant": Onward Latin American migrants and Brexit'. *Ethnic and Racial Studies* 45(16): 287–307.

Wilson, Thomas M. (2020) 'Fearing Brexit: The changing face of Europeanization in the borderlands of Northern Ireland'. *Ethnologia Europaea* 50(2): 32–48.

Zambelli, Elena, Benson, Michaela and Sigona, Nando (2024) 'Brexit rebordering, sticky relationships and the production of mixed-status families'. *Sociology* 58(3): 605–622.

Index

EU authorised representative for GPSR:
Easy Access System Europe, Mustamäe tee 50,
10621 Tallinn, Estonia
gpsr.requests@easproject.com

www.ingramcontent.com/pod-product-compliance
Ingram Content Group UK Ltd.
Pitfield, Milton Keynes, MK11 3LW, UK
UKHW021524090725
2321IPUK00001B/6

* 9 7 8 1 5 2 6 1 6 9 6 2 4 *